LABELLED WITH LOVE
A History of the World in Your Record Collection

T0323120

ANDY BOLLEN

The
History
Press

Cover illustration adapted from an image by iStockphoto/thenatchdl.

First published 2024

The History Press
97 St George's Place, Cheltenham,
Gloucestershire, GL50 3QB
www.thehistorypress.co.uk

British Library Cataloguing in Publication Data.
A catalogue record for this book is available from the British Library.

ISBN 978 1 80399 433 8

Typesetting and origination by The History Press
Printed and bound in Great Britain by TJ Books Limited, Padstow, Cornwall.

Trees for Life

CONTENTS

ACKNOWLEDGEMENTS

THANK YOU TO EVERYONE I have worked with on this journey, from band members to record shop colleagues, and to all the TV, radio and newspaper people I've worked for – especially the editors and producers from the BBC and the Comedy Unit.

I'd also like to thank my wife Sharron in particular for her patience and good humour; Adrian Searle; Danny Goldberg; and Mark Beynon and Jezz Palmer at The History Press for all their work.

ANDY BOLLEN
2024

INTRODUCTION

THIS IS A JOURNEY through your record collection. It is also a trip through the soundtrack and history of our lives. It's about two world wars, the Jazz Age and the blues. It's about the Great Migration when African Americans moved into industrial cities seeking work and filling the labour vacuum created by the First World War. It's about the segregation era and the civil rights movement. It's about the Wall Street Crash and the Great Depression. It's the rise of fascism, the Second World War, the Cold War, the Korean War, the evolution of rock 'n' roll, Elvis and the Vietnam War. It's about gangsterism and the Mob, the death of innocence with JFK. It's Beatlemania, the Swinging Sixties, peace and love. It's race riots and fighting in the streets across Europe. It's Nixon and Watergate. It's about punk rock and Reagan, it's about MTV and rap. It's Thatcherism, the miners' strike, the Berlin Wall and the internet, Nelson Mandela, Nirvana and New Labour. It's also about influential people who understood what constituted great music and knew how to promote and sell it, and those who could not.

2 TONE RECORDS

Founder: Jerry Dammers

Influential: The Specials, The Selecter, The Beat

IF STAX WAS THE soundtrack to the civil rights movement in the USA, 2 Tone was the urban, working-class sound of the UK in political turmoil. Backdrop and context are crucial. Leading up to May 1979, when Margaret Thatcher became prime minister, the preceding years saw race relations at crisis levels, the National Front was gaining traction, and immigrants were being attacked. After comments made by Eric Clapton, in 1976, along the lines that Enoch Powell was right, Britain had too many foreigners, a grassroots campaign led to the formation of Rock Against Racism.

RAR teamed up with the Anti-Nazi League and embraced the energy and spirit of punk. On 30 April 1978, they gathered from each corner of the UK, marching from Trafalgar Square to Victoria Park in London's East End, culminating in an open-air gig headlined by Steel Pulse, Tom Robinson and The Clash. It was a triumph for multiculturalism over the far-right and a pivotal moment for 2 Tone.

Thatcher's arrival in 1979, bringing along her belief that there was no such concept as society, ushered in a divisive period that presided over racial tension, riots in Brixton and Toxteth, the Falklands War, the Miners'

FANORAK FACT

Terry Hall and Jerry Dammers were arrested and fined £400 each after neo-Nazis showed up at a Specials gig in Cambridge. Hall and Dammers had been trying to break up a riot between security guards and fans.

Strike, Murdoch taking on Fleet Street, a culture of 'greed is good', and privatisation.

When ska and blue beat aficionado Jerry Dammers, of The Specials, formed the label in 1979, the band had been subject to an intense bidding war. The clincher in their contract with Chrysalis Records was the guarantee of their own label. Chrysalis signed The Specials to a five-album deal with a promise to release ten singles per year on their new 2 Tone label. This opportunity helped Dammers achieve a long-held ambition: to create his version of Motown – in the West Midlands. Coventry, like Detroit, had been suffocated economically and was suffering mass unemployment through the decimation of its car industry.

Musically, the sound was perfect. The timing was better. 2 Tone arrived as punk became jaded, losing its edge, softening and evolving into a more commercial product for mainstream consumption. The music was an amphetamine rush, merging the second wave of ska, marrying the Jamaican influence of reggae with a hard-edged sound, particularly in live shows. Again, it embraced aspects of punk – the anger, energy and frustration – and channelled it to an audience craving something new.

When a region or country struggles economically, the prevalence of the Far Right spreads amongst the disenfranchised. The talk becomes racist, and populist and clichéd rhetoric is used to stoke the political malaise and influence the youth. As a white kid, you're an easy target for these groups. Some refuse, they listen to records with their Black or white pal and form a band. Black and white, unite and fight.

They ignored punk's nihilism and will to destroy; 2 Tone wanted to fight for positivity, coming together and dancing. The central message was about unity. Even the artwork, the black and white, was a political statement, one of intent – bold and simple and cleverly executed.

FANORAK FACT

There's a 2 Tone museum in Coventry. Pete Waterman, who owned a record shop in Coventry called Soul Hole, helped Dammers and the band in the very early days, with gigs, advice and mainly transport – Waterman had a van.

The bands brought great English pop and political lyricism; the music was post-punk with a clever, new wave sound and twist. Jerry Dammers wanted the label to be socially aware, but it was also about fun: 'I just wanted 2 Tone to be like a little club and if you liked the music you became part of it.'

For two years, from 1979, the 2 Tone label engulfed the charts. Its first release was a double A-side of The Special AKA's 'Gangsters' and The Selecter's 'Selecter'. The first 5,000 singles were placed inside white sleeves and individually stamped with 'THE SPECIAL A.K.A. GANGSTERS VS. THE SELECTER'. The record stayed on the charts for twelve weeks, peaking at number 6. In September 1979, Madness doffed their pork pie hats to their hero, Jamaican singer Prince Buster, with 'The Prince'. The songwriter was a major influence on reggae, soul and Madness. (They later signed to Stiff Records and would go on to have a lengthy pop career.)

1980 dawned with The Special AKA live EP, which gave 2 Tone another anthem for doomed youth. 'Too Much Too Young' reached number 1. By November of the same year, The Specials, The Selecter and Madness appeared on the same edition of *Top of the Pops*. The Specials would split after their number 1 hit, the frenzied, unsettling, evocative 'Ghost Town'. Released in June 1981, for many it was the soundtrack to a summer of riots. 'Ghost Town' spent ten weeks in the charts, three of them at number 1. It was a brilliant, distinctive-sounding song, at times jazz, underpinned with a powerful reggae bass, a haunted-house Hammond and a weird Middle Eastern feel.

We may be wrong-footed by the quirkiness of the song and the pop sound, yet the message accurately conveys the feeling of having Thatcher's jackboot standing on your throat. It was more than a record on the radio. It mirrored what was happening across inner-city Britain and to society in general. It's difficult to convey the level of confusion, mistrust and anger around at the time. If you were 13, the next few years were uncertain, bleak and worrying. 'Ghost Town' became a portent of what would unfold over the following three or four years. Dammers wrote 'Ghost Town' after playing in Glasgow. He told *The Guardian*:

I'd written it after visiting Glasgow on tour. Thatcher's shopkeeper economics had closed vast swathes of industry. The recession and mass unemployment were so bad that people were on the streets selling household items, but the song could have been about anywhere in Britain.

Lack of diversification meant that the demise of the mining and steel industries ripped communities to shreds. It was a horrendous time and working-class towns and cities were hit hardest. In this scarred, embittered landscape, 2 Tone shone through. You lost yourself, escaping in songs like The Selecter's 'On My Radio', The Beat's 'Tears of a Clown' and The Specials' 'A Message to You, Rudy'.

In parallel with the strong, evocative music, the label's branding and design were equally distinctive, giving 2 Tone a unique identity. Jerry Dammers, a former art school student, was obsessive about detail. He wanted an indie look: black and white, simple and striking. The chequered, two-tone black and white symbolised racial harmony. It was bold and stands the test of time.

The famous dancing rude boy image (named Walt Jabsco) was derived from a photo Jerry Dammers had of Peter Tosh from the cover of The Wailers' debut 1965 album, *The Wailing Wailers*. The image was created by Dammers, Horace Panter and sleeve designers David Storey and John 'Teflon' Sims, who oversaw most of the label's artwork.

Along with its energetic music, political message and multiculturalism, 2 Tone should also be applauded for its approach to gender equality, witnessed in Rhoda Dakar and Pauline Black. The label practised feminism when it seemed unfashionable. A strong, talented woman, Dakar led a seven-piece all-female ska band, The Bodysnatchers. The wonderful Pauline Black was singer with The Selecter and also an actress and writer.

The egalitarianism at Rough Trade was also evident at 2 Tone and, arguably, held both labels back. The Selecter and The Specials had fourteen members between

FANORAK FACT

The name of the 2 Tone cartoon rude boy, Walt Jabsco, came randomly from a vintage bowling shirt Jerry Dammers was wearing when they needed a name.

them. Everyone had a vote and therefore a say on the label's output and direction. Despite the best intentions and a sustained musical assault on the charts, it's difficult for a business to function as a cooperative. In 2 Tone's case, pressure from touring the USA caused the most collateral damage. The Specials appeared on *Saturday Night Live*, performing a no-nonsense, particularly fraught version of 'Gangsters'. The pressure of touring was getting to them, as Jerry Dammers would later explain: 'It was a laugh to start off with, it was great. But it ended in chaos, total chaos.'

With bands splintering off to do their own projects, in 1984, 2 Tone had a hit with the anti-apartheid anthem 'Nelson Mandela', written by Dammers, produced by Elvis Costello and performed by The Special AKA. Soon, 1980s pop culture would be seduced and consumed by Stock, Aitken and Waterman. The label stopped operating in 1986.

It's testament to 2 Tone's peak period (1979–81) that the movement the label created still has a resonance today. Original label pressings are coveted; the fashion, sound and ethos continue to be popular, inspiring bands such as No Doubt, Rancid, Bombskare and Young Fathers. The death of Terry Hall of The Specials was announced on 18 December 2022. He was 63 and passed away after a short illness.

PLAYLIST: MY TOP 5 ALBUMS

The Special AKA: *In The Studio*
The Selecter: *Too Much Pressure*
The Specials: *The Specials*
Various Artists: *This Are 2 Tone*
Rico Rodriguez: *That Man Is Forward*

4AD

Founders: Ivo Watts-Russell and Peter Kent

Influential: The Pixies, The Breeders, Cocteau Twins

IT WAS 1977 AND, against the backdrop of punk, Martin Mills and Nick Austin set up Beggars Banquet. The label had evolved from a chain of five profitable record shops. Tubeway Army and Gary Numan hits funded a roster including The Associates, The Go-Betweens and The Cult. Ivo Watts-Russell and Peter Kent were Beggars Banquet record store employees. Watts-Russell in particular had proven, from the shop floor up, that he had a clear understanding of what constituted a Beggars band. His boss, Martin Mills, was impressed by how he understood the embryonic post-punk scene and funded an imprint, as a testing ground for Beggars Banquet. In 1979, Ivo Watts-Russell and Peter Kent started Axis, and after releasing four singles, they changed their name to 4AD.

The label existed as part of the Beggars Banquet Group. If bands did well, they would graduate to the main label. In 1980, they released two singles by Bauhaus, 'Dark Entries' and 'Terror Couple Kill Colonel', and the album *In the Flat Field*. Bauhaus moved to Beggars Banquet and, in late 1980, Watts-Russell and Kent gained full control of 4AD. Few record labels can lay claim to having been more enigmatic or influential.

4AD not only gave Beggars Banquet a run for its money but shook up the UK independent music scene. After a year, Kent sold his shares to Watts-Russell and set up Situation Two Records. Watts-Russell remained the sole owner of the label and went on to sign The Cocteau Twins, The Birthday Party, Wolfgang Press, Xmal Deutschland, Lush, The Pixies, Throwing Muses and The Breeders.

4AD not only created a record label; they conjured up a secret world, a parallel universe, set in a bewildering, maladjusted dreamscape. The artwork of 4AD sleeves had a distinctively stylised look. Designer Vaughan Oliver and photographer Nigel Grierson gave the albums a unique, idiosyncratic, haunted quality. Like works of art created in the psychiatric ward, these were the products of a fevered genius, paintings of great beauty and confusion, like Renoir on acid or Salvador Dali juggling on a unicycle. At the heart of Oliver's work for 4AD is an introspective dislocation and it worked. The capricious visual connections hinted at something magical; these metaphorical hinterlands provoked the already bemused music fan into asking, 'What on earth is going on here?' Oliver got it.

The brief was to envisage what the music looked like. At 4AD, he was part of the process, given the music before release and allowed time to work on it. Image and sound were everything. Oliver himself was less pretentious: 'I don't see myself as an artist. I work with artists and collaborate with them, but then it becomes graphic design. It's not art. I'm a graphic designer.'

At times, the artwork or graphic design was divorced from the music, yet the contradiction of image and sound, the distance, worked: the disturbed, otherworldly images and disparate elements gathered to create a cohesive image, like the Cocteau Twins' *Victorialand*, The Breeders' *Mountain Battles* and The Pixies' *Doolittle*.

These covers only added to the strangeness; a dark, surreal quality worked in tandem with the off-kilter nature of the music. The artwork was as crucial to the label's acts as the music inside. With the iconic sleeve art, you knew it was a 4AD act before you picked up an album. If ever a label was defined by its bands, branding and image, it was 4AD. I knew people who didn't care about the music but who collected 4AD releases like art. At the time, I found their behaviour troubling; now it looks like it may have been astute.

Their roster of acts embraced post-punk, alternative rock, shoegaze and dreamadelica. They were cinematic, melodramatic, atmospheric, iridescent, ambient and shimmering. They were also clever. Ivo Watts-Russell formed This Mortal Coil, an in-house label supergroup. The idea of a notoriously reclusive guy wanting to form a supergroup was outlandish but it worked. The label ethos focused on artists over bosses; it wasn't about execs but the artistic integrity of the bands. This is why Watts-Russell – being at the heart of and having to take centre stage in a supergroup – seemed so out of place.

One of the strangest artistic by-products of This Mortal Coil was being able to hear every word Liz Fraser of the Cocteau Twins sang on her hauntingly evocative rendition of Tim Buckley and Larry Beckett's 'Song to the Siren'. This Mortal Coil's 1984 album, *It'll End in Tears*, spoke to poetic girls with angular cheekbones, hung up on Sylvia Plath with a secret yearning to break out and dance to Kenny Loggins' 'Footloose'.

Watts-Russell made This Mortal Coil a lightning rod, a project which reflected his creative aesthetic and embodied the label's ethereal sound. It encapsulated 4AD as an artistic force. The message was about invention, experimentation and embracing creative collaboration. The concept would be fluid, changing the performers and contributors while keeping the name. This Mortal Coil became the label's statement of intent.

4AD highlights include The Breeders' *The Last Splash,* with the honeyed, whiskey vocal of Kim Deal and her melodic bass line on 'Cannonball', Throwing Muses, and Tanya Donnelly's later project, 'Belly'. The Cocteau Twins' *Heaven or Las Vegas* hit the spot the way only a bewildering symphony can. The Birthday Party released a couple of compilation albums: one of two EPs, *Mutiny/The Bad Seed* in 1983, and *Hee Haw* in 1989.

On their 1989 album, *Doolittle*, The Pixies perfectly captured the essence of 4AD – artwork, branding, the sound, the discordantly melodic and malfunctioning songs. Musically, it found the band perilously close to leaving the alternative independent underground for the bombast of stadium rock. I'm glad it didn't work out. They appeared happy in the niche they had carved out for themselves: popular, much loved and consistently performing to theatre and arena level sell-out tours, festival favourites — yet not quite that REM mainstream superstardom. Without *Doolittle*, there would have been no Nirvana, or at least no band which sounded

FANORAK FACT

The Cocteau Twins were named after a song by Johnny and the Self Abusers who became Simple Minds.

like they did in 1991. *Doolittle* and The Pixies inspired many people. The sound and artwork of *In Utero* by Nirvana was screaming out to be a 4AD record. It's one for debate. *In Utero* looks and sounds like a 4AD record: the dislocated music, the album title, the subject matter and the artwork (Steve Albini produced The Breeders' 1990 album, *Pod*). We can only imagine how Nirvana's story would have unfolded on a smaller label with less pressure: artwork by Grierson, Oliver and Cobain. If Nirvana had been on 4AD, they would have been allowed time with less pressure for a follow-up to *Nevermind*.

The best music bosses are fuelled by instinct; their decisions are based on hunches and not made by board meetings. They sign a band because they love something about them. When bands are contracted for purely financial reasons, it misses the point. Every label owner has a blueprint for the type of group he or she likes. Some enjoy hearing boy-meets-girl-falls-in-love-ends-in-heartache songs while others prefer 'Debaser', as Black Francis of The Pixies goes left-field. Why not write a song based on the French surrealist film *Un Chien Andalou* by Luis Buñuel and Salvador Dali? A film focusing on making art about nothing? In 'Debaser', Black tweaks the lyrics into French/English, 'I am un Chien Andalusia', while eulogising over the film, which is famous for a scene where an eyeball is sliced open. Most record company execs and bigwigs would call the doctor, turn around and walk out the door.

Such eclecticism made 4AD beloved by indie fans across the globe. Genius in art can nudge perilously close to mental illness. When, on *Doolittle*, The Pixies ask, 'Where is My Mind?' it summarises 4AD's shtick perfectly and is, perhaps, too close to the bone.

The kind of mind that seeks out perversely individualistic bands, ones that swim against the mainstream, while managing all the pressures of running a label, must have limits of endurance. All labels inevitably take on the identity of the person at the top; there's a brittle fragility central to 4AD's identity. In 1994, Watts-Russell paid the price with a nervous breakdown, linked to depression, arguments with artists, and sheer consternation at the music industry. Watts-Russell believed his original vision for the label was under threat.

4AD captures the true personality of independent art. It's the last chord of melody before the sorrowful darkness and the truncated, unresolved diminished minor chord before the crash into the abyss. It's music for unhappy dreamers. From a business point of view, its branding was distinctive, yet also pragmatic enough to make money. Few would guess its biggest seller was 1987's global smash, 'Pump Up the Volume' by M/A/R/R/S.

Watts-Russell left the label back in 1999, selling his half of 4AD to Beggars Banquet partner Martin Mills. In keeping with his perceived eccentricity, he headed off to the desert in Santa Fe, New Mexico, where he lives with his dogs. The current boss of 4AD, Simon Halliday, continues to prefer eclecticism. His approach chimes with the original owner's vision. They have artists with a divergent, independent quality who can create music close to the mainstream yet just veer towards a slightly strange, off-centre sound. 4AD continues as part of the Beggars Group, with artists like Future Islands, The National, Bon Iver, Grimes, St Vincent, Camera Obscura and Deerhunter.

Vaughan Oliver died aged 62 in 2020. Writing in *Design Week,* Molly Long said: 'Despite never writing a song or playing a note, Vaughan Oliver's contribution to the alternative music subculture of the 1980s and 1990s was considerable and, to many, genre-defining.'

PLAYLIST: MY TOP 5 ALBUMS

The Breeders: *The Last Splash*
Cocteau Twins: *Victorialand*
Throwing Muses: *House Tornado*
The Pixies: *Surfer Rosa*
Birthday Party: *Release the Bats*

A&M

Founders: Herb Alpert and Jerry Moss

Influential: Herb Alpert and the Tijuana Brass, The Carpenters, The Police, Joe Cocker

A&M WAS FORMED BY Herb Alpert and Jerry Moss in 1962. The A was for Alpert and the M for Moss. They were originally called Carnival Records, but had to change after realising there were a few other labels with the same name. Alpert was the musician, Moss the promotions man. Their first release, Herb Alpert and the Tijuana Brass's 'The Lonely Bull', sold 700,000 copies. A&M went on to become one of the best independent artist-friendly record labels, leaving a great legacy.

Alpert was a trumpeter, bandleader and a popular artist. Despite his comparative youth, in 1957 he had co-written hits with his writing partner Rob Weerts for Keen Records and in 1960 had a deal as a solo vocalist for Dot Records. In September 2012, during an interview for the label's fiftieth anniversary, Alpert told *Rolling Stone*, 'I was on a major label for a year and a half, and I had a real "a-ha" experience. I didn't like how artists were treated, and I filed that feeling away. I thought, "If I ever get a chance to have my own company, it'll be a true artist label, and revolve around the artist."'

Jerry Moss, from the East Coast, was schooled in radio work, looking after artists when he worked at the mainly Doo-wop label, Coed Records, based in the Brill Building, where he had learned the business. He was pivotal to a song called '16 Candles' by the Crest, which became a hit. Realising that his salary working for one company did not equate to his efforts or hit rate, Moss followed his instincts and moved to Los Angeles where he worked as an independent promotions man for various West Coast labels, helping them break into the East Coast radio circuit. Desperate to work for himself, he set up a small publishing company, moved into production, got to know producers and met Alpert.

They quickly became friends. Having similar ambitions, they decided to join forces. Moss suggested they put $100 each into an account and see if his contacts and Alpert's musicianship might come up with something. They recorded and released 'Tell It to the Birds', which received local radio airplay before Dot Records picked it up for $750; they sold 7,000 copies and suddenly had $2,000 in their account.

The pair then had their inspirational moment, at the bull ring. Both shared an interest in bullfighting, Moss in particular, because he had read and loved Hemingway's *The Sun Also Rises* (a modernist novel about ex-pats travelling to Pamplona to see the running of the bulls) and *Death in the Afternoon* (non-fiction about the ritual and traditions of bullfighting). While attending bullfights, they heard Mariachi bands and came up with 'The Lonely Bull' by Herb Alpert and the Tijuana Brass.

Due to the Tijuana Brass, they were considered an easy-listening label and were keen to broaden the roster. With the money generated from the sales of Tijuana Brass (over 13 million copies by 1966), they signed Sérgio Mendes. His fruitful relationship with A&M began with *Herb Alpert Presents Sergio Mendes & Brasil '66*, yielding a hit single with 'Mas Que Nada'. A further crop of huge-selling albums would follow from Mendes for many years.

With funding from the Mendes hits, they were able to diversify, and started taking chances on artists like Joe Cocker. His live album, *Mad Dogs and Englishmen*, released in 1970, was a huge success, and soon they were directly trying to sign or license artists from the UK such as Humble Pie, Peter Frampton and Supertramp.

With A&M, we have the singular vision, mindset and instinct that saw them pick up and sign an artist like The Carpenters.

FANORAK FACT

The famous Tijuana Brass that Herb Alpert fronted didn't exist at the start. He doubled up the trumpet parts himself when recording. It wasn't until he had hits with his singles and albums and had to tour that he formed the Tijuana Brass.

In hindsight, with Richard Carpenter's arrangements and skill as a musician and Karen's wonderfully melancholic contralto, it would seem obvious. However, at the beginning of their career, The Carpenters had many false starts. They were considered unusual at the time and were also competing against heavy rock bands. Their polished sound and smooth production would be viewed, even then, as too safe.

Moss and Albert had the instinct to sign The Carpenters in April 1969. They stood by them in October of the same year, despite their debut album *Offering*'s lukewarm reception. The LP only produced one minor hit, a ballad version of The Beatles' 'Ticket to Ride'. The song reached number 54 on the Billboard charts, and the album sold 18,000, leaving A&M with a loss. Despite this, again they remained loyal; Alpert knew all they needed was a hit single and everything would click.

Burt Bacharach was a fan and invited the duo to open a charity gala concert where they played a medley of Bacharach and David songs. Alpert had Richard Carpenter rework '(They Long to Be) Close to You'. A&M called it right and they had a hit, reaching number 1 and staying there for four weeks. After this breakthrough, *Offering* was reissued internationally in November 1970 as *Ticket to Ride* with a different cover, selling 250,000 copies. The Carpenters went on to have twelve Top 10 hits for the label, becoming global superstars. They were a great example of a label allowing artists to develop and breathe.

Cat Stevens, another artist with a unique style and a different take on the world, intelligent and articulate, was licensed from Island in the UK. The music business had changed and was about artists like The Carpenters, getting to know them as people, trusting them, and allowing them to develop at their own pace.

A&M remind me of my brother's Police albums and copying Stewart Copeland's drumming. Later, my taste developed for some old-fashioned country rock, the albums of Gene Clark, particularly *The Fantastic Expedition of Dillard & Clark*, where former Byrd, Gene Clark and banjo player supreme, Doug Dillard, created a quiet, majestically low-key piece of brilliance, filled with glorious vocal harmonies. Their second release, *Through the Morning, Through the Night,* has more cover versions on it, yet is worth hunting down for a listen. Another A&M favourite is the man behind some of The Carpenters' biggest hits, the excellent songwriter Paul Williams; some of his albums are spectacularly brilliant, especially *Just an Old Fashioned Love Song* and *Life Goes On.*

With A&M it was also about more than artistic freedom. You sensed they loved their job. When Wes Montgomery wanted to cover The Beatles' 'A Day in the Life', it was a left-of-centre move, yet his take on the tune is marvellous – a great insight into both the label and the jazz guitarist's skilled pace and intricate interpretation. (Our friends from Blue Note and Impulse! show up in despatches: the song was recorded in Rudy Van Gelder's studio in New Jersey with production by Creed Taylor.) This gives Montgomery's work a familiar warmth and vibrancy. So, with A&M attention to detail was also vital.

That they started out pulling resources in Alpert's small garage, with a piano, a two-track recording machine and a desk containing a phone with two extensions always endeared me to A&M. They ended up in Charlie Chaplin's old studio in Hollywood. Jerry Moss once said that if A&M had a big year, it would share the profits with its staff and the artists on the label.

A&M, particularly the UK side, is also remembered for signing the Sex Pistols ... then sacking them on 16 March 1977, after six days. As soon as it was released from its contract, A&M destroyed all 25,000 copies of the single 'God Save the Queen'. However, a few were salvaged and those in circulation are coveted by record collectors around the world. They are now among the most collectable and expensive pieces of vinyl and it's thought only nine remain. In 2015, an A&M copy of 'God Save the Queen' sold for £6,000.

The Police signed to A&M in March 1978. Again, here was a different kind of act – a post-punk trio with great pop and rock songs underpinned with reggae rhythms, who would sell big. The band found fame

> **FANORAK FACT**
>
> Jerry Moss found a hobby in horse racing, breeding and training a Kentucky Derby winner.

and fortune thanks to a prolific run of hit albums between 1978 and 1983, *Outlandos d'Amour*, *Reggatta de Blanc*, *Zenyatta Mondatta*, *Ghost in the Machine* and *Synchronicity*. They had five number 1 singles in the UK: 'Message in a Bottle', 'Walking on the Moon', 'Don't Stand So Close to Me', 'Every Little Thing She Does Is Magic' and 'Every Breath You Take', which also reached number 1 in the USA.

After selling A&M to PolyGram for $500 million, in 1989, Alpert and Moss stayed on as per their agreement for another four years. But they felt they had lost too much control: PolyGram changed the staff and hadn't kept their word, so A&M sued. A&M now exist as part of the Universal Music Group.

It might have started with a distinct middle-of-the-road, grown-up flavour, but by the end of its journey, A&M had signed and released a broad roster of acts from The Police to Carol King, Bryan Adams to Soundgarden, Peter Frampton to Supertramp, Cheryl Crow to the Flying Burrito Brothers, Procol Harum to Wes Montgomery, and from Janet Jackson to Elkie Brooks. The label treated its artists well and they reciprocated by delivering great work. Like many of the other great labels before them, A&M believed in the music and trusted in the artists to deliver. What has it left for us? Well, it's a wonderfully eclectic archive of over 600 albums, which has brought on an impossible headache when trying to decide my favourite five.

Jerry Moss passed away peacefully, aged 88, on 16 August 2023.

PLAYLIST: MY TOP 5 ALBUMS

Flying Burrito Brothers: *The Gilded Palace of Sin*
Joe Cocker: *Mad Dogs and Englishmen*
The Police: *Reggatta De Blanc*
Paul Williams: *Just an Old Fashioned Love Song*
Dillard and Clark: *The Fantastic Expedition of Dillard & Clark*

ALTERNATIVE TENTACLES

Founders: Jello Biafra and East Bay Ray

Influential: Dead Kennedys, NoMeansNo

FORMED IN SAN FRANCISCO in 1979 by two members of the Dead Kennedys, Jello Biafra and East Bay Ray, Alternative Tentacles was primarily an outlet to release their single, a satirical attack on 'zen fascist' senator Jerry Brown called 'California Über Alles'. Jello Biafra, the Dead Kennedys' frontman, was unrelenting and continues to be unique, with an absurdist approach to political activism. Alternative Tentacles would prove over time to be one of the most influential labels of the US punk scene.

Biafra was born Eric Reed Boucher in Boulder, Colorado in 1958. He changed his name to cause a reaction in 1978. It was the despairing juxtaposition of images: the starving people of Biafra and the consumerism of 'plastic America' with the Jell-O. He has been through it all, from obscenity lawsuits against the label to serious assault from baying punks accusing him of selling out. He is now a spoken-word artist and ran for the leadership of the Green Party of the USA, but it wasn't quite ready for his prankster approach.

Throughout his career, Biafra stuck to his mantra, 'Anything I can do to jar people's brain sediment, I'll do.' And jar people's minds he did. At the age of 21, he attracted media attention when he responded to a challenge from a friend and ran for mayor of San Francisco. His campaign highlights included a ban on cars within city limits and a law to make all businessmen wear clown suits from nine to five o'clock.

Eric's father was a psychiatric social worker and his mother a librarian. Somehow, he seemed to benefit from both, assembling an understanding of the susceptibility of the human condition and inheriting great language skills, with a fascination for poetry and literature from an early age. A love of music was also born from his father's eclectic record collection. As a kid, though, he struggled to mix at school, became insular and found his dreams and expectations were different from his peers. Biafra would explain years later, 'My heroes in those days were Batman villains. My other friends wanted to be nurses and firemen, but I thought the Riddler and Penguin were much better role models.'

If the Sex Pistols and The Damned were moved to action by the insipid sound of prog rock, in Colorado, country rock moved young Jello to seek out record stores selling the MC5, The Stooges, Nazz and 13th Floor Elevators. In 1978, he enrolled at the University of California-Santa Cruz but left after two months. It wasn't for him. Inspired by the sound and attitude of the bands he'd found in those record stores, he continued writing songs and poetry, and in the same year, formed the Dead Kennedys. After a week of solid rehearsals, they played their first show at San Francisco's Mabuhay Gardens and quickly gained a strong following.

Surprisingly, though, the band struggled to gain any traction. 'California Über Alles' didn't catch on in San Francisco but did in the UK after Bob Last of Fast Product in Edinburgh was given the record to listen to by New York promoter Jim Fouratt. It is seldom mentioned that the US West Coast explosion began on Scotland's East Coast. Last brought out the single and the Dead Kennedys took off in the UK. Cherry Red released their debut album *Fresh Fruit for Rotten Vegetables* in the UK and the IRS Records imprint, Faulty Products, released it in the USA. Alternative Tentacles would eventually release it too.

Alternative Tentacles was now the go-to hardcore punk label for bands like Bad Brains, Flipper and Black Flag. In 1981, Alternative Tentacles put out a compilation album featuring its bands, called *Let Them Eat Jelly Beans*, to introduce the label's artists to a more welcoming European audience. As with the Ramones, audiences in the UK and the rest of Europe seemed to get it quicker. The press especially tuned into the quirkier, quivering voice of the Dead Kennedys' crazed frontman; they were the US Sex Pistols, only more literate, more political and, well, more musical.

In 1986 the label became embroiled in a legal case, thanks to the Swiss artist H.R. Giger. His artwork, on a poster inserted in the fourth album *Frankenchrist,* led to the Dead Kennedys being up in court and on trial for obscenity. The band would win, eventually, but the collateral damage split the group and left Jello Biafra in sole charge of Alternative Tentacles. Instead of going into its shell and knowing it would upset and irritate the right-wing pro-censorship groups further, the label released Butthole Surfers' mini-album *Brown Reason to Live,* then albums by The Crucifucks and The Dicks.

Jello Biafra hit the university lecture circuit and released the first of his eight spoken-word albums. Apart from the Dead Kennedys, there would be Bad Brains, TSOL, D.O.A. and 7 Seconds. The label would produce the weird and wonderful and the strange. A personal favourite of mine is MDC's 'John Wayne Was a Nazi'. There was one point – the pre-grunge period, the late 1980s – when it was conceivable that the label could have been regarded as a success. It released work by the brilliant NoMeansNo, The Beatnigs and Alice Donut.

In the 1990s, the punk magazine *Maximum Rocknroll* accused the label and Biafra of hypocrisy for using Caroline for distribution. The problem was that Caroline was owned by EMI. The magazine banned Alternative Tentacles adverts and reviews, but the backlash reached the point where Jello Biafra was seriously assaulted by a group of punk fans squealing and yelling 'rich rock star' during a gig in 1994.

From 1998 to 2001, Biafra was in court taking on his former bandmates after the label and Biafra were sued by his band, claiming they were owed $76,000 – a decade's worth of album royalties. Biafra was no businessman and the oversight was blamed on an accounting error. In 2003, after an appeal, the label was forced to pay $200,000 in compensation and damages. The rights of the albums were returned to the band, which licensed them to Los Angeles label Manifesto Records. The decision was a crushing blow for Alternative Tentacles as the Dead Kennedys amounted to over 50 per cent of the label's sales.

After that, Jello Biafra implored people not to buy the repackaged Dead Kennedys music on Manifesto. Biafra described losing the band as 'like having your limbs blown off'. He took the situation badly: 'I've used my own money to keep the label afloat. Now many of our label peers are down to one or two employees or pulling the plug altogether. That scares the living shit out of me in some ways, but I think we're better equipped because we already know how to survive hard times.' Biafra and Alternative Tentacles have since flourished with the owner as a campaigner, calling out bankers and trying to save the planet. The label's biggest-selling acts are Leftover Crack and Pansy Division.

PLAYLIST: MY TOP 5 ALBUMS

Dead Kennedys: *Fresh Fruit for Rotten Vegetables*
NoMeansNo: *Wrong*
Jello Biafra & the Melvins: *Never Breathe What You Can't See*
Pansy Division: *That's So Gay*
Dead Kennedys: *Plastic Surgery Disasters*

AMPHETAMINE REPTILE RECORDS

Founder: Tom Hazelmyer

Influential: Helmet, Tar, Cows

AMPHETAMINE REPTILE RECORDS WAS formed in Washington state, in 1986, by Tom Hazelmyer (though its first release was not until 1988). He was born and raised in Michigan before, in 1980, his family upped sticks for Minneapolis. Here he worked by day in a foundry and performed by night with various punk bands. Growing bored with the underground punk scene, he took an unexpected leap (in our narrative at least) into the armed forces, when he enlisted in the Marines and was stationed close to Seattle in Washington state.

In the mid-1980s, his latest band, Halo of Flies (named after an Alice Cooper song), started to attract interest. They came close to securing a deal with a few major companies, but Hazelmyer felt it would be a better idea to set up his own label with the aim of releasing the band's albums.

Hazelmyer's is a dislocated All-American story. His tale is not all homemade lemonade and grandma's apple pie (perhaps if the pie was pumped full of apples laced with cough syrup and a heavy crust of 1960s garage ...). By now the label was based in Minneapolis and Amphetamine Reptile, or AmRep to their friends, were fast becoming a renowned label, particularly for those on the edge of town, artists and fans alike, who thrived on the periphery of the underground scene.

The first release sounded familiar. The revolutionary declaration, *Dope-Guns-'N-Fucking in the Streets*, was the rallying cry of the

MC5 manager, John Sinclair. The compilation hit the sweet spot and included Halo of Flies, U-Men (he had helped them out on bass several times), The Thrown-Ups and Mudhoney. Five hundred copies were pressed, of which around nine were coloured vinyl. Mudhoney's song 'Twenty-Four' was timed perfectly, before they started on the Sub Pop singles club as the Seattle label took off.

AmRep gained notoriety when it brought out Helmet's *Strap It On* and sold 40,000 copies. Hazelmyer's road to label boss was due to the situation he found himself in. Born in the mid-1960s, by the 1980s he found himself, pre-MTV and grunge, in a mix of noise rock, alternative metal and hardcore punk, just as Black Flag were splitting (for the first time). Things were so different before the internet. The weekly music press then was *Sounds, Melody Maker* and *NME.* It was here, mostly in *Sounds,* that you would find a nod to labels like Amphetamine Reptile in a singles or gig review; or perhaps you might hear something on a John Peel session on Radio 1.

As is often the way with such beautiful craziness, a person with good taste who is also no-nonsense can end up becoming boss by stepping up at the critical time. Wherever you find a scene, there's always a subterranean version of it, an underground take on the fake. The label captured that crucial pre-grunge dirty punk energy and inventiveness of mid-to-late 1980s Seattle.

Musically, the label is somewhere between Melvins groove grunge, Mudhoney's savage Stooges-fest and Helmet's heavy rifferama. Then, it's a hard left to the end of the dial for artists like Cows, Helios Creed, Servotron, Chokebore, Love 666 and Boss Hog. Categorising their artists is challenging, and that's how Amphetamine Reptile like it. Hazelmyer loved the 1960s psychedelia of UK bands, especially The Creation. He also fed off the UK punk and then post-punk bands, like the Sex Pistols, The Damned, Joy Division, Gang of Four, Wire, Killing Joke, Birthday Party, and Nick Cave and the Bad Seeds.

I've always liked Hazelmyer, which is primarily down to knowing about the label through Helmet and later, in 1994, the Melvins who released their sixth album, *Prick,* while they were under contract to Atlantic Records and were called ƧᴎIVꞀƎM (Melvins in mirror writing). To many, Hazelmyer is gruff, but under that persona lies someone who has an understanding of what he wants and the bands he likes.

He is scary and argumentative and at times over the top, but I'm from Scotland where everyone is like that – people in bands, tour managers, soundmen and record shop bosses. Usually, they're just creative people who understand the niche and become impatient when people don't maintain their standards. Hazelmyer was a different kind of entrepreneur, driven and relentless, and wanted things done a certain way. He readily admits to being influenced by Homestead Records and by the attitude of UK label Stiff Records, and its willingness to have fun and be cheap and inventive with its marketing.

Like many of our label bosses, he started setting up an outlet to release his own band's music, then one band he released changed the story. Helmet sold over 40,000 copies of their debut. Cows, who sounded like The Stooges, put on powerful and unpredictable live shows that were among the best around. Both received rave reviews. Hazelmyer claims it was all accidental, but if you do make records, unless you want to keep them in the loft and show them off at Christmas or at a party, you need to deal with the press, fanzines, promotion and distribution. It's hard work but he was good at it, and then others asked him to do it for them and suddenly he was running a label.

If you hear about people like Dave Grohl picking up vinyl in a record shop, they always speak in hushed tones about labels like AmRep. That's because the genuine guys who find themselves making it seriously big understand that the money's good, but it can be kind of soulless when all you ever truly wanted was to make a single. The decent guys who find unimagined mainstream fame never forget they got into music in the first place to make a record. They would love to release limited edition vinyl on the current version of AmRep.

FANORAK FACT

Hazelmyer owns and runs a bar appropriately called 'Grumpys'.

In 2015, Hazelmyer's story was the subject of a great Eric Robel documentary called *The Color of Noise*. Some years later, in December 2022, speaking on the *Veil of Sound* podcast, Tom Hazelmyer explained why his label was always assumed to be a bigger operation than it was. 'The perception always was that we were bigger than we were because we did shit right. Everyone thought we were this massive functioning thing, but it was just a bunch of efficient people up in the Midwest cranking it out and working really hard because we all loved what we were doing.' If the label's bands were touring, radio stations would play their records and record shops would carry the album they were promoting. They were professional. They had to be – only about five people were working there.

Hazelmyer puts his longevity down to doggedness, determination and stubbornness, and trying to prove wrong all those who wanted him to fail. He also takes great stock from the catastrophes that saw other labels crash and burn in unsuccessful business moves, while he was always focusing on one thing: making records. If you've ever been in a band, you'll know that many people think it's uncool to be overexcited to release a record. But once it's out there, anything can happen.

In recent years, Hazelmyer appeared to have scaled back his work, both running his pub and heading the label, after a serious illness. He wasn't quite shuffling off into semi-retirement, but he was stuck in Minneapolis and, until recently, releasing hand-carved limited edition vinyl – linocut artwork personally carved by Hazelmyer. But in 2022, he shocked everyone when he released *Bad Mood Rising* by the Melvins to critical acclaim.

Hazelmyer runs the label part-time now and loves it. The pace has changed and each project seems more like a pop-up company that is started and finished, its creation sent to a pressing plant and released. Things are more spontaneous. He's no longer interested in running the label the way it was done in the 1990s. The record is made, put out, no dramas. Current information about AmRep on the label's website is typical Hazelmyer – and funny: 'Old-school NOISE label. Recently resurrected. We make small run art releases and other shenanigans; they are usually priced accordingly, get over it. Based in Minneapolis.'

PLAYLIST: MY TOP 5 ALBUMS

Cows: *Daddy Has a Tail!*

Boss Hog: *Cold Hands*

Love 666: *Please Kill Yourself So I Can Rock*

Helmet: *Strap It On*

God Bullies: *Mama Womb Womb*

APPLE RECORDS

Founders: The Beatles/EMI

Influential: Badfinger, James Taylor, Billy Preston

THE BEATLES LAUNCHED APPLE Records in January 1968. The idea was originally suggested by their manager Brian Epstein (who died in late August 1967). He wanted to create a tax-effective business structure. John Lennon was clear about the label's intentions: Apple was a choice between paying tax to the government, or into a business. Like most of Epstein's business ideas, it would prove fraught. Apple's selection serves to remind us that every label, especially one with good intentions, requires a stringent fiscal strategy. At one point, the label was viewed as a soft touch and a creative free-for-all. Then, it was eventually turned around, spectacularly, by marketing the legacy of The Beatles.

John, Paul, George and Ringo threw off their *Sgt. Pepper* tunics and kaftans and donned city gents' and bankers' suits, and they looked happy enough at the launch. They announced Beatles Ltd was now officially changed to Apple Corps Limited, and registered as a trademark in forty-seven countries. Within a few weeks, they'd also registered Apple Electronics, Apple Films, Apple Music Publishing, Apple Records, Apple Retail, Apple Tailoring Civil and Theatrical, Apple Management, Apple Overseas and Apple Publicity. The Apple Building was based at number 3, Savile Row, in Mayfair, an area more associated with bespoke tailoring than rock 'n' roll.

The move to form Apple, however, highlighted the underlying problems affecting the band. They were now keen to take control. Each was a strong individual with unique tastes in art, literature, film and politics. Apple Records mirrored that creative tension. Paul was left as the main driving force. John was busy with Yoko. The Beatles, creatively, were no longer a group; they were a splintered, troubled band.

This would be reflected in their ninth studio album *The Beatles* (White Album) recorded between May and October and released in November 1968. The majority of the songs on the White Album were written in Rishikesh, India between February and April of 1968 at the Maharishi's Academy of Transcendental Meditation. Lennon and McCartney had met secretly during the retreat and worked together. Lennon wrote fourteen of the songs. Forty new songs were written and twenty-six recorded roughly and then demoed in Harrison's Esher home, Kinfauns. When The Beatles assembled at EMI's Abbey Road in May 1968, though, tensions were soon running high. John broke the band's working policy of no girlfriends or wives by taking Yoko Ono to work, and the number of takes and creative differences became so bad that George Martin left for an unscheduled holiday. He was followed by engineer Geoff Emerick who quit mid-session, and Ringo left the band for two weeks and flew off to Sardinia.

In 2018, on the release of a fiftieth anniversary Super Deluxe edition of the *White Album,* Giles Martin explained that dozens of unheard tracks reveal a friendlier studio atmosphere. Martin told *Forbes Magazine* perhaps a more company-friendly Apple version of events. In the same way, November 2021's *Get Back* documentary cast a different light on the recording process – it seems reports of tensions were over-egged. 'After the time of *Sgt. Pepper* the group was essentially taking back control and becoming a band again,' Martin elucidated. 'It is said to be a fractious time where the band was pulling itself apart, but if you listen to the outtakes, it is definitely not that. As opposed to having a sort of "architect of sound" overlooking them, they wanted to build the music from the ground up.'

Apple Records was a contradiction. It was viewed by many as a great artistic leap forward. The Beatles were taking control, taking care of business. If accounts in the

FANORAK FACT

Apple had a spoken word imprint called Zapple, run by Barry Miles. It planned to release a live UK performance of Lenny Bruce. It never happened.

book *The Longest Cocktail Party* by Richard DiLello are true, it was a crazy time, filled with the usual showbiz extravagance. There were so many hangers-on that the building was infiltrated with squatters, charlatans and every crackpot hippy under the sun.

The Beatles may have given the impression of a cultural utopia, but industry insiders viewed the project as EMI allowing the lads to let off steam and play grown-ups. This creative freedom would come at a cost. The trip was turning ugly. It created an atmosphere of backstabbing, paranoia and theft, which eventually saw the label dissolve into legal wrangles, while Apple crumbled in a sea of confusion.

After The Beatles split officially on 10 April 1970 (John allegedly told the others, unofficially, that he was leaving in September 1969), the label looked as though it existed to sue anyone and everyone. At one point, Apple Records announced the weekly legal writ instead of the week's latest release. It sued its distributors, EMI and Capitol Records, over unpaid royalties. Apple Computers was sued over trademark violations.

Apple may have defined the spirit of the 1960s – liberating, expressive and experimental. It was a great idea, ruined by egotistical power trips. This is what happens when far-out hippy millionaires, too naive to run a business, own the keys to the kingdom. Apple HQ at Savile Row attracted a collection of freaks.

The label continues to have both an emotional pull and intrigue for Beatles fans. Despite the business side being disorganised, there was always the music. The music saved Apple from becoming a nostalgic, 1960s artefact. The eccentric cast of characters was astonishing – people like engineer and Lennon's acid buddy, Magic Alex (Yannis Alexis Mardas), who spent over £300,000 on crazy inventions in Apple's basement, building a seventy-two track recording studio and flying saucers. Even sensible guys like BP Fallon had two jobs at Apple. His official role as a publicist was to write biographies on Apple artists; the unofficial one, to test the quality of Paul's grass from many suppliers, keen to serve the golden ticket. Then there was Chris Hodge, whom Ringo brought in as they shared a love of UFOs.

Undoubtedly, The Beatles' initial rationale with Apple was well intentioned. They even ran an ad campaign inviting artists to send their demos and had an open submission policy. They were ahead of the game, trying to change the creative environment for artists. However, a combination of awful business practice, naivety and misplaced trust saw the venture becoming farcical. The Beatles' inner sanctum was normally tight, with the same staff throughout their careers; business was always kept in-house. It would be a safe assumption that the project also went off-kilter due to recreational pharmaceuticals.

The label might best be distilled in a singular sketch from the mockumentary, *The Rutles: All You Need Is Cash*, where George Harrison (reporter) is interviewing Michael Palin (Eric Manchester) while behind him the contents of Rutle Corps HQ are being stolen mid-interview. The sketch depicts the public perception of the chaotic way Apple was run.

From an early age, Apple had a major effect on me. The label was one of the major driving forces behind my fascination with music and record labels. When I was 6, I had something of a musical epiphany when I realised the singer in Wings was the man from The Beatles. I had the Wings single 'Hi, Hi, Hi' b/w 'C Moon' (it was a New Zealand release; don't ask me how we came to have it – theft no doubt). It had a full Granny Smith apple on the A-side and a half on the B-side. I thought the Apple Records logo, designed by Gene Mahon, was a work of genius. Somewhere else in my inherited suitcase of records from my Aunt Ellen was the first official Apple Records single, 'Hey Jude'.

Paul McCartney placed Pete Asher as head of A&R. In Peter and Gordon, he had scored both a US and a UK number 1 with McCartney's 'A World Without Love'. He was now more interested in the recording, production and business side. Apple allowed each of The Beatles to nurture and mentor their own projects, which created an eclectic roster of talent. Each member of the band would actively be involved in the recording sessions.

They had James Taylor (brought in by Asher, who produced Taylor and would eventually leave for the USA to manage him), Mary Hopkin, Billy Preston, the Modern Jazz Quartet, Badfinger (originally named The Iveys), Jackie Lomax, soul singer Doris Troy, the Black Dyke Mills Band, Radha Krishna Temple and John Tavener.

Ron Kass was installed to sort out the business – then was forcibly removed after being falsely accused of 'financial impropriety' by the next character in the band's managerial soap opera, Allen Klein. After Allen Klein's contract expired in 1973, Apple eventually became a holding label for The Beatles' back catalogue and the solo projects of ex-Beatles. Many of the original acts signed by Apple had fruitful careers. It wasn't all doom and gloom. Over the period from 1968 to 1975, Apple released fifty singles and over sixty albums, including each of The Beatles' solo projects.

The label had a resurgence in the 1990s with many of the original Apple artists' music remastered and issued on CDs containing bonus tracks. Neil Aspinall – the man said to be the closest ally and confidant of the band, who had been with them from the start and was running Apple – organised the lucrative *Beatles Anthology* series.

The Apple company today has recoiled from the financial wreck of the 1970s. Neil Aspinall retired as head of Apple Corps in 2007. In business terms, circa 2009, the once money-wasting vanity project was having the last laugh, thanks in the main to renowned industry reissuing expert Jeff Jones, who replaced Aspinall.

In 2009, to tie in with *The Beatles: Rock Band Video Game* and with a worldwide release date of 9 September 2009 (09.09.09), Apple reissued a remastered version of each Beatles album. Every album was repackaged with mini DVD documentaries, and the first four albums were issued in stereo for the first time. Two box sets with sixteen remastered stereo albums and a limited-edition box set of mono mixes of all albums up to and including *The Beatles* were also released.

By the end of 2010, the compilations, *1962–1966* and *1967–1970* had been reissued. An additional box set, *1962–1970*, included photo cards and a stamp. The Beatles' entire remastered catalogue, after a protracted legal wrangle, finally became available for download on iTunes. They even found time to release a much-needed label compilation of twenty-one songs called *Come and Get It: The Best of Apple Records*.

Apple continues to amaze and confuse in equal measure. Moving on from its hippy beginnings, when Apple was a sticker EMI stuck on The Beatles' plaything, the label has, after being skilfully restructured by Jeff Jones, become a wonderfully run, profitable business.

PLAYLIST: MY TOP 5 ALBUMS

Badfinger: *No Dice*
Doris Troy: *Doris Troy*
Billy Preston: *That's the Way God Planned It*
Jackie Lomax: *Is This What You Want?*
Mary Hopkin: *Postcard*

ATLANTIC RECORDS

Founders: Ahmet Ertegun and Herb Abramson

Influential: Aretha Franklin, Ray Charles, The Rolling Stones, Led Zeppelin

FEW LABELS HAVE HAD such a broad and lasting impact on R&B, soul, jazz, rock and pop as Atlantic Records, founded by Ahmet Ertegun and Herb Abramson in New York in 1947. The Atlantic logo is less a corporate trademark and more a birthmark, granted to the greatest names in the rock, pop and soul canon – names such as Led Zeppelin, The Rolling Stones, Aretha Franklin and Ray Charles.

Ahmet Ertegun was the son of a Turkish ambassador and had grown up in London, Paris and Washington. He knew a bit about the world. He was erudite, well mannered, a class act – a perfect fit for everything that oozed from every pore of his label. He became a jazz lover having been transfixed by the elegance of Duke Ellington and Cab Calloway when his brother Nesuhi dragged him to watch jazz concerts as a child. They eventually became so besotted with jazz and soul that they promoted concerts for Lester Young and Sidney Bechet.

His friend, Herb Abramson, was studying to be a dentist. Both were passionate jazz and soul record collectors and also organised and promoted jazz concerts. On top of root canals and extractions, Abramson also had experience working in A&R and production for the jazz label National Records, where he produced Joe Turner and signed Billy Eckstine.

By 1947, Ertegun was looking to create a label and turned to Abramson. The intention was to record blues and jazz. Their passion for music was matched with an unusual approach to their artists – because they had funding from a family friend, a Turkish dentist by the name of Dr Vahdi Sabit, they could afford to place less pressure on the artists to turn a profit. This meant that, unlike other labels, they could pay and look after their talent. Atlantic was one of the first labels to embrace artist development. Until then, it was common practice for music companies to cheat acts out of money. The simple process of paying artists what they were owed worked for them. They attracted better and bigger stars, happy to sign if it meant getting paid royalties on time.

The label was run by three people, Abramson as president, Ertegun as vice-president and Herb Abramson's wife, Miriam, who managed the day-to-day office business, paying bills and wages. When Abramson was called up to serve in the US Army in 1953 (in the dental corps; wonder if he was a drill sergeant?) Ertegun retained him on full pay.

One man down, Abramson and Ertegun agreed to bring in Jerry Wexler. He was a music journalist at *Billboard* magazine, where he was famous for coining the term 'Rhythm and Blues' to replace the term 'race music'. As Barney Hoskyns explained in his 2003 book *Ragged Glories* (Pimlico): 'It was Wexler who suggested to its [*Billboard*'s] editor, Paul Ackerman, that they change the label on their Black music charts from "Race Records" to "Rhythm and Blues" thus providing a neat tag for the Black sound that had evolved out of urban blues and big-band swing.'

At this point, Atlantic was an independent label working hard to push its product. Wexler, while on the road as a record plugger, had enjoyed the music coming out of Memphis, and when he heard Carla Thomas, he was mesmerised. This brought him to the Memphis-based label, Stax. Wexler couldn't believe his luck. Here was a company creating a sound with its tailor-made studio, a converted movie theatre, one which had a sloped floor, giving the sound an added kick. It had an amazing house band called Booker T. & the M.G.'s and a modest label, well run by Jim Stewart. (See Stax.)

Initially, the relationship was a perfect arrangement. Atlantic obtained the tight, influential, Black soul sound of Stax. Stax and Stewart were happy to have a cool New York label interested, able to provide wider distribution and license artists. Recording away from New York or Los Angeles, artists performed with freedom, loving the laid-back nature of the studio. The chemistry was magical. Wexler brought his newly signed Florida duo, Sam and Dave; they would be released via Stax, yet remain owned by Atlantic.

By 1965, Wilson Pickett had been through various studios and producers; the process had been fraught. 'In the Midnight Hour' was his third single for Atlantic. Despite Pickett's demands, with the help of Donald 'Duck' Dunn on bass, Steve Cropper on guitar and Al Jackson on drums (Booker T. wasn't present for the session), and with Wayne Jackson's horns, 'In the Midnight Hour' became a smash hit – number 1 on the R&B charts, number 21 on the *Billboard* pop charts and number 12 in the UK.

Pickett had three separate sessions at Stax in 1965. By now he was testing the patience of the normally easy-going session men working there. The musicians and staff, perhaps more streetwise than owner Jim Stewart, convinced him that Wexler might love the sound from the studio, but Atlantic and not Stax were benefiting from the hits. Stewart valued the relationship; the musicians in the studio felt Wexler was less a soul visionary and more a mercenary. Something clicked with Stewart and by December 1965, he had stopped outside sessions.

If we assume that, originally, Jerry Wexler was a soul whose intentions were good, one who knew how to feed off the soul music in the South, it is still difficult to imagine a lanky, white, Jewish New Yorker inhabiting the Deep South; yet by all accounts he bled R&B and soul. He was attuned to the struggle and understood the sensitivity and depth of it, the authenticity. He was also a businessman and knew what was being produced would sell. He appreciated that something special happened when his acts recorded at Stax. Wexler had a great gut feeling for it.

He signed Aretha Franklin when Columbia decided not to renew her contract. Franklin was at a crossroads, aged 24, and her career needed direction. It changed trajectory and, with some Memphis love, the queen of soul was reborn. From the moment he arrived at Atlantic, Wexler's business nous was obvious. As well as being a talented producer, he would get out to radio stations and pay them to get Atlantic acts on the air. He was forward-thinking in his approach to employing independent songwriters and producers, and creating subsidiary labels. He pored over facts and figures and knew the importance, from his *Billboard* days, of sales – the numbers.

Ertegun had given him a clear remit: rhythm and blues. He wanted Wexler to produce R&B music for the Black population. Wexler's appointment proved prudent and fruitful. Over the subsequent fifty years, besides Wilson Pickett and Aretha Franklin, he would sign Bob Dylan, Dusty Springfield, Ray Charles, the Allman Brothers, Led Zeppelin and Dire Straits.

It was back in 1949 that Sticks McGee gave the label its first hit with 'Drinking Wine Spo-Dee-o-Dee'. Sticks McGhee's brother, Brownie, sang backing vocals on the track and it sold 400,000 copies, reaching number 2 on the *Billboard* charts. It would turn out to be an eventful and busy year with Atlantic recording 187 songs. This year saw Ruth Brown sign to Atlantic Records and score a hit with her first record, 'So Long', which reached number 6 on the R&B charts. This was only after an elongated recuperation, Brown having been badly injured in a car crash on the way to audition nine months earlier. She would become the label's first best-selling artist with a prolific run of hits.

In 1950, Joe Morris had a hit with 'Anytime, Anyplace, Anywhere', the label's first 45rpm-format hit. Ertegun penned the company's first R&B chart number 1, The Clovers' 'Don't You Know I Love Him', in September 1951. Ruth Brown launched a remarkable run of form with the label's first million-selling single, 'Teardrops from My Eyes', followed in the spring of 1952 by another number 1 smash, '5-10-15 Hours'. This run would continue with 'Daddy Daddy' and 'Mama He Treats Your Daughter Mean' reaching Number 1.

FANORAK FACT

Wexler and Ertegun signed Led Zeppelin to the label on the recommendation of Dusty Springfield. On the subject of Dusty, one of her finest moments, *Dusty in Memphis*, was a bit of a misnomer. Used to performing with sumptuous orchestras in lavish studios, she had a tantrum at the American Sound Studios in Memphis – she's Dusty, she's allowed. She fell out with engineer Tom Dowd and stormed off, refusing to sing. Jerry Wexler recorded the backing tracks by tight soul band The Memphis Cats, and had Dusty come in to do the vocals in New York, when she had calmed down.

This was her last hit for Atlantic, though one song called 'Oh What a Dream' would continue to sell for years.

In 1952, Atlantic signed Ray Charles. 'I Got a Woman', 'What I'd Say' and 'Hallelujah I Love Her So' followed. The Clovers' 'One Mint Julep' was next. When Ertegun found out Clyde McPhatter was forming his new band, The Drifters, he signed them. Their first single, 'Money Honey', was the biggest R&B hit of 1953.

The collaboration between Ertegun, Wexler and Atlantic studio engineer Tom Dowd created over thirty hits; songs such as 'Splish Splash' by Bobby Darin, 'Yakety Yak' by The Coasters, 'Tweedle Dee' by LaVern Baker and 'Shake, Rattle and Roll' by Big Joe Turner.

In 1955, Ahmet Ertegun's brother, Nesuhi, took a job at Imperial Records that was perfectly suited to his jazz expertise. Soon after, Ahmet and Jerry Wexler convinced him to move to Atlantic, where he would become a partner. He was made vice-president in charge of jazz and immediately got to work improving and adding to the label's already extensive jazz LP line. His remit was to improve the quality of artists as well as update the style and branding of the sleeves. He would produce John Coltrane, Charlie Mingus and Ornette Coleman. When Herb Abramson returned from the army in the same year, he was made head of Atco (an Atlantic Records subsidiary, which housed The Coasters and Bobby Darin). Maybe Abramson had lost his hunger or edge, but after he failed to produce hits for Bobby Darin, Ertegun and Wexler bought Abramson out.

Not only did Atlantic have Wexler and Tom Dowd producing and engineering, but partly through the efforts of Nesuhi, it also hired writers Leiber and Stoller, who churned out hits for The Coasters and The Drifters. Wexler was the talent spotter; he famously bid $25,000 for Elvis when Sun Records' Sam Phillips decided to sell his contract to the highest bidder. RCA (see RCA) signed the King for $35,000 (plus $5,000 to pay back royalties that Sun owed Presley). Years later, Wexler admitted he didn't know how Atlantic would have found the money to pay for its offer.

The 1960s dawned, with the emergence of the civil rights movement. This saw Wexler and Dowd get to work producing acts such as Stax/Volt artists, Otis Redding (Atlantic pressed and distributed the records), Wilson Pickett, Solomon Burke, Percy Sledge and Aretha Franklin. Meanwhile, Ertegun stuck to the pop and rock side, finding Sonny and Cher and Buffalo Springfield.

In 1967, at Jerry Wexler's and Nesuhi's insistence, Ahmet Ertegun sold Atlantic Records for $17.5 million to Warner Seven Arts Corporation. Warner Bros. was insistent he, Wexler and Nesuhi should remain, and a deal was made to secure their services. In 1968, the label signed Led Zeppelin and Cream.

With The Rolling Stones' contract to Decca now honoured, Ahmet Ertegun made an audacious approach to sign the band. In 1970, after protracted negotiations, they signed to Atlantic Records. The 1970s would see further rock 'n' roll releases from Led Zeppelin, Yes, Crosby, Stills, Nash & Young and Bad Company.

Atlantic (and its subsidiaries) made, produced and distributed great-sounding music. Led Zeppelin's 'Whole Lotta Love', Dusty Springfield's 'Son of a Preacher Man' and Aretha Franklin's 'Respect' are all classics, songs close to perfection. The label's acts remain a broad church, and today Atlantic is home to Missy Elliott, Metallica, Genesis, Ed Sheeran and Bruno Mars. It is part of WEA, with Warner Bros. and Electra, and collectively owned by Time Warner.

PLAYLIST: MY TOP 5 ALBUMS

MC5: *Back in the USA*
Dusty Springfield: *Dusty in Memphis*
Archie Bell and the Drells: *Tighten Up*
AC/DC: *Back in Black*
Les McCann and Eddie Harris: *Swiss Movement*

BELLA UNION

Founders: Simon Raymonde and Robin Guthrie (left 2000)

Influential: Midlake, Fleet Foxes, Father John Misty, John Grant

SIMON PHILIP RAYMONDE AND Robin A. Guthrie formed Bella Union as a means of providing an outlet for their band, the Cocteau Twins. It was a brilliant idea in principle, as it allowed Raymonde and Guthrie creative freedom. Not only would they issue Cocteau Twins material, but they would also release different collaborations and projects, as their previous label, 4AD, had with This Mortal Coil. It sounded like the perfect idea, at the time.

The original line-up of the Cocteau Twins, formed in Grangemouth, was Elizabeth Fraser, Robin Guthrie and Will Heggie (Heggie left in 1983 and Raymonde joined in 1984, staying until they split). They were young, naive teenagers, without a lawyer or a manager, and like many bands of this era they eagerly signed poor contracts. They had reached a crucial point in their career with 4AD. Their main problem was their closeness to the label. It was a complex and claustrophobic relationship. Robin Guthrie and Liz Fraser were a couple and lived with 4AD boss, Ivo Watts-Russell. They were not only friends, but had also become like family, so any business discussions made the relationship with 4AD fraught.

They had signed to the label on a ridiculous deal and had to watch on, having sold millions of records, as lesser bands were paraded to the public on bigger advances from the cash the Cocteau Twins themselves had generated. It's probably best summarised by saying the Cocteau Twins weren't in a good place, professionally or personally. They left 4AD to sign a major deal with Universal – Mercury – and regretted it before the ink was dry.

By 1997, they were experienced artists, well schooled in the pitfalls and dangers of the music industry, and decided to take control of their own affairs. They set up Bella Union with a unique selling point: the band was the label and the label was the band. We should recognise the prominence the Cocteau Twins held in the music industry at this point. They were one of the most original acts in the UK for decades. By then, they were mentioned in parallel with bands like The Smiths, The Cure and New Order.

Bella Union now had the office, the branding, the logo, the letterhead and the staff. On paper, it seemed like the perfect decision. This is the music industry, though, and like life it rarely, if ever, goes to plan. Within six months, Liz Fraser informed Simon Raymonde and Robin Guthrie she didn't want to be in the band anymore. She'd had enough. Once the singer left, they had no other option. They had to look for other bands and make the label work. Instead of spearheading a glorious new creative chapter for the Cocteau Twins, they hastily became A&R men and set out on a journey that saw the label develop into one of the UK's most popular independents.

Raymonde, like many label bosses before him, started out working in a record shop. He worked at Beggars Banquet Records Shop in Earl's Court. The manager of the shop then was Peter Kent, who set up 4AD with Watts-Russell but was now running his own label, called Situation Two. Kent had released Raymonde's previous band, The Drowning Craze.

Fast forward to 2017 and Bella Union was celebrating twenty years of invention and innovation, with Raymonde sticking to his outrageously obvious approach – he released music by people he liked. This was imperative to the business relationship. He only worked with acts he got on well with. It was two decades that introduced the UK to artists like Midlake, The Fleet Foxes, Ezra Furman, Father John Misty and John Grant, while solidifying the label's roster with acts such as The Flaming Lips, Mercury Rev and Spiritualized, to name a few.

Bella Union started with The Dirty Three, Françoiz Breut and The Czars, who

> **FANORAK FACT**
>
> Simon Raymonde's father co-wrote 'I Only Want to Be with You'.

featured John Grant. After a few years, by 2000, Guthrie left the label to move to France. It would have prompted incredulity if anyone had told Simon Raymonde his acts would be nominated for Brit Awards and headline festivals and that Bella Union would win 'Music Week Award Independent Record Company of the Year' four times. Around this time, he would have laughed in their face; on some occasions, while close to a nervous breakdown in dealing with managers, he more likely would have cried in their face.

Raymonde liked to rely on introductions and referrals from other bands. While out at Austin, Texas, for the influential music industry festival and conference South by South West (SXSW), Raymonde signed the Denton, Texas band, Lift to Experience. They recorded *The Texas Jerusalem Crossroads*. Due to personal issues their career imploded, but not before they had enthused about their friends, fellow Denton band, Midlake. Raymonde caught them at SXSW and signed them.

Their debut, *Bamnan and Silvercork*, was cherished but the love didn't transfer into sales. This changed with their second, *The Trials of Van Occupanther*, an album that proved to Bella Union that the label was capable of handling a product that was starting to move, establishing one of its acts as serious players.

The signing of Fleet Foxes was something of a coup. While in Iceland, watching Midlake play Øyafestivalen (best described as Iceland's Glastonbury), Raymonde was beginning to realise he'd hit his ceiling. Frustrated at never breaking that crucial 30,000 album sales barrier, which guaranteed bigger tours, more extensive radio airplay and a higher profile, he was at his lowest ebb and decided to close down the label. But when he left Øya and was back at his hotel, he checked an email from an American friend, an agent and a booker who sent him a MySpace link. He was blown away by Fleet Foxes when he heard 'White Winter Hymnal'. These are the fine margins. Raymonde was on the verge of quitting, then heard a band and realised he had to sign them.

FANORAK FACT

The name Bella Union was suggested by Robin Guthrie when he said Native Americans used to create 'Bella Unions' as a place for entertainment.

Raymonde was desperate to secure the band, but they were signing to Sub Pop. He convinced them to sign for Bella Union in the UK and Europe. A few weeks before their album was due for release, Pinnacle (distributor) and V2 (licensing) went bust. The van carrying 50,000 of the Fleet Foxes' album was heading over from Germany and, if it had reached the Pinnacle warehouse, the albums would have been impounded. Raymonde managed to get the name of the driver, make a call and avert calamity.

From Fleet Foxes' eponymously titled debut in 2008 to *Helplessness Blues* in 2011, they were a commercial success for the label. Fleet Foxes' drummer, Josh Tillman, aka Father John Misty, would add his elegantly debauched swagger to Bella Union's output. Father John Misty's albums, *Fear Fun, I Love You Honeybear, Pure Comedy, God's Favourite Customer* and *Chloë and the Next 20th Century,* along with his great live shows, have delivered global popularity. Tillman's prolific output looks set to keep on rolling.

Bella Union comprises music fans; it has a small staff, who completely adore the artists they work with. They believe in them, so find it easy to tell everyone how great they are. They play to their strengths, finding it easy to market, share and spread the word. It sounds simple, yet labels often fail by getting the simple parts of the process wrong. Business, selling anything when it's boiled down, is about convincing the public your product deserves to be bought. So their energy and positivity come through.

Bella Union's story is one of perseverance, pivotal signings, chance meetings and a focus on the long view. When you add in an obsession with music and the label's bands, you have a recipe for success. It's also about keeping it small, well organised and having a family feel to the label. Along with loyal staff, especially its press and A&R people, Bella Union has international distribution and promotional staff across the world with whom they have worked from the start. There's a dedication and loyalty to the label.

John Grant is an artist who sums up the care, love, concern and loyalty integral to

FANORAK FACT

John Grant co-wrote the Icelandic entry for the Eurovision Song Contest, 'No Prejudice' by Pollapönk.

the label's DNA. After recording two albums, his band, The Czars, folded and Grant went into something of a downward spiral; it was his friends Midlake who got together and saw him through, helping him to record his first solo album, *The Queen of Denmark*. This, along with the second album, *Pale Green Ghosts*, brought acclamation and Brit nominations. In 2014, Bella Union released *John Grant and the BBC Philharmonic Orchestra: Live in Concert*, and in 2015, *Grey Tickles Black Pressure*.

Other label highlights worthy of mention are the 2006 release of Fionn Regan's *The End of History*, Beach House, Explosions in the Sky, and Warren Ellis, Mick Turner and Jim White in the Dirty Three, together with the work of Lanterns on the Lake. Bella Union's path started in 1997 with the implosion of the Cocteau Twins. Perhaps Raymonde's experience of being part of a band, more akin to a force of nature, with a filmy, ethereal, otherworldly sound who seemed irascible and mercurial gave him the skill set required to handle the setbacks, misfortune and calamity that would come his way.

In the end, you marvel at his survival instincts, then the good taste, ear for an artist, dedication to the cause and the support staff he had around him, which gave the label longevity and stability. From an uncertain start, Bella Union has placed itself in a strong position globally through a clever mix of breaking new bands and releasing established ones, and again, the label has done it on its own terms. For surviving alone, Raymonde should be applauded. He's also provided us with a broad canvas of artists as well as many who now sit happily around the interesting parts of the mainstream.

PLAYLIST: MY TOP 5 ALBUMS

Dirty Three: *Toward the Low Sun*
Father John Misty: *Fear Fun*
Midlake: *The Trials of Van Occupanther*
Lanterns on the Lake: *Beings*
John Grant: *Pale Green Ghosts*

BLUE NOTE RECORDS

Founders: Alfred Lion and Max Margulis

Influential: Art Blakey and the Jazz Messengers, John Coltrane, Thelonious Monk

Blue Note Records are designed simply to serve the uncompromising expressions of hot jazz or swing, in general. Any particular style of playing which represents an authentic way of musical feeling is genuine expression. By virtue of its significance in place, time and circumstance, it possesses its own tradition, artistic standards and audience that keeps it alive. Hot jazz, therefore, is expression and communication, a musical and social manifestation, and Blue Note Records are concerned with identifying its impulse, not its sensational and commercial adornments.

Alfred Lion, 'Statement of Purpose' of Blue Note Records, 1939

This mission statement perfectly captures the spirit of the jazz label, eloquent, clean, stylishly purposeful and focused on controlled expression. Blue Note has a distinctive nuanced élan and grace; its core identity exudes and conveys a natural self-assurance. Alfred Lion wanted to bring jazz to the masses, on his terms. His label had to epitomise the effortlessly cool nature, honesty and truth of the art form. By keeping it real, the label captured the quintessence of jazz, making it one of the leading labels to emerge from the genre.

The label was formed in New York, in 1939, by Alfred Lion, a Jewish-German immigrant American, and US musician and writer, Max Margulis. They would later be joined by Lion's childhood friend from Berlin, Francis Wolff. Both Lion and Wolff had escaped the Nazi regime, travelling to the USA to make a fresh start, and they were intent on making the most of the opportunity.

Lion was pursuing a dream. The journey began with the release of boogie-woogie pianists Albert Ammons and Meade Lux Lewis. The intervening years would bring hits for Sidney Bechet's 'Summertime', the genius of Thelonious Monk's 'Round Midnight', Art Blakey and the Jazz Messengers' 'Moanin'' and John Coltrane's 'Blue Train'.

Blue Note refers to the 'blue notes' of jazz and blues. These musical notes symbolise pain, heartache, love and loss, yet have come to define so much more – civil rights, social unrest and economic hardship. The blue note may also represent poor African-American musicians, frequently suffering from heroin, cocaine or alcohol addiction, many of whom died through a lack of proper medical supervision. These musicians were playing in a broken, racist and divided society, and despite this environment, managed to play with dexterity and skill. Fortunately, labels like Blue Note gave them a platform, a refuge and a form of escape to express themselves.

Like the best labels, Blue Note's style and graceful design closely reflected its music, giving the label a strong identity. It was one of the first companies to consider aesthetic fusion: the look and the sound. It was about the sound of the record and the look of the sleeve. For Lion, Margulis and Wolff, the artwork had to reflect the emotional charge and dynamism of a perfect solo. It had to mirror the phrasing with an elegant flourish, a blistering piece of improvisation and the meandering beat and groove.

FANORAK FACT

The pre-1966 Blue Note recordings by Rudy Van Gelder have the 'P' symbol in the vinyl's run-out ('P' for Plastylite). If you've any, keep them.

Blue Note releases were a creative contradiction; the sleeves at times looked both modern and traditional. The image of the artists performing or in moody contemplation, matched with clean typography, made the product instantly recognisable and deeply desirable. Even the idea of moody contemplation was new. Until then, artists would pose in staged action shots or bland studio publicity shots. Blue Note was one of the first to understand that the visual representation of the musician had to convey the intensity and emotional impact of the music.

The label became as important for its look as for its groove. It understood the importance of a strong identity in the marketplace. While Francis Wolff masterminded the cover photography, he also brought in Reid Miles from *Esquire* magazine to work on the design, layout and artwork of the label's albums.

Blue Note's sleeve design would mean nothing without the contributions of producer Creed Taylor and renowned recording engineer Rudy Van Gelder. Both recorded most of the albums and singles from around 1953 onwards. Taylor was an independent producer. He would later sign John Coltrane to the cool and brilliantly branded – with the exclamation mark – Impulse! Records, and managed the Verve label before going on to set up CTI (Creed Taylor Incorporated).

Not only a top producer, Taylor was also savvy with marketing. He worked with leading musicians and soloists, the best in their field. This is why he would be so closely affiliated with Blue Note and work with the label's main recording engineer, Rudy Van Gelder.

Creed Taylor and Rudy Van Gelder clicked from the start. If Taylor's strength was putting together a concept and selling it, Van Gelder's was about the sound and duplicating the energy from the musicians in the studio. He was innovative, particularly embracing multi-tracking technology. Known for bringing recordings alive with the use of reverb, giving them a warmth and a presence, he was also notoriously secretive about his studio mastery.

Van Gelder did reveal one of his recording secrets – the efforts made to source the best and most advanced microphones of the day. From there, it was about mic positioning, capturing the sound, and pushing the boundaries both in the studio and in the recording of live shows. He paid particular attention to detail during the mastering process, transferring tape

FANORAK FACT

Lee Morgan's *Search for the New Land* is thought by jazz aficionados to be the inspiration behind John Coltrane's *A Love Supreme*.

to acetate, before getting it to the pressing plant: the Plastylite Corporation in North Plainfield, New Jersey.

Jazz purists consider the 1950s and 1960s the label's peak. At this time, Blue Note was issuing material by tenor sax player Dexter Gordon, pianist Sonny Clark and trumpeter Lee Morgan. Morgan, an astounding bop trumpeter, arguably one of the best ever, was also fighting heroin addiction (he even pawned his coat and beloved horn to feed his habit). Lee Morgan joined Dizzy Gillespie's group at the age of 17 and was allowed space on stage to perform solo. He was a virtuoso with an uncanny ability to make the horn sing and repeat vocal phrases. Morgan was to trumpet playing what Hendrix was to guitar or Buddy Rich to drums. His playing – bebop mixed with a cool, strutting, funky swing – had a powerful exuberance, entertaining the real jazz aficionados who appreciated that he was showing off. As with many of the greats, his spellbinding ability and mercurial nature would come at a heavy price.

Sadly, it would be over for Morgan at the age of only 33. He had been making a comeback, getting clean and returning to form when he was tragically shot by his wife while performing in a club called 'Slugs' in Manhattan, in February 1972. Snow on the road and the undesirable location of the jazz club meant an ambulance took too long to arrive. Had it been on the scene quicker, Morgan's life might have been saved.

Blue Note was taken over by Liberty Records in 1965 and, over the years, was passed around like an unwanted pup. By the early 1970s, the label was in flux. In 1973, the release of Donald Byrd's *Black Byrd* saw a move towards jazz and funk fusion; one which was met with disapproval by jazz fans. Despite this, the label survived. Blue Note Records is currently in the hands of EMI and the Universal Music Group.

Though nowhere near its halcyon days, today it thrives on nurturing emerging talent. Traditionalists wouldn't have approved of any singing on a Blue Note album, yet one of its recent big-selling artists is Norah Jones. The Los Angeles indie electro-pop duo The Bird and The Bee released their first EP on Blue Note in 2006 and their album in 2007. Greg Kurstin of the band has become one of the most sought-after producers in the music industry. Since 2012, under the somewhat shamanic auspices of Don Was as president, the label has undergone something of a renaissance with artists Robert Glasper and Gregory Porter and a roster of emerging young talent; there's still a simple desire to produce great-sounding music. Porter's third album, *Liquid Spirit*, won the Grammy for Best Jazz Vocal Album in 2014.

PLAYLIST: MY TOP 5 ALBUMS

Lee Morgan: *Search for the New Land*
John Coltrane: *Blue Train*
Donald Byrd: *Black Byrd*
Dexter Gordon: *Our Man in Paris*
Art Blakey and the Jazz Messengers: *Moanin'*

BUDDAH RECORDS

Founders: Art Kass, Artie Ripp, Hy Mizrahi and Phil Steinberg

Influential: 1910 Fruitgum Company, Ohio Express, Captain Beefheart

BUDDAH WAS THE EPITOME of a New York label. It evokes nostalgia – the city buzzing, stifling, overwhelming, laughing, swearing and arguing; yellow taxi cabs with car horns blaring. Thinking of Buddah recalls movie scenes like the plumes of steam sensuously sizzling from the subway grate below Marilyn Monroe in *The Seven Year Itch*, the opening of Woody Allen's *Manhattan*, or *Broadway Danny Rose*. Somewhere in my cinemascope version of New York, with its Brill Building, Brooklyn Bridge and Carnegie Deli imagery, amid the hustle and bustle, there's Buddah Records pumping out bubblegum pop hits like there's no tomorrow, in a city full of insomniacs.

The setting might be the cool, happening metropolis with a swinging party in every penthouse. Yet there were always millions of ordinary people, waking up tired, wrapping up in their winter coats and heading to work. Like Buddah, there was the glamour, yet there was also the reality. In amongst the vision and excitement, New York stories were authentic.

Let's meet the star of this particular label. His name is Art Kass: he was a boss at Kama Sutra Records. Our main protagonist is disgruntled. One of his acts there, The Loving Spoonful, are generating life-changing amounts of money. They're hitting it big, yet their income is propping up and bailing out MGM Records. Art's problem is that Kama Sutra – despite doing the work – is a subsidiary of, and distributed by, MGM. As well as having an obvious flair for the music industry, Kass is intuitive, with a real eye for what's swinging and what's dead in the water, and he knows MGM is fading.

In the 1950s, MGM was considered a major label, similar to Columbia, Capitol and RCA, chiefly because MGM owned its manufacturing facilities. Art Kass was brought from MGM to Kama Sutra because he knew the music business from top to bottom and the cost of everything. Most importantly, Kass had reached this level in the music business because of his accountancy background. He knew numbers and at the time was unhappy with what he saw at MGM.

Kass split from MGM and formed Buddha Records with Artie Ripp, Hy Mizrahi and Phil Steinberg. This allowed him to select and release artists without rewarding MGM. Kass, most importantly, knew that his friend and former MGM colleague, the 24-year-old music industry superstar Neil Bogart (who would soon be credited as the 'Bubblegum Kid' and go on to form Casablanca Records, breaking Kiss, Donna Summer and Village People) had left his job as vice-president and sales manager of Cameo-Parkway. Kass also knew Bogart when he was a young buck general manager at MGM and had an instinct for sales and what teenagers loved. He was also connected to Super K Productions (Jeff Katz and Jerry Kasenetz), a pop production factory that churned out the popular genre of bubblegum music.

When Buddah was formed in 1967, it was a time of great flux in the music scene. Musically it felt lopsided, lacking coherence. On the West Coast, San Francisco was tripping out in the Summer of Love. Elsewhere, Aretha Franklin was recording in Muscle Shoals, Alabama and releasing 'I Never Loved a Man (The Way I Loved You)'. Psychedelic rock had evolved into the pop mainstream and The Doors were banned from the *Ed Sullivan Show*. In the UK, at the beginning of June, The Beatles released *Sgt. Pepper's Lonely Hearts Club Band* and by the end of the same month were broadcasting 'All You Need is Love' to the world.

Back in New York, the hits were churning out of the epicentre of the music industry: the Brill Building. You couldn't swing a baby grand piano without hospitalising Carole King and Gerry Goffin, Cynthia Weil, Barry Mann, Mort Shuman, Doc Pumas, Ellie Greenwich and Jeff Barry, Neil Sedaka,

> **FANORAK FACT**
>
> Buddah was misspelt, accidentally. Its original logo was of a Shiva deity and not a Buddha.

Howard Greenfield, Burt Bacharach, Hal David, Tommy Boyce, Bobby Hart, Jerry Leiber and Mike Stoller. In Downtown Manhattan, the once-thriving folk scene in Greenwich Village was slowing down. Artists inspired by Fred Neil, Tim Hardin and Dave Van Ronk (he nurtured and helped a budding Bob Dylan) had figured out that, with a subtle change in style and approach, they might be able to make a living. By 1967, artists from this scene such as The Byrds and The Lovin' Spoonful had gone on to become household names.

Buddah moved quickly with Super K Productions. Kasenetz and Katz were happy as they were scoring hits with Ohio Express and the 1910 Fruitgum Company. The label loved bubblegum pop; it was studio-based, cheap to make and sold big.

Kass, always eager for income streams, realised the quick turnaround of bubblegum hits meant they would need an effective distribution network to get product to the shops. With this in place, they were able to offer distribution deals with many influential independent labels. They distributed Curtom, Charisma, Chrysalis, T-Neck, Bell and Hot Wax. This meant artists as diverse as Curtis Mayfield, Monty Python, Genesis, Rory Gallagher, The Isley Brothers, Baby Huey, The Partridge Family and Honey Cone would be involved with Buddah. Honey Cone are a classic example of how Buddah Records worked. The wonderfully sassy 'Want Ads', the band's third single on Holland Dozier Holland's Hot-Wax label, was distributed by Buddah Records, reaching number 1 on the *Billboard* charts in 1970 and selling over a million copies.

Buddah's first number 1 single came from the brilliant psychedelic bubblegum pop of a band hailing from Oxford, Ohio called The Lemon Pipers with 'Green Tambourine'. The success left the band with something of a creative dilemma. They were a full-on rock 'n'

FANORAK FACT

The Lemon Pipers split in 1969. Bill Bartlett formed a band called Starstruck and wrote a song based around a Leadbelly number called 'Black Betty'. This was picked up by New York producers who reworked it around Bartlett's riff, released it under the name Ram Jam and had an international hit in 1977, proving they were indeed a full-on rock 'n' roll band.

roll band with their own brilliant material. They were frustrated at being given hits from the Brill Building and being told what to do in the studio. Their excellent second album, *Jungle Marmalade*, was overshadowed by the label's desire to have the band stick to the bubblegum genre.

There was something of an elephant in the room. Maybe it would be more the horse's head in the bed, with Buddah too: the rumours around the topic of Mob connections. In the 1950s and 1960s, any popular cash business with quick turnover – like casinos, strip joints and the music business – often had links to the Mafia, whether they chose to or not. It's well documented that the reputed underboss of the Colombo family, John 'Sonny' Franzese, had a financial interest in Buddah. He was allegedly approached by his friend and Buddah boss, Phil Steinberg, who needed help after being threatened by Morris Levy. Levy was connected to the boss of the Genovese family, Vincent Gigante. Gigante famously feigned insanity while he roamed around the streets of Greenwich Village in his bathrobe mumbling to himself. He would later admit it was an elaborate scheme to avoid arrest. At this point, Gigante would have been a powerful and serious threat to Steinberg had Franzese not intervened. It is said, Franzese received a cut of the label in return. It is also alleged he used the label to launder funds and was partial to the odd piece of 'payola'.

Through Bogart's hard work, as a master promoter, the label's hit single ratio was incredibly high. He left in 1973 to form Casablanca Records. Shortly after Bogart left, Gladys Knight and the Pips left Motown and signed with Buddah. They became the label's biggest act with hits 'Midnight Train to Georgia' and 'You're the Best Thing That Ever Happened to Me'. In 1976, the label brought in jazz drummer and producer Norman Connors as musical director. Connors steered the label towards R&B and disco, with songs like Andre True Connection's 'More, More, More' and Chic's 'Dance, Dance, Dance (Yowsah, Yowsah, Yowsah)'. This became a hit in 1977 after it was reissued by Atlantic.

FANORAK FACT

John Sebastian from The Lovin' Spoonful was the first choice and nearly joined the supergroup Crosby, Stills, Nash & Young (Crosby, Stills, Nash & Sebastian).

Buddah called it a day in 1983 after financial problems saw Arista take over distribution. Art Kass sold the label to Essex Entertainment. Buddah was relaunched in 1998 by BMG with the correct spelling of Buddha, before morphing into a reissue label, BMG Heritage Records, in 2002. Today it is owned by Sony Music Entertainment and run by Legacy Recordings.

PLAYLIST: MY TOP 5 ALBUMS

1910 Fruitgum Company: *Simon Says*
The Lovin' Spoonful: *Hums of The Lovin' Spoonful*
Baby Huey: *The Baby Huey Story – The Living Legend* (Curtom)
Honey Cone: *The Best of Honey Cone Collectables* (Soul Wax)
The Lemon Pipers: *Jungle Marmalade*

CAPITOL RECORDS

Founders: Johnny Mercer with Buddy DeSylva and Glenn Wallichs

Influential: Frank Sinatra, The Beatles, The Beach Boys

FEW RECORD LABELS EPITOMISE old-school record industry style like Capitol Records. Maybe it's the fading Hollywood glamour, the label's building, Sinatra, The Beatles and The Beach Boys. Capitol was more than a record label, at times transcending music itself; it was of huge cultural significance in the second half of the twentieth century. Capitol is a historical and musical time capsule, a soundtrack to the last eight decades.

Capitol Records was formed in 1942, in Los Angeles, by Johnny Mercer, Buddy DeSylva and Glenn Wallichs. The label would become a force in popular culture with some of the most important artists of the twentieth century. The foundations were solid with Mercer, DeSylva and Wallichs in control. They played to their strengths, used their collective talents and extensive music industry experience and, by keeping it simple, they were successful.

Mercer was a songwriter, born in Savannah, Georgia, who came to New York aged 19, made it big in Tin Pan Alley and moved to Hollywood in 1935 to work at RKO studios. DeSylva was also a popular songwriter who, along with George Gershwin, had written the musical *Blue Monday*, though, more importantly, he was an experienced producer who had cut his teeth at Paramount Studios. He was equally adept at sourcing and raising money. Wallichs was a record shop owner who ran the Hollywood store, Music City. Here, customers would listen in booths to a recording and, if they liked it, would buy the record and even the sheet music. If they had any cash left, they'd buy a radio too. In effect, DeSylva was the money man (he was responsible for raising $25,000 to set up the company), Mercer was A&R and talent spotter, and Wallichs took care of day-to-day commercial operations.

In early 1942, Capitol released its first 78, on shellac, 'I Found a New Baby' by Paul Whiteman and His Orchestra. Later in the year, they were celebrating two *Billboard* Top 10 hits, with 'Cow Cow Boogie' by Ella Mae Morse and 'Strip Polka' written by Johnny Mercer. Mercer's first big signing was Nat King Cole. He signed to Capitol in 1943, and the Nat King Cole Trio's 'Straighten Up and Fly Right' sold over 500,000 copies. The revenue from Cole's record sales would bankroll the burgeoning label with a roster of artists including Bing Crosby, Peggy Lee and Billie Holiday.

Allied to switching from shellac to vinyl and with the growing popularity of albums and 45s, Capitol would soon be in a position to take on East Coast rivals Decca, RCA and Columbia. Capitol has always had a stylish groove and swing. Perhaps it's the spirit of Sinatra, those impeccably stylish photographs, the movies and those timeless melodies. Even the logo triggers immediate memories and emotions for many generations of music fans across the world. The decades after the Second World War were a peerless time for Capitol.

The 1950s started with a penchant for movie soundtrack albums. *Oklahoma*, *The King and I* and *Carousel* proved popular, adding considerably to Capitol's coffers. Artists like Judy Garland, Dean Martin and Les Paul added to the profits. EMI bought the label in the mid-1950s, in time for the birth of rock 'n' roll. Capitol's smash hit was Gene Vincent's 'Be-Bop-A-Lula'. This period also saw arguably the label's best and brightest star, Frank Sinatra, recording a prolific nineteen albums between 1956 and 1962 including *Songs for Swinging Lovers!*, *In the Wee Small Hours* and *Come Fly with Me*.

FANORAK FACT

The label's thirteen-floor building is a famous landmark, designed by architect Welton Becket. The blinking light on the building spells Hollywood in Morse code. The building itself is said to be the shape of records stacked up on a turntable, at least according to urban myth.

The Beach Boys released their debut in 1962, *Surfin' Safari*, beginning a stellar career at Capitol. Four years later, their eleventh album, the era-defining *Pet Sounds*, was one of the best albums ever recorded, if not *the* best. Capitol Records, the spirit of California and West Hollywood will be forever entwined with the pop genius of Brian Wilson and this album. Among the same photograph archive that captured Sinatra, we have images that perfectly chronicle the baby-faced Brian Wilson singing on, producing and arranging the album. *Pet Sounds* was released on 16 May 1966.

It's difficult to distil such a great piece of art into a few sentences. Several components made it special: the arrangements and the songs, and the fact it forced The Beatles to write *Sgt. Pepper's Lonely Hearts Club Band*. The mutual appreciation between McCartney and Wilson began when Brian heard *Rubber Soul* and was inspired to write an album as good. The first song he wrote was 'God Only Knows'. There's also Wilson's precocity and stunning virtuosity. He was only 23 years old when he recorded *Pet Sounds*.

Yet the album was not universally embraced. On hearing the record for the first time, the label bosses were unhappy, some even furious with the band's change in direction. They believed Brian had taken The Beach Boys too far off-kilter and responded by rush-releasing two best-of albums to distract fans. It took time for the album to be truly appreciated. On release, *Pet Sounds* charted at a disappointing – for them at least – number 10 on the *Billboard* charts. The first best-of album reached number 8.

Capitol Records was more than The Beach Boys. Bobby Darin, Glen Campbell and Bobbie Gentry were highly respected stars, selling vast numbers of records. When EMI bought Capitol in 1955, it became the US home for its international acts. This meant that EMI brought The Beatles to the party. Capitol had first refusal on 'UK EMI' acts released in the USA. It declined The Yardbirds, Manfred Man and The Hollies. It's hard to believe Capitol was initially reluctant to release even *The Beatles*. It was as late as November 1963 when Capitol finally exercised its option to pick up the Fab Four, in time to unleash Beatlemania on the USA in 1964.

Capitol had several issues to sort out ahead of launching *The Beatles* in the USA. It had previously been released on an independent label called Vee-Jay, while 'She Loves You' was on Swan. Capitol bosses were also concerned about the sound of The Beatles' records. They sounded too flat; they weren't energetic, clear or bright enough for the US market. They had their producers alter the sound of the albums with the use of an echo chamber. This added more life when they were played on American radio. Whatever they did worked. For the rest of the decade, the band delivered for Capitol.

The 1970s began with The Beatles' *Abbey Road* at number 1. Inevitably, with thirteen top-selling albums, Capitol had grown used to the profits The Beatles generated in the USA. When Paul McCartney officially announced the band were splitting up on 10 April 1971, the economic impact on the label was substantial. That the band spent almost three years splitting up should have left Capitol better prepared. McCartney's famous self-interview was interpreted by the media as confirmation it was over.

When the accountants picked over the receipts of a Beatles-free year, Capitol had taken a hit of $8 million, the equivalent of $54 million today. Fiscally, it would slowly get better. In 1973, the release of Pink Floyd's *Dark Side of the Moon* turned the business around (in 2023 this was estimated to be nudging close to 50 million copies, and at one point in 2011, it was selling 10,000 a week). The label also released Beatles compilations, known as The Beatles' 'Red' and 'Blue'

FANORAK FACT

On 3 February 1966, The Beach Boys visited San Diego Zoo for the *Pet Sounds* album cover photo session. According to Al Jardine, the big white goat on the cover was one of the most obnoxious animals he'd ever met in his life, and working in the music industry, he'd met a few. The song 'Pet Sounds' was originally called 'Run James Run' and was meant for inclusion on the soundtrack for the James Bond movie *You Only Live Twice*. When it wasn't selected, it was added to the record.

'best-of' compilations. These albums weren't only greatest hits collections, they revisited the group's best work. It was a shrewd piece of business and introduced the band to a whole new generation of fans. The albums were expertly packaged. They were presented in two distinct career sections, from 1962 to 1966 (red) and 1967 to 1970 (blue).

As they were contracted to EMI/Capitol, all four of The Beatles released solo albums in 1973. Ringo Starr, who had maintained strong friendships with all three of the others, had invited them to appear and write on his album, *Ringo*. Harry Nilsson, Marc Bolan and Nicky Hopkins also took part in the sessions. His album had two number 1 hits, 'Photograph' and 'You're Sixteen'. *Band on the Run* by Paul McCartney and Wings had two hit singles, 'Jet' and 'Band on the Run'. *Mind Games* by John Lennon and *Living in the Material World* by George Harrison both significantly added to the Capitol solo Beatles' 1973 fund.

The label of today represents music across most genres, from R&B, pop and indie to hip-hop. The label has evolved with acts like Beck, Coldplay and Sam Smith. Capitol Records is now owned by Universal Music Group.

PLAYLIST: MY TOP 5 ALBUMS

Bobbie Gentry and Glen Campbell: *Bobbie Gentry and Glen Campbell*
Frank Sinatra: *In the Wee Small Hours*
The Beach Boys: *Pet Sounds*
Frank Sinatra: *Songs for Young Lovers*
The Stone Poneys: *The Stone Poneys* (featuring Linda Ronstadt)

CASABLANCA RECORDS

Founders: Neil Bogart and Larry Harris

Influential: Kiss, Parliament, Donna Summer

CASABLANCA RECORDS WAS FORMED in 1973 by the charismatic Neil Bogart (real name Neil Bogatz) and his cousin Larry Harris (Harris was his sidekick and confidant when they were radio promotions guys for Buddah). Casablanca was the embodiment of every 1970s stereotype when it came to music business hedonism and excess. Camels and palm trees adorned the vinyl art. Everything from the acts on the roster to the branding screamed fun and plenty of it. Fun doesn't come for free, though; eventually, someone has to pay.

Bogart's first job was in sales, at the now-defunct music business trade magazine *Cashbox*. He then moved to an executive job at Cameo-Parkway Records. In 1967, he became general manager of Buddah Records. At Buddah, he was credited with creating bubblegum acts 1910 Fruitgum Company and Ohio Express, made the label millions and was nicknamed 'The Bubblegum Kid'.

In a few years at Casablanca, with hits from Village People and Donna Summer, he'd become 'The Disco Kid'. By 1973, the label concept was in shape and the industry was keen to see what he was doing. Bogart's reputation preceded him and, needing both cash and distribution, he was soon dealing with the wily Mo Ostin at Warner Bros. Eventually he was able to negotiate a deal and secure funding. Bogart's proposal to Mo Ostin was simple and astute. Casablanca would become a subsidiary of Warners, benefiting through financial backing and their extensive distribution network. Ostin knew he held the trump cards: cash and distribution. He also knew Bogart would whip up publicity for his signings and keep Casablanca high profile – so to Ostin, it was low risk.

It became problematic with Warner Bros. for several reasons. Staff didn't appreciate Bogart's arrogance, brashness and style of working, or his misguided confidence with Kiss. Casablanca almost went bust trying to break them. Warner Bros. didn't get the band. When they wouldn't sell, Warner Bros. demanded Bogart had Kiss remove their makeup to see if it would improve sales. Bogart didn't ask the band, convinced this was their major selling point. He knew Kiss haemorrhaged money, especially at the beginning of their career. He also knew the band would come through. One of the biggest spends came on breaking them live. Kiss had to be the main act, which meant taking the unusual step of promising full guarantees to promoters to cover the costs of Kiss headlining.

The promotions team at Warner Bros. refused to give any special treatment to Casablanca, seemingly sticking to their own artists and placing Bogart's acts way down the pecking order. The main stumbling block for Bogart, though, was his frustration at the amount of time that Warner Bros. took to record an album. The label was cumbersome, moving too slowly, so Bogart decided to leave and go it alone. Ostin allowed Casablanca to leave with the proviso that it repaid what Warner Bros. had paid to bankroll the label, $1.5 million, and Bogart managed to do so.

At the label's lowest ebb and facing bankruptcy, Bogart was determined not to show weakness. He famously would have the building painted or give everyone a wage rise. If people assumed the label was flourishing, they would treat Casablanca accordingly, he reasoned, and it worked. It was about profile, being seen with the hippest people, in the coolest places, at the best parties.

After three indifferent Kiss albums, *Kiss* (1974), *Hotter than Hell* (1974) and *Dress to Kill* (1975), Bogart decided to cash in on the band's live performance by releasing *Alive!* The album reached the Top 10, but better still, the band's earlier albums started selling.

Following on from 1974's *Up for the Down Stroke*, Parliament were creating a

> ### FANORAK FACT
>
> 'Last Dance', from the movie *Thank God It's Friday*, sung by Donna Summer and written by Paul Jabara, won an Oscar for best original song.

buzz. In 1975, they released *Chocolate City* and the mothership had well and truly landed. This didn't happen by luck. Bogart was a master of promotion. All of the label's staff were promotions people. He was P. T. Barnum, a showman, from the 'there's a sucker born every minute' school of promoting. He'd do anything to break bands. He'd hire planes to advertise and launch an act. He used merchandising tie-ins, board games, dolls, picture discs, anything to increase exposure and sales. He would do the same later with the films they produced.

Casablanca was based on hype and Bogart was the main attraction, every bit the star and figurehead. Bogart had been a student at the High School of the Performing Arts, the school made famous by the TV show *Fame*. He was full of inner desire and self-belief, and refused to give in. He was in the entertainment business and it was show time; hit the lights, it's time to perform; profile, perception and payola. Instinctive, intuitive and great fun to be around, Bogart was probably one of the most charismatic bosses the music industry has ever produced. For Casablanca, the ends justified the means. Amid the overindulgence and chaos, they eventually delivered, at an enormous cost.

Casablanca scored a commercial hit when it licensed Giorgio Moroder's Oasis label. One of the songs featured a Boston singer named Donna Summer. The song was 'Love to Love You' and it was so popular at one of the label's many parties that the crowd asked for it to be played and played again. Bogart called Moroder that same evening and begged him to make a longer version and change the title to 'Love to Love You Baby'. He obliged and made a seventeen-minute epic, ostensibly announcing the arrival of the extended 12in single format.

In 1976, Casablanca joined forces with Filmworks Inc., becoming Casablanca and Filmworks Inc. They produced *The Deep*, *Midnight Express* and *Thank God It's Friday*. In 1977, the European major PolyGram, owned by Philips and Siemens, followed up its 1975 $8 million acquisition of RSO by acquiring a 50 per cent stake in Casablanca for $15 million. On paper, from afar, both labels appeared an attractive proposition. They were selling truckloads of records and having worldwide hits. This was the height of the movie soundtracks for RSO, *Saturday Night Fever* and *Grease*, and the sales of Donna Summer and Village People for Casablanca.

In 1978, they posted wonderful results – something close to a $407 million combined turnover. The release of Village People's run of hits started with 'Macho Man'. The label signed Lipps Inc. in 1979. The writer, producer and musician Steven Greenberg, along with vocalist Cynthia Johnson, released the album *Mouth to Mouth*, delivering the worldwide disco hit 'Funkytown'.

In Larry Harris's entertaining tome *And Party Every Day: The Inside Story of Casablanca Records*, there's a memorable vignette where he describes how Parliament's George Clinton and his 'assistant', Archie Ivy, arrived at an executive meeting with uncut cocaine. Clinton claimed it was the most potent he'd ever had, so potent, 'anyone who tried it would speak Spanish as the stuff hadn't cleared customs yet'. Clinton would hold court in full stage outfit, discussing plans about the band's stage show and the zillions they'd require to realise his interplanetary live show. Harris claimed Clinton 'would ramble on, giving voice to every thought that came into his head, stream-of-conscious style, like William Faulkner gone jive'.

There's a notorious party, one of those music business parties that have entered industry folklore. Tales of epic levels of hedonism have been added over the years, making them sound even more apocryphal. The party was held to celebrate the release of Kiss's debut album and Warner Bros. buying Casablanca. It was held in Los Angeles's Century Plaza Hotel. It's allegedly the most expensive and extravagant music business party ever, the perfect balance of opulence and decadence. This characterised both the brilliance and, at the same time, the Achilles heel at the centre of the label. Casablanca was selling millions of records a year. Employees were treated to first-class travel; staff had the best cars and everyone from top execs to clerical staff at the label shared in the spoils.

Bogart's mantra – especially when it came to promo and breaking new bands – was always 'whatever it takes'. At the start of his career, one of the toughest nuts to crack

FANORAK FACT

Larry Harris concedes that one of his regrets was not signing Rush, who impressed while supporting Kiss. He considered the band too ugly – and thought Geddy Lee's nose was too big.

was WABC programme director Rick Sklar. The influential no-nonsense boss could not be bought, swayed or convinced, so Bogart had his brother-in-law hide in the WABC toilets with a battery-operated record player and wait until Sklar had to pay a visit, then play the record.

Casablanca Records burned brightly and crashed dramatically. During the short-lived peak (1974–80), the company embodied the clichéd image of rock 'n' roll excess. In the entertainment industry of the 1970s, this wasn't unusual, but Casablanca took it way beyond oblivion and the cost was astronomical. The label also had Angel, deliberately marketed as the antithesis of Kiss. Dressed in white, good-looking, each member stepped out of a pod – allegedly inspiring the famous scene in *Spinal Tap*. Millions were spent on the band, who were expected to be the next big thing, but they failed. Casablanca also had the melodic rock of Trigger, who typified late-1970s formulaic radio-friendly rock, but whom radio stations were radio-unfriendly towards and refused to play. They also signed comedian Rodney Dangerfield.

With *Saturday Night Fever* taking off and the world going crazy for disco, just when all seemed lost for both Casablanca and Donna Summer, someone listened to the B-side of her fifth single, 'I Feel Love'. It was originally the B-side to 'Can't We Just Sit Down (And Talk It Over?)'. It was Moroder again, experimenting with a Moog synthesizer along with English songwriter Pete Bellotte, who came up with it.

The Hudson Brothers presented a Saturday morning kids' TV show. Neil Bogart loved their demos so much that he went behind their back and released an album called *Hollywood Situation*. One song, 'So You Are a Star', about Bill Hudson's ex-wife Goldie Hawn, was a hit. The band longed to be treated as serious musicians, but they couldn't shake off the kids' TV show tag.

Casablanca had spent a crazy amount of money getting to this point. The factors that made the label attractive – the sales, the craziness, the entertainment, and the parties – shone the spotlight on the label and gave Bogart a high profile. But while Casablanca may have been selling records, it was costing them too much to make them.

PolyGram failed to take a deep dive into the detail and costs, helped in no small way by Bogart's skill at hiding 'expenses'. A great example of the label's hara-kiri involved being contractually bound to the release of all four members of Kiss's solo albums on the same day. The promo alone cost $750,000 and how likely was it that Kiss fans would buy *all four* albums on the one day in 1978? PolyGram saw the hits but not the debts. In a few years, disco had peaked, Donna Summer was suing and heading to Geffen, and Angel were splitting up. Harris quit Casablanca in 1980 before PolyGram learned it had lost $220 million, seized the label and sacked Bogart.

Bogart went on to set up a label called Boardwalk. By 1985, Casablanca had been shut down, many artists had been dropped, and others had been absorbed into Mercury Records. Casablanca was briefly resuscitated by former industry stalwart and CEO of Columbia and Sony Music Entertainment, Tommy Mottola, in 1998. The label then lay dormant from 2009 but was relaunched in 2012 and now operates as a thriving EDM (electronic dance music) label. Brett Alperowitz currently runs Casablanca, with dance acts Tiësto, Martin Garrix, Dimitry Vegas and Nicky Romero. It exists as a subsidiary of Republic Records under Universal Music Group.

When we look at labels famed for their partying and drug culture, the rock 'n' roll drug-fuelled labels like Creation and Factory pale into insignificance compared to Casablanca. Neil Bogart would die prematurely, aged 39, in 1982, from lymphoma. In his short time on earth, he packed more into his life than 100 mere mortals could.

PLAYLIST: MY TOP 5 ALBUMS

Parliament: *Mothership Connection*
James and Bobby Purify: *You and Me Together Forever*
Fanny: *Rock and Roll Survivors*
Gloria Scott: *What Am I Gonna Do?*
Hudson Brothers: *Hollywood Situation*

CHESS RECORDS

Founders: Leonard and Philip Chess

Influential: Chuck Berry, Muddy Waters, Howlin' Wolf, Etta James

IT'S 1947 IN CHICAGO and the windy city is hustling and bustling. A young Jewish immigrant from Motal, Poland (now part of Belarus), Lejzor Shmuel Czyż, has changed his name to Leonard Chess. He is a businessman and invests in Aristocrat Records, becoming a partner alongside Charles and Evelyn Aron. After gaining experience, he continues to add to his holding, eventually buying the others out and forming Chess Records. He would eventually be joined by his brother, Philip.

Leonard wasn't a music business natural but already had an innate understanding of what people wanted. He had spells working in his father's junkyard business, then in a couple of small bars, best described as dives – but made his money in some profitable discount liquor stores. From here, customers bought their alcohol and he watched them dance and party after working hard all week.

The next logical step would be to invest in a rundown restaurant, convert it into a nightclub and generate income from a bar. This would become the Macomba Lounge. It wasn't the Playboy Club, but a tough venue, which, despite being frequented by hookers, pimps and drug dealers, was renowned for the energy and authenticity of its blues music.

This was south-side Chicago, home to the poorest African-Americans, a great many of whom had come up from the South to escape racism. Those who had migrated had reported back in praise of the more liberal atmosphere in Chicago and the chance to live a better life. There were jobs in the city and opportunities for those willing to work. It was tough, yet for those from across the Deep South, Chicago was the Promised Land. It had plenty of work for African-Americans and was packed with clubs playing jazz and blues.

Leonard wanted to record some of the acts who played at his club, predominantly these jazz and blues groups. The music was loud and powerful; it had to be to cut through the noise. And yet there was something else. It was more guttural and primal. Leonard was excited by an artist called McKinley Morganfield who, under his blues moniker Muddy Waters, fascinated and mesmerised in equal measure. This was when he met Evelyn and Charles Aron, the husband and wife team behind Aristocrat Records.

Leonard remained unsure if the excitement and energy felt in the club would translate into record sales. The sound was maybe too niche. It was Evelyn Aron who convinced him that the vast number of Black people now working in Chicago would love it. Muddy Waters kicked off by releasing his first single, 'Gypsy Woman', on Aristocrat in August 1947. It was his second single, 'I Can't Be Satisfied', which provided the label with a minor hit: all 3,000 copies sold out in a day. There would be eight single releases from Muddy Waters on Aristocrat. In Waters, Aristocrat had an artist born in Mississippi and steeped in the essence of the Delta blues, someone who would come to the city and not only define Chicago blues, but tower above the genre. Waters was a pivotal artist who bridged the gap between the Delta blues and rock 'n' roll.

In 1950, Leonard Chess bought out Aristocrat completely, changed its name to Chess Records and brought in his brother, Philip. The first release on the new label was 'My Foolish Heart' backed with 'Bless You' by Gene Ammons in June, on a 78rpm format. It became the label's biggest hit

FANORAK FACT

Leonard Chess had no musical training whatsoever. If he or the label was unsure, the brothers famously adopted their bus stop test. When they had something freshly recorded, they opened the windows and gauged the reaction from the queue at the bus stop. If they were bopping, they knew they had something. The bus stop test was 99 per cent accurate.

of the year. The next release was 'Rollin Stone' backed with 'Walkin' Blues' by Muddy Waters. The Chess brothers proved they meant business by releasing some twenty singles by the end of the year.

Ike Turner was a teenager in 1951 when he recorded 'Rocket 88' in Sam Phillips' studios in Memphis. Phillips hadn't yet properly set up Sun Records, so the single was issued on Chess. The Chess brothers had an agreeable business relationship with Phillips and contacted him to help find more blues acts from the South. Meanwhile, Phillips licensed Howlin' Wolf, Rufus Thomas and Doctor Ross to Chess.

Muddy Waters and Leonard Chess continued to have a great working relationship. Waters tried to convince Chess to let him record with a band. This move brought in the precocious Little Walter, whose microphone blues harmonica phrasing and amplified technique were revolutionary. The dynamic of the label changed when Little Walter plugged his mic into a guitar amp. His virtuosity on harmonica, along with the innovative new sound, has, over time, made him a genre-defining artist. This was a significant moment in the history of blues music, as the harmonica was no longer a bit-part player; it was now a central part of the blues sound.

In 1952, Little Walter had a number 1 hit with the instrumental 'Juke'. Up until then, he had been in Muddy Waters' band. From 1952 to 1958, he had fourteen hit singles with Chess including another number 1 with 'Babe'. He also appeared as a session man on many recordings.

In 1955, Waters introduced the label to a musician from St Louis named Chuck Berry, whose stellar career was launched with the single 'Maybellene'. Sonny Boy Williamson was also signed (on subsidiary Checker Records). Bo Diddley signed in this year, releasing a single with 'Bo Diddley' on one side and 'I'm a Man' on the other, also released on Checker. More names followed to either Chess or their affiliates, including Ike Turner, John Lee Hooker, Fontella Bass, Etta James, Koko Taylor and Little Milton. Willie Dixon was also involved at the label as a bass player, writer and producer. He wrote 'Hoochie Coochie Man', 'I Just Want to Make Love to You' and 'Little Red Rooster' among many others.

The story of Chess and the 'Chess Sound', though, is one of the stripped-down sound of bluesmen escaping from the Mississippi Delta to Chicago. It's also down to two tough, white, Jewish guys, doing business in a rough, Black ghetto. Leonard was the aggressive, more intense, mercurial partner, driven by instinct, who dealt with Muddy Waters and Etta James. Philip was the more sensitive brother, less uptight, who dealt with the doo-wop bands. Philip focused more on the jazz side whereas Leonard did the blues. Philip was happier to run the business side from the office and Leonard was more at home with his acts in the studio.

The blues aficionados loved the authenticity of the Chess sound. The reality is that the Chess brothers wouldn't pay for anything fancy. In the case of Muddy Waters' 'Rolling Stone', the benchmark bombast and booming echo effect was due to the strategic placing of a mic rigged at one end of the sewer pipe with an enormous speaker at the other.

They were hard-nosed businessmen and the sound held in such high regard by so many influential acts through the decades occurred because Leonard Chess wanted it cheaply recorded: a basic, simple, effective sound. Their approach was to capture the strained aggression, heartache and anger and to get it down on tape, mastered and out to radio stations to play it. Then, they would sell it to their willing Black audience. However, in common with Blue Note, Verve and Atlantic, Chess made sure the artists were paid.

Few labels have had such reach and influence as Chess Records. The Rolling Stones, Led Zeppelin, The Yardbirds and The Kinks all are indebted to Chess. Chess Records is the reason the Rolling Stones exist. A teenage Keith Richards approached Mick Jagger at Dartford railway station because he was carrying Chess LPs. The Rolling Stones' influence and debt of gratitude extended to naming a song in honour of the label's address at the time, '2120 South Michigan Avenue', an instrumental that appeared on 5 by 5, their second EP.

In 1969, Philip and Leonard Chess sold the label to General Recorded Tape (GRT), which paid the brothers $6 million for the company. Leonard Chess died shortly after the deal went through; Philip lived until October 2016, dying at the age of 95. Chess is significant for the sound it delivered and the staggering number of greats who appeared on the label. Marshall Chess, Leonard's son, ran the company briefly as vice-chairman before founding Rolling Stones Records.

There are many great, personal moments and artists from which to choose, beginning with Gene Ammons on sax, who, as the label's first release, delivered a hit between jail sentences for narcotics. Ammons was an incredibly significant talent known for his harmonic substitutions, Lester Young influences and great fluidity of expression. Before his premature death from cancer aged 49, he had evolved into a chirpy jazz funk fusion cat on the release of 1970's *Brother Jug!* (Prestige), another one recorded at Rudy Van Gelder's studio at Englewood Cliffs, New Jersey.

Chess produced post-war blues and R&B stars who changed the world. Imagine being a teenager in 1956 and hearing Howlin' Wolf's 'Smoke Stack Lightning' for the first time. My favourite Chess artist was Koko Taylor. Her voice is drenched in something magically luxuriant, part Ella Fitzgerald, part Etta James, part dynamite. Koko brings the depth of expression, anger and frustration that can only emanate from the blues. For the sound of the genre personified, listen to the depth and power of her singing on 'Wang Dang Doodle'.

The label ceased to exist in 1975, though the music lived on. In the 1980s, Marshall Chess noticed the back catalogue was being ignored and approached All Platinum to reissue it. When All Platinum went bust, Chess was acquired by MCA Records, which merged into Universal Music imprint Geffen Records and was owned by the Universal Music Group. The Chess brothers were inducted into the Blues Hall of Fame in 1995.

PLAYLIST: MY TOP 5 ALBUMS

Muddy Waters: *Folk Singer*
Koko Taylor: *What It Takes: The Chess Years*
Chuck Berry: *Greatest Hits*
Gene Ammons: *Soulful Saxophone*
John Lee Hooker: *Plays and Sings the Blues*

COLUMBIA RECORDS

Founder: Edward Easton

Influential: Bruce Springsteen, Leonard Cohen, Bob Dylan

TODAY, WHEN WE PICK up a smartphone to record a voice memo or leave a message, we do something Thomas Edison set in place in 1887. While he was working on the telegraph messaging system, it occurred to him to transcribe sounds onto a cylinder wrapped in tinfoil. From that, the patent for the phonograph was issued in 1878. It was in this era that the Columbia Phonograph Company and the American Graphophone Company evolved into Columbia Records.

The Columbia Phonograph Company was founded in 1889 by stenographer and lawyer Edward Denison Easton, originally to sell Edison phonographs and its phonograph cylinders. He and a group of investors concentrated on the Washington DC, Maryland and Delaware areas. The company was named after the area where it was based, the District of Columbia, in Washington DC.

These businesses had to adapt to advances in technology, the rapid growth of commercial radio stations and the widespread availability of radios – nearly 3 million in the early 1920s. They also suffered the loss in phonograph sales that radio's popularity created, all the while contending with the Wall Street Crash and the Great Depression, and bookended by two world wars. Columbia is the longest-surviving record label in the music industry and has had many firsts and so many great artists.

The company immediately recognised its artists and realised that the music only sounded as good as the engineers and technology they had. Behind the scenes, its engineers worked on innovative electrical microphones which opened up recording, taking the process to another sonic level. Suddenly, instead of being limited to recording tight vocal groups, they were able to expand. Now they were recording orchestras and vocal choirs while maintaining a subtle, clear sound. In 1925, Columbia released a choir of 850 Associated Glee Clubs of America singing 'Adeste Fideles' at the Metropolitan Opera House. With this ambitious event, the label proved it had the knowledge, skill, commercial capability and technology to recreate high-quality recordings.

Then the music started to swing. From the 1920s, Al Jonson's 'Swanee', Bessie Smith's 'Downhearted Blues', Louis Armstrong's 'St. Louis Blues' and Ethel Waters' 'Dinah' set the bar high. Duke Ellington and his orchestra, the Washingtonians, recorded their first song for Columbia in 1927. They were popular due to appearances on a popular weekly radio show from Harlem's Cotton Club. Ellington would record for Columbia and its subsidiaries for the next thirty years.

Ragtime and Sousa marches ushered in the 1930s. Then, there was the 'king of swing', Benny Goodman. The clarinettist, composer and renowned band leader was one of eleven children born to Russian immigrants. He was, in the vein of many bandleaders of the era, something of a champion of civil rights, breaking taboos by allowing Black and white performers to play together in the deeply segregated and racist south.

When Louis Sterling decided to merge Columbia Gramophone Ltd, the Columbia operation in the UK, with RCA Victor-owned HMV Gramophone Ltd, he created the biggest record conglomerate in the world – Electrical and Musical Industries Ltd, EMI. This made RCA Victor part owner of American Columbia.

In 1938, Alex Steinweiss, a graphic designer, effectively invented the record album sleeve by creating the first illustrated 78rpm record cover. In 1953, he would do the same for the 33⅓rpm album sleeve. Until then, artists had a brief line or two on the cover of their sheet music. With Steinweiss, both the album sleeve design

FANORAK FACT

Doris Day's 'Secret Love' from the film *Calamity Jane* won an Academy Award for Best Original Song; the song reached number 1 on the *Billboard* chart in 1954.

and packaging changed. He was responsible for placing the discs inside a folded cardboard sleeve with artwork on the front and notes on the back, which would soon become industry standard. He was famous for his personal lettering style, 'The Steinweiss scrawl'.

Record label fans adore Columbia. There's nothing more aesthetically pleasing than looking at each of Columbia's vinyl release logos, from the sixteenth note semiquavers of the famous 'Magic Notes' releases and the 'Columbia six-eye', to the 'Walking Eye', not to forget the red label in the 1950s and the CBS logo outside the USA.

In 1943, Frank Sinatra signed for Columbia. Originally, he was the heartthrob pop idol of the day, delivering hit after hit. Sinatra had seventeen Top 10 chart hits from 1943 to 1946. The Bobbysoxers made a megastar out of Sinatra, but the end of the war saw the return of GIs and a change in tastes. Sinatra's popularity waned; he was reluctant to release the novelty material Columbia pushed upon him and was dropped.

Nathan Milstein, performing one of the most famous violin pieces, Mendelssohn's Violin Concerto in E minor with the New York Philharmonic in June 1948, was Columbia's first LP release. This was followed by one of the first musicals on LP, *South Pacific*. The album's sales made Columbia the main Broadway cast recording label. One of my favourites is *West Side Story*, another of those musicals that remind you of wet Sunday afternoons and BBC 1 film matinees. It's Bernstein and Sondheim at their best. The Columbia cast album was number 1 on the *Billboard* chart for fifty-four weeks.

The label released Edith Piaf's 'La Vie en Rose' in 1950, selling a million copies in the USA. Then in 1954, Doris Day had a hit with 'Secret Love'. March 1957 brought Miles Davis to CBS with the release of *'Round About Midnight*. Originally, the album was regarded as mediocre at best. Yet over the years, it has become rightly viewed as a masterpiece of the hard bop genre and one of the finest jazz records of all time.

FANORAK FACT

Until 1948, when Peter Carl Goldmark of Columbia Records created the LP, music was recorded on shellac. Shellac is a resin secreted by the female lac bug and found on trees in India and Thailand.

More classics such as *Milestones*, *Kind of Blue* and *Sketches of Spain* would follow, defining Davis and the label. The 1950s would also see the release of Duke Ellington's *Ellington at Newport*. This album is considered a significant moment in jazz due to the spectacular and electrifying performance of the band. It also revitalised Ellington's faltering career.

In 1960, Clive Davis joined Columbia and by 1966 had become general manager. The same decade saw Bob Dylan, Simon and Garfunkel, Johnny Cash and Barbra Streisand sign for Columbia. In 1968, CBS and Sony joined forces.

Flicking through vinyl from Columbia and CBS is like curating a history of music from Benny Goodman to Beyoncé, Louis Armstrong to Adele. There are just so many great names, including (apart from all those already mentioned) The Byrds, The Clash and AC/DC. You get the impression that those in charge at Columbia, CBS and Sony, across the decades, knew what they were doing. As a label, CBS was always a good example of big business doing its job well.

Columbia evolved from reverential jazz label into country, classical, folk, rock and pop. Currently, acts like The Vaccines, Civil Wars, First Aid Kit and George Ezra coexist with experienced acts like Dylan, Springsteen, Depeche Mode, Neil Diamond and The Foo Fighters. The label is part of the Sony Music Entertainment Group.

PLAYLIST: MY TOP 5 ALBUMS

Leonard Bernstein/Sondheim/Laurents: *West Side Story*
Duke Ellington: *Ellington at Newport*
Bob Dylan: *Blonde on Blonde*
The Byrds: *Younger Than Yesterday*
Miles Davis: *Kind of Blue*

CREATION RECORDS

Founders: Alan McGee, Joe Foster and Dick Green

Influential: Oasis, The Jesus and Mary Chain, Primal Scream

I BLAME KOJAK FOR Creation Records. Anyone of a certain vintage, able to recall the show, will be familiar with the opening credits. It featured early 1970s shots of New York – the pre-gentrified streets of pimps and hookers, the same streets shared with The Velvet Underground. There has to be a reason why so many Glaswegian musicians looked across the Atlantic and fell in love with The Velvet Underground. The opening credits to Kojak are as good a reason as any. Maybe it was Lou Reed's sunglasses? At the time, before New York underwent urban regeneration, the city and Reed shared an equally dystopian, ferociously bleak cityscape and a penchant for cool shades.

To fully understand the fraught narrative of Creation Records is to understand The Velvet Underground. It's also about Syd Barrett, 1960s garage psychedelia, The Beatles, Big Star, The Clash, Joy Division and The Jam. It's also to appreciate a dysfunctional creative phenomenon, one of unbelievable highs and devastating, bitter lows. It's about one man's intuition for music and a journey that took him from Mount Florida in Glasgow to the centre of government and Downing Street.

Creation was a label built by music fans, musicians and outsiders, not businessmen. Alan McGee formed Creation (named after one of his favourite 1960s bands), with Dick Green and Joe Foster, in 1983. The seeds of the Creation story, in truth, began in Glasgow back in 1978, when two school friends, Alan McGee and Bobby Gillespie, formed a band called The Drains and recruited guitarist Andrew Innes (Gillespie and Innes would go on to form Primal Scream).

McGee and Innes ventured to London and, after briefly being in H2o, formed The Laughing Apple. They released three singles between 1981 and 1982: two on the Autonomy label and one on their label, called Essential. It was at this moment that McGee cut his teeth, getting a taste of the whole process, from the manufacturing to the promoting and selling of records, and realised he could do it. Something must have clicked: he quit his job at British Rail, formed a band called Biff Bang Pow (a song by The Creation), started running club nights for fans of 1960s psychedelia and set up Creation Records.

He found himself in the middle of it, a Svengali, a mover and shaker, akin to Malcolm McLaren or Kim Fowley. As Bruce Pavitt did with Sub Pop (see Sub Pop), McGee started Creation with a fanzine: his was called *Communication Blur*. He then ran a night called 'The Communication Club' before establishing The Living Room on Tottenham Court Road. These small nights showcased indie bands, interspersed with 1960s garage punk. Anything that was an antidote to the synth-pop prevalent at the time was the order of the day.

The events brought together like-minded outsiders who loved this music. At the same time, McGee placed an ad in *Melody Maker* looking for bands with 'perfect pop songs who hated the current pop scene'. It was with the money made from these nights, and with a loan for £1,000, that he launched Creation. McGee sensed there was a burgeoning scene for discerning, independent music fans. For the bands, it would provide a platform and the thrill of having their work released on vinyl. The first releases featured regular performers at The Living Room.

Let me tell you about someone I know called Nick Low. He's a quiet, unassuming guy, a radio producer, and is accidentally responsible for one of Creation Records' most influential bands, The Jesus and Mary Chain. I know Nick both from my days in bands and from his work as a successful independent producer for BBC Scotland. He set up an indie label called NoStrings Records and launched the careers of Del Amitri and Kevin McDermott. Like a *Zelig* figure, he quietly hung around while these great events took place around him. He, along with Stephen Pastel, ran a night called the *Candy Club*. If it wasn't for him, it's likely The Jesus and Mary Chain (or The Daisy Chain then) would still be in a bedroom in East Kilbride fighting with each other.

They gave Nick a demo (on the other side were obscure Syd Barrett songs), but Nick knew the band were the wrong fit for him:

> They handed me their demo at the Candy Club and it wasn't for NoStrings Records but I thought Alan McGee might like it and they were looking for a drummer. I gave it to Bobby to give to Alan. Had the Mary Chain been on NoStrings I fear they would have disappeared without a trace – I believe they needed the Alan McGee chutzpah, he could take that rawness, chaos and energy and really market it. I feel McGee is a huge part of their initial success.

Nick was mates with Andrew Innes from school and he came around with Bobby Gillespie to visit. He was just starting Primal Scream and gave him the demo of the Mary Chain for McGee and told him there was some great Syd Barrett stuff on the other side too, if he didn't like the band. Gillespie loved the Mary Chain and was hooked. He couldn't stop listening to the band, rang them and pleaded with McGee to get them out of East Kilbride to London and play The Living Room – which at the time was above the Roebuck pub.

Originally based upstairs in the living room of the Adams Arms pub on Conway Street (now The Lukin), The Living Room moved to above the Roebuck (now The Court) at 108 Tottenham Court Road. The first Creation album (CRE LP 001) was released in August 1984 and was a live compilation from the Adams Arms days called *Alive in the Living Room* and included, The Television Personalities, The Pastels, The Loft, Three Johns, Mekons, The June Brides, The Jasmine Minks, Alternative TV and The Legend!

It was at this same gig in 1984 that Alan McGee signed them at the soundcheck. He was captivated while watching them and immediately felt the tension between the brothers. It was the familiar sibling rivalry, central to some of the best artists, that can either unite or destroy but makes them special; artists capable of awe-inspiring

FANORAK FACT

The feedback that propelled The Jesus and Mary Chain's sound was accidental, caused by the low ceiling and vocal PA with one microphone at their soundcheck at The Living Room.

rock 'n' roll but who can easily self-destruct. The Kinks, The Everly Brothers, the Bee Gees, Creedence Clearwater Revival. It was the same friction and sibling rivalry at the centre of The Jesus and Mary Chain that later drew McGee to Oasis. He recognised their influences, the groups and classic rock 'n' roll moments that inspired them. The Jesus and Mary Chain were The Velvet Underground and Suicide. The music? It was a weird lovechild of The Beach Boys and The Ronettes, delivering barbed-wire candyfloss in a wall of high-octane chaos, leather trousers and sunglasses.

Later, with Oasis, he'd appropriate the mod look: feathered Paul Weller haircuts, the fashion of the street; the same mainstream pop culture and the melodic well-trodden path built by The Beatles, The Kinks, Bowie, Slade, The Jam and The Stone Roses. With both Oasis and The Jesus and Mary Chain, the unpredictability was the attraction. Central to the notoriety of both bands was that they stood out musically from their contemporaries. The Jesus and Mary Chain were up against synth pop, while Oasis delivered nonchalant guitar anthems at a time when acid house and techno were de rigueur.

Creation's implausible triumphs and frenzied failures reflected McGee's nature. He was a stubborn nonconformist who survived on raw instinct. Life was a whirling, unbridled state of pandemonium. The label was run like a bad soap opera and the drama was toxic; funds were always low and drugs ubiquitous. It was *Coronation Street* on crack, *EastEnders* on ecstasy.

By the 1990s, Creation had a wealth of critical acclaim based on albums like Primal Scream's *Screamadelica* and Teenage Fanclub's *Bandwagonesque*. They weren't making significant amounts of cash. Primal Scream took six years to have a hit. By 1991, when the cost of producing My Bloody Valentine's *Loveless* almost bankrupted the label, McGee had decided to sell to Sony.

Like the best soaps, when scriptwriters run out of ideas, someone wins the lottery. In Creation's case, on 31 May 1993, an unsigned band from Manchester was playing at King Tut's Wah Wah Hut on St. Vincent Street in Glasgow. They were called Oasis and would turn around the label's fortunes. I should add that I was standing beside McGee while he watched this band. I'd love to say I thought they were the future of rock 'n' roll. They were okay, loud for a support act with a great sound. Alan McGee was bouncing up and down with excitement. He saw something in the chemistry, the enigmatic frontman, the look and the songs. In June 2013, McGee told the *Daily Record*:

> The music business had already passed on Oasis by this point. They had done a gig at *In The City* showcase in Manchester that year. Noel and Liam had a tiff on stage, so nobody had bothered to check out if they were any good. Six months later, I get the opening times for King Tut's wrong and happen to see them play four songs in Glasgow. It's like it was meant to be. It was that random. It was a bit like walking to a bus stop and discovering Elvis Presley.

With their eventual manager, Marcus Russell (who managed Johnny Marr and Bernard Sumner), Alan McGee was able to gain the band's trust and mentor them. I've always had a special relationship with Oasis and Creation, simply because I was there the evening they were signed. It is beyond belief how McGee looked at the band we both watched and for it to turn out as it did.

After their first two albums and the Britpop stand-off with Blur, everything changed for the label. Despite Oasis's achievements, Creation was cracking under the strain, with reports in the music press of a culture of jealousy, infighting, rival factions and bitterness.

The label shut down in November 1999. There were heady moments on the journey: Primal Scream's *Screamadelica,* Teenage Fanclub's *Bandwagonesque* and Sugar's *Copper Blue*; Britpop, McGee and Noel Gallagher in Downing Street, Oasis at Knebworth; honourable mentions in despatches for BMX Bandits' *Life Goes On,* Super Furry Animals' *Fuzzy Logic* and Arnold's *Hillside* album.

From CRE001 The Legend!'s '73 in 83' to CRE333 Primal Scream's 'Acclrtr', from the first single to the last, Creation delivered on its own terms. In the beginning, it merged punk and psychedelia, then evolved through acid house and into mainstream stadium anthems with Oasis. Whether it was cranking it up a level while managing The Jesus and Mary Chain or his sheer unbridled enthusiasm for the early bands on his roster, like The Pastels, Jasmine Minks and Television Personalities – or finding and launching Oasis – McGee's ethos for the label was always consistent. Creation had to be a label of punk rock spirit with the melodies of 1960s psychedelic pop.

If you look at any record label's singles release schedule, it's always an accurate indicator and guide to the quality of artists. For Creation, there's one intense period with releases by Swervedriver, The Cramps, BMX Bandits, Oasis ('Shakermaker'), Primal Scream, Ride, Oasis ('Live Forever'), Sugar, the Boo Radleys and 18 Wheeler. The Verve were telling lies; the drugs clearly did work.

Alan McGee set up the label Poptones in 1999 and wound it down around 2007. He now lives in Wales, runs a label from home called 359 Music and finally appears happy in his skin. He relaunched Creation Management with business partner Simon Fletcher in 2014 and looks after The Jesus and Mary Chain, Wilko Johnson (before his death in November 2022), the Happy Mondays and Cast. You get the feeling there's more to come. The wonderfully tasteful Joe Foster runs Rev-Ola Records, and Dick Green, Wichita Recordings. Dave E. Barker, who set up Glass Records before setting up Paperhouse for Fire Records, joined Creation and in 2015 resurrected Glass Modern.

Today, Alan McGee is a millionaire many times over and has survived – just. At one point in 1994, he reached his low after ingesting a colossal line of coke before flying to the USA. Speaking to Lisa Higgins of the *Mirror* in January 2014, McGee said:

> I knew when the guys in orange jumpsuits were putting the oxygen mask on me and carrying me out that I'd f***ed up. They measured my blood pressure and decided my life was at risk. They thought I might be having a heart attack. They were really worried that I was going to die.

Creation sold over 54 million records before selling to Sony for £30 million in 1999. It remains the benchmark for any music fan in how far you can take your love of music, with some raw ambition and a £1,000 loan. Oh, and the gift for a sarcastic quote to whip up the press, boundless enthusiasm, crazy inventiveness and a keen understanding of what the public wants – well before the public knows. However, according to Noel Gallagher of Oasis, knowing how to handle artists was perhaps Alan McGee's best attribute. On the front of McGee's book *Creation Stories: Riots, Raves and Running a Label* (Pan Macmillan, 2014) Gallagher was unequivocal: 'McGee is a true believer in the power of music and more importantly a believer in the people that make music. He gave me, and many more like me, a chance to change my life.'

On the band that changed his label's fortunes and his own life, McGee vividly remembers the moment he saw Oasis. Speaking to the *Daily Record*'s John Dingwall in November 2013, he said:

> I could hear all these Manc accents arguing. I looked over and saw Liam Gallagher for the first time. He looked amazing. A proper, Adidased-up mod. He had hair like a young Paul Weller. And I thought, 'He's got to be the drug dealer.' Because nobody in a band looks that good.

On the alleged suspicion around his random showing up at the venue on that Bank Holiday in May, Alan McGee is still amazed: 'People don't like to believe in luck – they assume it's too much of a coincidence, that Sony sent me to the gig on a tip, but I really thought I was just going to surprise my mate.' I believe him. I saw his face and reaction. I was there too.

PLAYLIST: MY TOP 5 ALBUMS

My Bloody Valentine: *Loveless*
Teenage Fanclub: *Bandwagonesque*
Primal Scream: *Screamadelica*
Ride: *Going Blank Again*
Sugar: *Copper Blue*

DEF JAM RECORDINGS

Founders: Rick Rubin and Russell Simmons

Influential: Public Enemy, Run DMC, Beastie Boys

NEW YORK'S INFLUENTIAL RAP and hip-hop label was set up by Rick Rubin in 1984. The label, which would go on to become a global phenomenon, was started in Rubin's New York University dorm room with a loan from his parents. Its fortunes changed when Rubin, aged 21, a former punk rocker from Long Island, teamed up with Russell Simmons, a manager and promoter, to start hip-hop's worldwide revolution.

In keeping with most of our label stories, there's an auspicious moment – Def Jam's occurred by accident – at a party. The hip-hop artist DJ Jazzy Jay went to a party with his pal, Russell Simmons. Simmons was managing rapper Kurtis Blow and his brother's band Run-DMC. Jazzy Jay had released a song with T La Rock called 'It's Yours' on Rubin's label, Def Jam. He loved the sound of it and was desperate to meet and talk to the producer. He was expecting to meet a Black producer and met an amiable, long-haired, white punk rock fan. They hit it off and when Simmons brought his business acumen to Rubin's small label, everything changed.

From a business perspective, Def Jam identified its audience and within a few years the label found a winning formula, shape and identity. In James Todd Smith (LL Cool J), they had the label's heartthrob. With the Beastie Boys, they had frat rock chaos and monster riffs, and with Public Enemy, the controversial sound of an act that vocalised the sentiment held by a vast majority of young, angry, African Americans.

Def Jam Recordings, like most fledgling indie labels, started with guys who were music fans who had a sixth sense, a feeling something was brewing. Like the real nonconformists of pop, Malcolm McLaren, Seymour Stein and Alan McGee, they sensed there was something in the water and change was afoot. As with punk, new wave and then Britpop, the signs were there if you were attuned to the moves and trends on the streets and at the edges of the counterculture.

The label found itself perfectly aligned with the sound and attitude emerging from the downtown New York art, punk and club scene. When this merged with the embryonic sound of hip-hop and the attitude of the South Bronx streets, Simmons knew it was on the verge of going from a local scene to a major movement. He had watched the fashion on the street and the sound in the clubs evolve. After years of being ignored, hip-hop was moving out of the fringes and gate-crashing the mainstream.

Def Jam, simply by its timing, belonged to a bizarre and complex era of acquisitions and mergers in the music industry. Giant companies such as Seagram, a Canadian beverages conglomerate, fancied some music business action. It made inroads into becoming a media empire, with deals to take over MCA and Universal Studios. It bought PolyGram from Philips for $10 billion. Then, Seagram was bought out by Vivendi, a French multimedia conglomerate, for $33 billion. The actions rippled down the food chain and many bands were unsympathetically dumped when accountants trawled through the spreadsheets.

Def Jam worked well for several reasons. Timing was critical, as was a supremely talented producer with an attuned ear and a clear notion of the sound required. Crucially, Simmons had a great business mind and was already managing and promoting acts. He had street smarts and had put on block parties and understood what was emerging musically. This gave Def Jam an edge. Later, in interviews, Simmons claimed he had learned the basic business principles of supply and demand, markup, profit and distribution as a former small-time drug dealer. This was a business built from the street into a global brand.

But the perennial problem that strikes most ambitious labels is cash flow. How do you attract those bands you want to sign? Cash is king.

When the margins are stretched, you are left vulnerable to cashflow problems. So when Def Jam signed a distribution deal with CBS, it could attract talent.

It started with LL Cool J, and the 17-year-old didn't disappoint. His first single, 'I Need a Beat', sold a million. LL Cool J, the Beastie Boys and Public Enemy would become influential figures in hip-hop. (The Beastie Boys left in 1987, signing to Capitol and setting up their own label, Grand Royal.) Def Jam housed hip-hop and dance superstars like Jay Z, Rihanna, Ja Rule, Kanye West and Method Man & Redman. But you readily identified with and immediately recognised aspects of the Def Jam punk rock attitude as much as their Led Zeppelin and James Brown drum loops.

I've always been fond of Def Jam because of its motto 'Respecting DJs since 1984'. I was a DJ and got their attitude. Admittedly, my DJ-ing didn't involve decks or the ghetto. Any US sounds would be 1960s psyche, garage punk, Pebbles' compilations, The Seeds, Big Star, The Byrds, Gene Clark, Love, Buffalo Springfield, Tim Buckley, The Chocolate Watchband, Lee Hazelwood, The Buckle and The Dovers, then a nod to Motown and Northern Soul.

Rubin was becoming an in-demand producer, and with his popularity growing, he started more independent production work. In 1987, he produced The Cult's classic, *Electric*, giving them a sparse, raw, sound. The only remnant of any hip-hop was the thundering bass drum sound. This signalled a change of direction for both the band and himself. It was Rubin's first non-hip-hop album. He would, over the next thirty years, go on to reinvent many top names of popular culture. When The Cult approached him, he was still living in his NYU dorm room and far from acting the hotshot producer.

In 1991, Kurt Cobain said, 'Rap music is the only vital form of music introduced since punk rock.' It's easy to draw parallels. A new generation of disenfranchised, disaffected youth. An underground genre from the periphery, smashing into the mainstream while changing the game as it

FANORAK FACT

Rick Rubin was in a high-school punk band called The Pricks. At university he befriended Jazzy Jay, who taught him some basic hip-hop production tips.

seeks a voice to express itself. As a fledgling producer, Rubin loved confrontation and punk. Nirvana were excited to be sharing the bill at Reading in 1992 with Public Enemy.

The history of Def Jam Recordings is astonishing. It's the multi-conglomerate started from college digs. It's Apple or Facebook, something making it big through passion and drive. *Forbes Magazine* loved Simmons. Def Jam Recordings kicked off, or at least helped solidify and highlight, a sub-genre in hip-hop. If the music was game-changing, Def Jam's importance was also about identity. Now young, Black, urban America had a voice, one of creativity and entrepreneurship, one presented positively to the world.

In an interview with *The Guardian*'s Gareth Grundy in 2011, Russell Simmons stated: 'Without hip-hop, we wouldn't have had Obama.' He was also convinced, in the same interview, that white kids loved hip-hop: 'It's not just black kids. White kids who grew up on hip-hop have progressive politics. Hip-hop influenced a generation who helped put Obama in the White House.'

In November 2017, Russell Simmons was accused of over a dozen cases of sexual assault or sexual misconduct. He admitted being inappropriate and apologised but vehemently denied all allegations of rape, telling the *New York Times*, 'These horrific accusations have shocked me to my core and all of my relations have been consensual.' He stepped away from his business interests and has since kept a low profile.

The label became a more commercial mainstream label when Jay Z was appointed CEO in 2004, bringing Rihanna and Kanye West to the party. But for me, it was all about the formation of the label – a white punk and heavy metal fan and a Black rap fan from the streets setting in place an influential and unparalleled label, from nothing. As part of the merger between MCA and PolyGram, the Island Def Jam Music Group was created to house over fourteen labels. In 2014, it was announced that IDJMG would be split into

> **FANORAK FACT**
>
> The engineer on The Cult's *Electric* was Andy Wallace, who four years later would mix *Nevermind* by Nirvana.

three individual entities, Def Jam Recordings, Island Records and Motown Records.

Simmons, until late 2017, was a high-profile, inspirational business-man, entrepreneur and philanthropist. Rubin formed a new label, Def America, later changing the name to American Recordings, and produced Tom Petty, Johnny Cash, Neil Diamond and Neil Young. In 2007, he was named co-president of Columbia Records, and in 2012, he won a Grammy for album of the year with Adele's *21*.

PLAYLIST: MY TOP 5 ALBUMS

Public Enemy: *It Takes a Nation of Millions to Hold Us Back*
The Roots: *Then Shoot Your Cousin*
Public Enemy: *Fear of a Black Planet*
Beastie Boys: *License to Ill*
Method Man & Redman: *Blackout!*

DERAM

Founders: Deram was part of Decca

Influential: David Bowie, Cat Stevens

INITIALLY, DERAM WAS SET up as an outlet for artists who would showcase Decca scientists' Deramic Sound. Formed in London in 1966, it quickly evolved from an out-there prog imprint into a happening home for exciting artists. Deram became Decca's cool subsidiary and arguably found a fruitful niche by accident. The label had an unintentional elegance, capturing the beat, vibrancy and fresh optimism of a happening London sound. It also quickly became a costly incubator label from which most of the artists moved on and became stars elsewhere.

Decca engineers worked tirelessly, investigating ways to give more space, to broaden and soften the sound of recording tracks, to combat the limitations of four-track reel-to-reel tapes (machines widely used by most professional studios at the time). To boil down some extremely complex physics, Decca scientists and engineers took two four-track recorders and doubled-up stereo tracks. Recordings had to be mixed to the left, centre or the right-hand side. Previously, instruments had been placed at specific points in the stereo field.

Thanks to the work of Decca engineers, a more natural, panoramic stereo spread was produced, called Decca Panoramic Sound, subsequently shortened to Deramic, then to Deram. Their research was happening at a time of rapid advances in the field and the system quickly became obsolete due to the widespread commercial availability of eight-track recording consoles.

In between releasing singles from emerging talent, Deram issued a series of easy-listening orchestral albums in 1967 to demonstrate the stellar work and advances in its panoramic stereo sound. Despite the quality of the sound being bright, powerful and clear, the subject matter was unexciting.

However, Deram's star shone briefly from the mid-1960s, augmented by a quirky roster of artists. Among the talent were Cat Stevens, Procol Harum and David Bowie. They would go on to be internationally renowned artists. Bowie, in particular, influenced the music industry like few others.

It was commonplace in the 1960s for major record labels to create subsidiaries for alternative-sounding bands. EMI had Harvest; Philips used Vertigo. Decca created Deram to house their more alternative artists, those the established main brand considered too uncommercial. It would develop artists who didn't fit with the major label philosophy of Decca's chart-topping groups: The Rolling Stones, Small Faces, Them and The Zombies.

From a business point of view, this must have been a frustration. Procol Harum, for example, scored a hit with 'A Whiter Shade of Pale', reaching number 1 in the UK charts and number 5 in the USA. They only released one album and a single before signing to Regal Zonophone in the UK and A&M in the USA. Cat Stevens was another case in point – he had three hit singles on Deram before signing to Island Records and finding global success.

Deram started in 1966, with 'Happy New Year'/ 'Where the Good Times Are', by Beverley, as its first release, a song written by Randy Newman and produced by Danny Cordell. Cat Stevens was the second label release with 'I Love My Dog', which reached number 28 in the charts. Between September and December 1966, Deram released music by David Bowie with 'Rubber Band'/ 'The London Boys', The Move with 'Night of Fear' / 'Disturbance' and Cat Stevens with 'Matthew and Son', which reached number 2 in December.

FANORAK FACT

Deram albums bore a DML prefix for mono and an SML prefix for stereo releases.

David Bowie's self-titled debut was released on Deram on 1 June 1967. However, the label's first album hit was the 1967 album *Days of Future Passed,* by The Moody Blues. Deram's first international best-selling hit single was the quirky and infuriatingly catchy 'I Was Kaiser Bill's Batman', by Whistling Jack Smith.

Despite the Deram roster having a great range of psychedelic, beat and mod bands producing wonderful sounding songs like The Move's 'I Can Hear the Grass Grow', and 'Bend Me, Shape Me', by Amen Corner, the label also suffered collateral damage from a scattergun approach. It released a procession of artists producing great songs that never became hits. The classic Northern Soul favourite from Timebox, 'Girl Don't Make Me Wait', The Syn's 'Created by Clive' b/w 'Grounded', Warm Sounds' 'Birds and Bees', The Eyes of Blue's 'Heart Trouble', The Gibsons' 'The Magic Book', The Quik's 'Bert's Apple Crumble', Tintern Abbey's 'Vacuum Cleaner' and Grapefruit's 'Elevator'.

I was hooked on Deram from an early age because of two bands. My introduction to the label was a mysterious single called 'The Magic Book' by The Gibsons. Written by the top songwriting team Cook and Greenaway, it followed their familiar compositional shape, opening with a killer chorus and hooking you in. It sounded like the theme from a kids' TV show. This single was found discarded and dirty in the bottom of a box at a church fête in Airdrie, in the early 1970s. It was in such bad condition that the friendly woman at the stall gave it to me for free. It was from the Netherlands. Consequently, I always thought the band were Dutch ... I imagined a cool, hip, well-attired, stylish band like The Monkees or The Lovin' Spoonful.

Research threw up a couple of issues. When I finally saw what the band looked like, they were more in keeping with the back four at Feyenoord or Ajax circa season 1969/70. Oh, and more noteworthy, they hailed from Australia. When I hear it, I get goose pimples. It's one of those childhood nostalgia tunes that evokes the same warmth as the theme music to *Trumpton*, *The White Horses*, *The Flashing Blade*, *Banana Splits* or *The Clangers*.

The second was a band called Honeybus. I had heard of their hit, 'I Can't Let Maggie Go', released in 1968, though I became more familiar with them around the winter of 1991. They were a psychedelic/ baroque pop band, regularly mistaken for Badfinger (especially by me) and often compared to The Beatles at the time of *Rubber Soul*. Sadly, they only ever released one album, called *Story*, and if you're lucky enough to have a copy, it's worth a fortune. This was because the band split in 1969. *Story* was released in 1970. With no band to promote it, the album failed to chart. The fact it didn't sell made it highly collectable and rare.

Deram consistently released great artists with powerful, fresh-sounding singles. In the end, though, as a label concept, it was destined to be flawed. It's included to remind us that great music can come from experimentation. With too much focus on the sound and science along with its short-term approach, the business model was wrong. Deram was a one-night stand instead of a meaningful, long-term arrangement. So many great acts fell through its hands. If the label bosses had been as efficient with contracts as the lads in the lab were at pushing the sound barrier, it might have been a different story.

Deram was relaunched with Bananarama, Bronski Beat, Fine Young Cannibals, The Mo-Dettes and Splodgenessabounds in the early 1980s. But returning the label to its heady heights would prove impossible. Deram's trademark was based on artists with phenomenal cutting-edge records. By then, the rest had caught up. It's a reissue label now.

PLAYLIST: MY TOP 5 ALBUMS

David Bowie: *David Bowie*
Honeybus: *Story*
White Plains: *My Baby Loves Lovin'*
The Moody Blues: *Days of Future Passed*
Cat Stevens: *Matthew & Son*

DOMINO RECORDING COMPANY

Founder: Laurence Bell

Influential: Franz Ferdinand, Arctic Monkeys, Hot Chip

I LOVE DOMINO RECORDS for many reasons. It's not just the great music from an interesting and eclectic array of bands; it's the way the company allowed its acts time to develop, taking a long-term view. Many record labels over the past eighty years set out with an artist-led policy. It's so much more difficult to maintain this aspiration when none of your acts are selling and everyone's in the studio recording and you need money fast and, try as you might, the whole lot is going one way.

Domino Records was founded by Laurence Bell, in Putney, south-west London, in 1993. Bell, from an early age, was a passionate pop fan. As a teenager, he started fanzines, was heavily involved with the local music scene, helped bands, booked gigs, did the merchandising and helped local groups release records. He moved into London and, with the same enthusiasm, worked at Tower Records. There, he was spotted by someone at Fire Records and offered a job. He was determined to have a career in the music business.

Domino's initial strategy focused on licence agreements. This made sense from a business perspective as it meant studio and production costs were wiped out. The label's first UK release was the Massachusetts band Sebadoh, featuring the Dinosaur Jr. bassist, Lou Barlow. With the single 'Soul and Fire', from the Sub Pop album *Bubble and Scrape*, Domino introduced the UK to the delights and warmth of melodic lo-fi.

Laurence Bell's story is one of a music-mad aficionado, funded by £5,000 plus £40 a week from the Enterprise Allowance Scheme. He had enthusiasm, a phone, a fax machine and the phone numbers of influential people at labels in the USA who already trusted him, contacts he'd picked up while working at Fire Records. He did it his way and remained true to his original vision of working with bands he loved. His shrewdness, allied with sharp marketing ideas (he called it 'pop terrorism'), allowed a diminutive independent to take on the majors, not only punching above its weight, more like David taking on Goliath and whipping major company ass.

The US bands he'd worked with at Fire Records spoke positively about Domino. The label always paid bands what it promised to pay, when it said it would, the full amount, and on time. Laurence Bell's US connections would deliver artists like Will Oldham and Jim O'Rourke, and it was Oldham and Sebadoh who brought in Bill Callaghan's Smog. Bands remember people who look after them, treat them well and pay them. They tend to talk about agents, bookers, promoters and companies that honour contracts. Bands like to pay the rent and eat. Domino delivered. Bands signed.

FANORAK FACT

Franz Ferdinand and Sparks got together when Alex Kapranos was looking for Huey Lewis's dentist: 'I was in San Francisco, looking for Huey Lewis's dentist,' he said. 'I hear this voice behind me saying, "Alex, is that you?" I turn around and it's Ron and Russell from Sparks.'

Domino expanded its enterprise, licensing Royal Trux, Smog and Will Oldham from US label Drag City. The kinship with Drag City continues. In the mid-1990s, when the world was getting its soiled knickers in a twist over Britpop, as Oasis and Blur were slugging it out in full view of an expectant media, Domino signed The Pastels, Flying Saucer Attack and The Third Eye Foundation.

In 1997, Domino released Pavement's *Brighten the Corners*. It was deemed a return to form by the last great and true independent American underground band and was produced by Mitch Easter, REM's first producer, at his Drive-In Studios in Winston-Salem. Domino released Elliot Smith's third album, *Either/Or*.

This included songs that appeared in the Oscar-winning movie *Good Will Hunting*. Will Oldham as Bonnie Prince Billy released *I See a Darkness*. Oldham's wounded, aching, figurative Appalachian folk is not going to make it onto *X Factor* or a *Top Gear* dad-rock compilation. It was a beautifully crafted, spacious, hypnotically paced narcotic – a delicious depression.

Bell also focused on homegrown acts like Kills, Clinic and Four Tet. Showing wilful disregard for the bottom line, he continued to go against the grain, cherishing and coveting anything that would be eschewed by a mainstream audience. However, in those acts, especially those imported from the USA, he offered something to the independent music lover: a sense of what they craved, something special no one else was interested in.

Independent labels sensed from around 2001 that it was the perfect time for expansion. If you look at the record industry in the 1990s, you have grunge with Nirvana and Pearl Jam, then in 1994, veer into Britpop, with Blur, Oasis and Pulp. By the end of this cycle, and music is always cyclical, you have a ridiculously vacuous era of bad mistakes.

The record industry hadn't had it so good, probably since the 1980s with the advent of CDs, and acts like Dire Straits and Queen selling millions. As former A&R man and now writer John Niven explained in a piece celebrating the twentieth anniversary of Britpop, in the *New Statesman*:

> A decent hit meant you were selling over a million albums at 13 quid a pop. As opposed to today, when you're celebrating doing 100,000 at £7 per unit. We were selling ten times the volume at twice the price. It did not lead to reasonable behaviour or sane decisions.

The music industry continued to lick its wounds from the hubris of Britpop. A time of exuberant advances on many bands who couldn't deliver, followed by humiliating culls as artists were dropped, had made bands wary of the major label route. Artists started to believe independent labels would provide a safer career and a more sympathetic creative platform. Labels such as Domino showed they had the infrastructure and agility required to compete against the majors.

A&R-wise, Laurence Bell took a unique approach, preferring to go on word of mouth and recommendation. He encouraged his bands to perform constantly. Groups like Franz Ferdinand created a scene with their warehouse gigs, starting something themselves. By 2004, Domino had released Franz Ferdinand's self-titled album. It would eventually sell nearly 4 million and win the Mercury Music Award. Further accolades followed, yet Domino refused to rest on its laurels and used Franz Ferdinand's multiplatinum sales to sign Sheffield's Arctic Monkeys.

The Arctic Monkeys played the gig circuit in Sheffield, building up a following, yet remaining relatively unknown outside their home base. Bell loved them and their attitude and the fact they were like a gang. He spent time watching the band perform live, getting to know them before they signed. He preferred artists who were happy playing live, generating a buzz, making it happen; they were perfect for him.

The band were mates and school friends, had great songs and were musically tight. They were acerbic and fed into the same indie seam as The Libertines and The Strokes. What marked them out and made them move so quickly was their use of early social media and peer-to-peer file sharing. They distributed demos they had burned to fans at gigs. The band then actively encouraged fans to upload and share them on the internet; this excitement among the fans created a downloading frenzy. This marketing blitz was the modern incarnation of a 'buzz around a band'.

Instead of live reviews in the music press, referrals from agents to A&R staff, recording demos and meetings in London with record companies, Arctic Monkeys flipped the process of getting a deal on its head. Their approach created an instant fan base. The traditional approach was gone; they had changed how it was done. Bell quickly realised, from the reaction among fans, that the internet was changing the rules for the music business. Everything would culminate in October 2005, when Franz Ferdinand's second album, *You Could Have It So Much Better*, gave the label its first number 1 album and the Arctic Monkeys' 'I Bet You Look Good on the Dancefloor' a number 1 single. Knowing the Arctic Monkeys' album was in the warehouse and the stock ready to go, Laurence Bell brought the release of the album forward by a week and caught the music industry on the hop. *Whatever People Say I Am, That's What I'm Not* broke records for a debut album, selling 363,735 copies in its first week.

Domino left its rivals dumbfounded not only with the sales, but with the sheer momentum and scale of Franz Ferdinand's and Arctic Monkeys' success. The majors knew Domino was able to convince artists that its independent infrastructure was resolute. They also knew the label nurtured its acts, allowing them to take risks, something major labels didn't have the patience for.

Domino Records has offices in Wandsworth, Berlin, Paris and Brooklyn. It owns a publishing arm and a series of labels, including Geographic, an imprint run by Stephen McRobbie and Katrina Mitchell of The Pastels. It releases Maher Shalal Hash Baz, Bill Wells Trio, Future Pilot AKA, International Airport and The Royal We. It has an ongoing reissue catalogue featuring Orange Juice, Joseph K, The Fire Engines, Sebadoh and Young Marble Giants. It has also invested in the latest crop of US talent, like Animal Collective, Dirty Projectors and Real Estate.

In 2012, Domino (Geographic) released Lightships, the then side project of bassist, songwriter and founder of Teenage Fanclub, Gerard Love. (Love announced in August 2018 that he would leave the group at the end of the year.) The Domino roster includes Robert Wyatt, Hot Chip and King Creosote.

From the start, Domino approached the business with the long view. Most bands are slowly nurtured, with passion, a minimum of fuss; the approach is kept simple, and the artists are allowed to develop. The music is made with care and love, and ultimately, the results yield a bumper musical crop. Profits are reinvested in artists and the process begins again. The future looks bright for a label that started out with nothing more than a contact book, avoided genres and refused to be pigeon-holed. With Anna Calvi, Franz Ferdinand, Arctic Monkeys and The Kills, Domino Records is pushing the boundaries as a leading independent record label in the UK.

Laurence Bell and his label continue to outgun and outthink the majors with a unique and idiosyncratic approach. One of its signings, the Isle of Wight's Wet Leg, have already scooped two Grammys and won two Brit awards. A run of hit singles including 'Ur Mum' and 'Chaise Lounge' and a hugely popular eponymous debut album witnessed Wet Leg enter the UK and Australian album charts at number 1 and the US *Billboard* album chart at 14.

PLAYLIST: MY TOP 5 ALBUMS

Pavement: *Crooked Rain Crooked Rain*
The Pastels: *Mobile Safari*
Animal Collective: *Honeycomb/Gotham*
Lightships: *Electric Cables*
Franz Ferdinand: *You Could Have It So Much Better*

ELEKTRA RECORDS

Founders: Jac Holzman and Paul Rickolt

Influential: Love, The Stooges, The Doors, MC5

DISCUSSING ELEKTRA MAY DEVELOP into a sustained dramatic piece. One of revenge, a tale of unspeakable vengeance and torment rained upon people I once called friends. Sometimes I have an Elektra night. Don't get too alarmed, it's not some weird book club night where we discuss the Greek classic, *Electra*. (Jac Holzman loved the name and gave Electra the 'k' to make it sound harder.) No, my Elektra nights are far less bloodthirsty. I would play music from the label all evening.

As time passes by, I'm finding it more difficult. Of all the albums I've loaned out and never had returned, most were on Elektra. As much as it's an irritation to a record collector and music fan, it's the ultimate compliment too. It means people have enjoyed the albums so much that they deliberately avoid your phone calls, for fear of an updated version of the Greek tragedy.

Elektra was founded in 1950 by Jac Holzman and Paul Rickolt at St John's College, Annapolis, Maryland. They were into folk, classical and baroque. Holzman's taste was more scholarly and this is reflected in his approach. He began releasing folk music out of his college dorm room and hence the label was born, admittedly a tiny one, but a label, nonetheless.

It's difficult to play an album from Elektra's roster of acts and not be inspired. There is a fascination and allure to the label and this era, starting with folk music, then moving into the psychedelic pop and baroque of the mid-to-late 1960s. Jac Holzman had an unambiguous vision: he had to love the artist, or he wouldn't sign them. The bands and artists the label had at its peak – Love, The Doors, The Stooges, MC5 and Tim Buckley – have been influential and still hold sway today.

Holzman's first release on Elektra was with John Gruen orchestrating and Georgiana Bannister singing German poetry. Holzman had pressed 500 copies of the LP but sold just over a hundred. In October 2020, the 89-year-old admitted in a *Rolling Stone* interview, it didn't go too well: 'It was a mess, and I was very discouraged,' Holzman says. 'The repertoire wasn't right, and I didn't know how to connect it with people.'

Undaunted, Holzman refocused and continued. It was a great time to start a label. In the 1950s, the LP record format was breaking through and FM radio was increasing in popularity (invented by Edwin Armstrong in 1933; licences were granted in 1940 and took off over the next decade).

For Holzman, the parts were falling into place. Sensing a profitable future could be developed, he dropped out of college, returned to New York and focused entirely on the nascent enterprise. The exciting and diverse artists – the coolest of the day – with elegantly designed, eye-catching sleeves? Well, those would have to wait. It wasn't all cool and hip; not at the beginning. Before establishing the brand and reaching the point when he signed acts he loved, things were more pragmatic. At first, Holzman focused on generating cash, stumbling upon an unusual income stream. He found a sizeable and lucrative market releasing albums featuring songs by the armed services, which sold well.

In 1958, he released an album entitled *The Wild Blue Yonder ... Songs of a Fighting Air Force*. He quickly moved on to find hits in other areas of the military. Another popular seller was an innovative series of sound-effects albums: 1960 witnessed the release of the first in a series of thirteen albums called ... *Authentic Sound Effects Vol. 1: Sound Effects*. Here you were able to listen to meticulously accurate recordings of a car door closing, a lawnmower (handheld) or, my favourite, a passing marching band. The records were popular with the punters at home but more so with radio, TV and filmmakers who saved on expensive recording sessions and overdubs. Holzman and Elektra loved the album series as they profited financially by not having to pay performers' royalties.

Into the early 1960s, the label expanded with folk artists Josh White, Jean Ritchie's Appalachian folk and the lucrative Israeli folk of Theodore Bikel. Holzman signed Judy Collins, who would release seventeen albums for the label in twenty-two years. Elektra signed Phil Ochs, though Holzman's greatest career disappointment was missing out on Bob Dylan. When Dylan was making waves in New York, Holzman had moved to Los Angeles and they kept missing each other. Ochs was a star from the Greenwich Village folk scene. Tom Paxton and Tom Rush also signed, as did Bleecker Street's Fred Neil.

In 1963, Holzman set up a budget classical imprint called Nonesuch, created to make classical music more accessible and affordable to the masses. The profits from these releases would go towards funding Elektra's mid-1960s pop acts. In 1965, Elektra tried a brief venture with Survey Music called Bounty Records. This was Holzman's first move into pop. Their biggest act was the Paul Butterfield Band; when Bounty Records folded, Butterfield became part of Elektra.

The label started to command attention with the advent of psychedelic rock and pop, establishing itself at the forefront of the counterculture. It signed a host of acts who would become household names, contemporary artists from Los Angeles such as Love and The Doors.

Love's version of Bacharach and David's 'My Little Red Book' gave Elektra its first chart single. This came from their debut, *Love*. The folk, psychedelic baroque pop would continue on *Da Capo*, then in 1967 on *Forever Changes* which, despite failing commercially at the time, has been re-evaluated as a classic.

It was The Doors, though, who brought the label commercial success, releasing eight albums between 1967 and 1971. They also had three singles that sold over 1 million copies: 'Light My Fire', 'Hello I Love You' and 'Touch Me'.

Holzman's focus moved to Detroit and the signing of MC5 and The Stooges, two unyielding proto-punk rock groups. Along with Paul Butterfield's Blues Band, the label had The Incredible String Band and cult acts Rhinoceros, Crabby Appleton and Clear Light. Hardly million sellers, yet Holzman loved them, so they were signed.

In the 1970s, the label hit gold with sales from Carly Simon, Harry Chapin and the million-selling soft rock band, Bread. It signed New York's Television, whose studio debut, *Marquee Moon* in 1977, is a 100 per cent bona fide masterpiece. Queen also signed with Elektra for the USA (staying with them until 1982, when they moved to Capitol).

Holzman surrounded himself with sharp, music-minded people whom he trusted, people who would turn him on to other acts. Tastemakers such as Arthur Lee of Love dragged him along to see their support band play the Whiskey a Go Go four nights in a row. The band were The Doors. The label's press and publicity man, Danny Fields (who would later manage the Ramones and The Stooges, and seemed at the very epicentre of pop, punk and rock culture), encouraged him to listen to and sign the MC5. Lenny Kaye, who would later play guitar in the Patti Smith Group, was an ideas man and music enthusiast. The pop and rock historian was hired by Holzman to curate the influential Nuggets series. The first album was called *Nuggets: Original Artyfacts from the First Psychedelic Era*.

For the sound, he had the label's in-house producer Paul A. Rothchild and engineer, Bruce Botnick. The records sounded powerful and clear, kicking through the hippy dross. All of these people connected with Holzman's label ethos. With the MC5, The Stooges and Tim Buckley, Elektra simply oozed cool.

FANORAK FACT

Ahmet Ertegun attended the same college as Holzman, St John's, and formed Atlantic records in 1947.

Holzman sold Elektra for $10 million in 1970 to Kinney National (now Warner Music Group). As part of the agreement, he stayed on until 1973. Despite leaving Elektra, Holzman is highly regarded within the music industry. As a director of Pioneer, and then as a chief technologist at Warner Communications, he was involved in the early pioneering of cable and the development of CD. Now in his nineties, Holzman, the record company exec, is embracing technology. In April 2016, Warner Music Group announced that Holzman was its new Senior Technology Advisor, 'a wide-ranging technology scout exploring new digital developments and identifying possible partners'.

Labels have had to evolve, from vinyl when they were kings, to the CD, when they were able to sell everything again at twice the price. Sounds like a shrewd business model to me. The advent of the internet and downloading brought a shuddering drop in income and forced the industry to develop innovative ways of making money. Elektra could have done with Holzman at the helm.

In 2004, Warner Music Group merged Elektra and Atlantic, and 40 per cent of Elektra and 60 per cent of Atlantic went into a new company called Atlantic Records Group. Within the group, Elektra broke off into a subsidiary that lay dormant for five years. In 2009, Atlantic announced Elektra Records would be revived as an independent entity within WMG. In October 2012, Jeff Castelaz was announced as president of Elektra Records. The label currently operates with artists like Little Boots, Cee Lo Green and Bruno Mars. You know who you are. If you're reading this, can I please have my albums back?

PLAYLIST: MY TOP 5 ALBUMS

Love: *Forever Changes*
Nuggets: *Original Artyfacts from the First Psychedelic Era, 1965–68*
The Stooges: *Funhouse*
MC5: *Kick Out the Jams*
Television: *Marquee Moon*

EMI

THE WORLD-FAMOUS CONGLOMERATE EMI is (or was until 2013) widely viewed as the consummate embodiment and cornerstone of everything British – but, like another high-profile British institution, it's German. The label was founded in 1887 by German-born American inventor Emile Berliner. EMI, from its inception, was linked to the development and technology of music.

It was Berliner who invented the gramophone method of recording and reproducing sound, mocked and ridiculed as a gimmick by performers of the day. But he persevered, eventually forming the Gramophone Company in London in 1897. It built up a roster that included Nellie Melba and Adelina Patti. The business changed significantly when it signed its first superstar, Enrico Caruso. The bestselling Italian tenor released over 240 records for the Gramophone Company. When artists realised what he was earning in royalties, they flocked to sign with the company.

In the UK alone, Caruso sold over 3.5 million records, earning £162,345 in royalties (the equivalent of £25 million today). In the USA, details from his Victor earnings revealed he was paid a flat fee for each song recorded. His royalty rate was 40 cents per record (records went for around $1 to $1.50 each), netting a career tally of over $5 million. By 1906, the company had subsidiaries in Europe, Russia, Africa, India, China and Australia.

Meanwhile in London, the US-owned Columbia Phonograph Company, the future partners (in the 1930s) of the Gramophone

Company, was formed. It traded in the cylinder records and 'grapho-phones' that played the actual gramophone records.

The First World War hit both companies badly. Before the war, the Gramophone Company was selling 4 million records per annum. Columbia's factories were used to manufacture munitions and the Gramophone Company lost a substantial amount of German business (it operates today as the renowned classical label Deutsche Grammophon). The Gramophone Company also lost all its interests in Russia.

After the war, it was boom time again. Columbia Phonograph Company had top conductors like Sir Thomas Beecham, and the Gramophone Company signed Sir Edward Elgar. They both worked with top-selling orchestras, the Berlin and the Vienna Philharmonic. The Gramophone Company had its first million-selling release with Ernest Lough, a 14-year-old choirboy, singing 'O for the Wings of a Dove' from Mendelssohn's 'Hear My Prayer'. The 1920s also saw Columbia expand, buying up Pathé in France, Parlophone in London and Odeon in Germany. The Parlophone deal included the leading tenor of the day, Richard Tauber.

Just when both businesses were achieving great sales and their profits were up, they were both hit by the Great Depression. Sales fell by 80 per cent. In 1931, the Gramophone Company and the Columbia Graphophone Company merged and the result was named Electric and Musical Industries or, as the Sex Pistols would later immortalise in song, EMI.

The merger had many upsides. One was the crucial work of super scientist Alan Blumlein in the EMI labs. The electronic expert invented the first system for recording and playing stereo sound. He also advanced electrical television by developing circuitry that allowed an electronic method of picture transmission for television, convincing the BBC to adopt the electrical instead of the mechanical version. He was involved in the advancement of radar and was killed during the Second World War while overseeing secret tests on the H2S airborne radar system in a Halifax bomber.

EMI was at the forefront of major advancements in recording, with magnetic tape recorders allowing artists multiple takes. In 1948, the first vinyl long player was released and the following year saw the introduction of 45rpm singles. Both formats were cheaper and more robust than the brittle and fragile shellac 78s. Now, LPs had twenty-five minutes on either side. Albums and singles caught the public's imagination.

The 1950s shaped up well and EMI licensed product for RCA Victor and Columbia. When Columbia decided to stop their deal in 1952, to release their own artists internationally, EMI countered by targeting US talent. In 1955, EMI bought Capitol Records, a move that gave the label Sinatra, Nat King Cole, Dean Martin, Peggy Lee and Gene Vincent. The licensing agreement with RCA Victor in the UK meant that EMI released Elvis Presley from 'Heartbreak Hotel' in 1956 on its HMV Pop label. It would release over a dozen Elvis hits including 'Blue Suede Shoes', 'Love Me Tender', 'Hound Dog' and 'All Shook Up' (his first UK number 1). Profits from the Capitol and RCA Victor deals allowed EMI to reinvest in the UK with artists like Adam Faith, Shirley Bassey and Frankie Vaughan. In 1958 it released 'Move It' by Cliff Richard, one of the most celebrated artists in the history of British pop music.

The label was in good shape as it headed into the 1960s. EMI (via Parlophone) recorded hit after hit with The Beatles, Gerry and the Pacemakers and Cilla Black. In the USA, EMI had Capitol Records, therefore The Beach Boys, and a licensing deal with Tamla Motown which, at one point, was giving EMI two hits for every three singles released.

In 1969, the label created Harvest to house their left-of-centre bands, including Pink Floyd, Syd Barrett, Deep Purple, The Move, Barclay James Harvest and Be Bop Deluxe. Harvest significantly boosted the EMI coffers with sales from *The Dark Side of the Moon*. Meanwhile, EMI signed the future million-selling band Queen.

On 8 October 1976, EMI signed the Sex Pistols to a two-year record deal for £40,000. The Sex Pistols' first and only single on EMI was 'Anarchy in the UK'. It was released in November 1976 and only

FANORAK FACT

There is no official mention of the Sex Pistols in the EMI timeline.

reached number 38 on the charts. On 1 December, Queen had to pull out of a TV appearance and EMI booked the Sex Pistols as a last-minute replacement. Their appearance on the *Today* show, presented by Bill Grundy, became the inciting incident in the band's career. No stranger to drink, Grundy was impatient towards the band and their entourage and was contemptuous of the assembled yobs. When the bored host goaded them into swearing, Johnny Rotten and then Steve Jones obliged, and the Pistols hit pay dirt. The next day the band were headline news. In January 1977, EMI had enough and sacked the band, gave them £40,000 and sent them on their way.

Despite wonderful success in 1978 from both Kate Bush and Olivia Newton-John, EMI were in acquisitions mode from as early as 1979, when they purchased Liberty/United Artists in a deal that included Blue Note. The 1980s would bring something for everyone, with Iron Maiden, Kraftwerk and Duran Duran.

When EMI Music Publishing acquired SBK World Entertainment, a publishing company that owned 'Santa Claus Is Coming to Town', as well as the *Singin' in the Rain* and *The Wizard of Oz* soundtrack albums, the tills were ringing. They managed to gain 50 per cent of Chrysalis, which meant half of everything from Jethro Tull, Blondie, Ultravox, Spandau Ballet and Billy Idol.

In 1990, EMI Music Publishing acquired the Filmtrax catalogue, which allowed it to buy the remainder of Chrysalis. EMI then bought the Virgin Music Group in 1992, a takeover that included The Rolling Stones. EMI had invested in Food (see Food Records), an indie set up by former Teardrop Explodes keyboard player Dave Balfe. Throughout the 1990s and into the millennium, EMI continued to release great rock and pop music with Radiohead, Blur, the Spice Girls and Robbie Williams.

In 1996, the company continued to build its wealth and power with some shrewd business moves, including 50 per cent of

> **FANORAK FACT**
>
> The Smiths signed to EMI – Morrissey was even given a list of imprints to choose from and signed for Nipper's HMV. The band's acrimonious split in 1987 put paid to the idea, but it meant EMI had two acts for the price of one.

Berry Gordy's music publishing company, Jobete, which included 15,000 Motown songs. It also bought a majority stake in the publishing company Hit and Run, which held songs by Genesis, Peter Gabriel and Mike and The Mechanics. Then there was the acquisition, for a mere $200 million, of more than 40,000 copyrights from Windswept Pacific, including titles such as 'Louie Louie', 'The Twist', 'Barbara Ann', 'Mony Mony', 'Why Do Fools Fall in Love?' and 'Hot Legs' – all songs that would earn millions from TV, film and advertisers. Spend! Spend! Spend! What could possibly go wrong?

In 2007, EMI was bought up by the private equity firm Terra Firma. The next six years were probably the most turbulent and uncertain in its history. The company was downsized across the globe, fell out with its bankers, Citigroup, and was sold to its rivals, Universal and Warner Music. In 2013, US-based Universal bought EMI worldwide; however, the EU forced it to sell the UK company. (EMI Records was renamed Parlophone purely for the sale to Warner Music.) EMI Music Publishing was then forced into selling to Sony Music.

EMI should always be remembered for two important reasons: its wonderful assortment of artists and its efforts to lead in terms of technology. From inventing the gramophone method of recording and reproducing, to then inventing stereo recording, it was a trailblazer in sound. EMI was also the first to release a digital album download with David Bowie's *Hours* in 1999.

PLAYLIST: MY TOP 5 ALBUMS

Glen Campbell: *Glen Campbell's Twenty Golden Greats*
Queen: *News of the World*
Kate Bush: *The Dreaming*
Pink Floyd: *Piper at the Gates of Dawn*
Gang of Four: *Solid Gold*

FACTORY RECORDS

Founders: Tony Wilson and Alan Erasmus

Influential: Joy Division, New Order, Happy Mondays

MANCHESTER AROUND 1978 OFTEN conjures up memories of TV documentaries about eastern European-style town planning gone wrong – places like Hulme, where urban regeneration initiatives were imposed in haste, while Victorian streets, full of charm and character, were designated slums and bulldozed. Those living there, perceived by the planners as slum dwellers, were rehoused into badly conceived visions of modern living and packed together into decks. The urban dream became a nightmare; the new landscape evolved but was now rife with crime, violence, theft and drug abuse. The vision was laudable, yet the execution fell short, much like the rise and fall of Factory Records, a quixotically unrealistic, utopian project that spectacularly meandered off course.

In the first month of 1978, over in a posher part of town, on Palatine Road, Didsbury, TV presenter and Cambridge graduate Tony Wilson, with his actor friend and band manager Alan Erasmus, officially launched Factory out of Erasmus's flat. By May of the same year, they were running a music club to showcase local talent: The Russell Club, Royce Road, Moss Side – it's long gone now, replaced by flats.

Wilson was a high-profile face in the north-west, presenting the music and arts 'What's On' section on the regional TV news programme *Granada Reports*. This would later evolve into his pop show, *So It Goes*. Wilson was viewed as the label's main man and his media savoir-faire meant he wasn't shy when it came to talking, continuously, about Factory, Manchester and the north-west.

When the club started creating a buzz among local bands and music fans, Wilson invited designer Peter Saville and record producer Martin Hannett into the fold at Factory Records. From the start, Wilson was clear about the importance of cultivating a brand, and the importance of mood and aesthetics. In the post-punk era, it was highly unusual for bands to release anything other than hastily stuck-together, roughly hewn music. Until then, if you wanted to make your own records, half the fun involved staying up all night, gluing and folding sleeves, and stamping the entire run with your primitive artwork. Then you'd run to the Post Office to post 45s to radio stations and newspapers in the hope of some airplay or a review. This would not be the case for Factory. From the off, it would be a cut above the rest.

FANORAK FACT

Factory was known for its unique cataloguing system, which added to the mystique. FAC or FACT was used, followed by a number. It released catalogue numbers for everything, including unfinished movies, pipe dreams and even menstrual eggs. One memorable number was a lawsuit brought by Martin Hannett. Antony H. Wilson died in 2007; his coffin has the final catalogue number, FAC501.

Wilson's appointment of Peter Saville gave a unique look to the single and album sleeves, his cool minimalism the antithesis of punk's graphic, disposable, DIY pin-up art. He added an element of postmodernism to post-punk. Saville was inspired by books like Herbert Spencer's *Pioneers of Modern Typography* and Jan Tschichold's *The New Typography*. The latter's design manifesto is viewed as a significant benchmark, a definitive book on graphic design. When you pore over Factory's artistic output, Saville's influence is evident. There's a form and shape, a natural evolution that overlaps between neoclassical and postmodern that reflects the music within. He would eventually give the label's roster an atmospheric and distinctive look that helped define Factory's sophistication. It was an image that ran counter to the prevailing taste and its origins are visible in even the earliest gig posters Factory produced.

The label's first release was called 'A Factory Sample', a sampler containing tracks from local bands, such as The Durutti

Column, Joy Division, Cabaret Voltaire from Sheffield, and a comedian named John Dowie. This was released on Christmas Eve 1978, which probably seemed like a good idea at the time. While the boldness is to be admired, anyone with experience in the music industry will know it was probably the worst day of the year to release anything.

In 1979, Factory released Joy Division's *Unknown Pleasures*. The album was well received and the band made the front cover of the *NME*. Trailed and hailed in equal measure by Radio 1's John Peel, they were invited to record a prestigious session for his show. Around this time, the band's manager, Rob Gretton, was also invited to join the label as a partner.

Saville created his most memorable and evocative artwork, drawing on neoclassicism, for the second Joy Division album, *Closer*. The signature image is a black and white photograph of a marble tomb in Genoa by Bernard Pierre Wolff. Wolff's choice foreshadows the tragic death of Ian Curtis, the band's lead singer, on 18 May 1980. Suffering from depression, he took his own life shortly before a US tour. The remaining members then formed New Order.

The label's reputation may have been predicated and affirmed by Joy Division and New Order; however, it was also about the Happy Mondays, Durutti Column and A Certain Ratio. In the late 1980s, Factory remained influential and profitable with the Happy Mondays and the label's participation in the Madchester era. It was still capable of going head-to-head with other key labels of the time, like Creation.

Factory Records is another example of a label understanding the importance of regional association. It had a great name, artistic angle and image. In Joy Division, it had the perfect band to launch the label. The city of Manchester was in Factory's DNA; the music and bands were a personification of north-west defiance. The label was also an example of how to run a business badly, exemplified by its policy of not making bands sign recording contracts; they were able to leave when they wanted. This was down to Tony Wilson, who wanted a more avant-garde approach, a Manchester version of the Situationist philosophy. (The Situationists were an avant-garde group from Paris, made up of intellectuals who believed in artistic and cultural revolution and thought modern industrial society and capitalism were creatively exploitative.) His championing of this philosophy made great copy, though the bank managers and accountants were none too impressed.

The label lays claim to one of the most ridiculous of pop's financial anomalies. New Order's 'Blue Monday' became the best-selling single 12in in the UK. Due to the cost of making it, the label lost money on each copy of the original release. The Peter Saville sleeve design contained three die cuts and cost £1.10 to make, while the vinyl record sold for £1.00.

The band remain dismissive of the song itself. Bassist, Peter Hook, is disparaging about 'Blue Monday', openly claiming it's a rip-off from a Donna Summer B-side. The band were influenced by the New York club scene, and this was their homage. (The song in question is Donna Summer's 'Our Love', the eight-minute extended version of which is on Casablanca. The original version sounds like Sparks. It's worth checking out.)

If you want to run a label as a career, don't look to Factory for inspiration. For a party, yes, not for a business. While in New York to showcase New Order, Wilson, Rob Gretton and Martin Hannett often frequented clubs like Danceteria either for New Order gigs or to socialise. It was staring them in the face: a coolly designed nightclub that could also be a live music venue, a disco and a style lounge. Gretton wanted the same in Manchester. Rob Gretton, New Order's manager, opened The Hacienda (FAC 51) in 1982. It helped define the 1980s dance scene and surprised many observers by lasting a whole fifteen years before finally being shut down by the drugs squad in 1997. The club, according to legend, was costing its owners, New Order, £10,000 a month to keep afloat. The clubbers didn't buy a drink; they were too busy with ecstasy. Once again, it was possibly a great idea ruined by poor execution.

> **FANORAK FACT**
>
> Madonna played her first UK gig at The Hacienda in January 1984, appearing on *The Tube*.

Perhaps you'd prefer to open a pub? Factory did: the Dry Bar (FAC 201). If this wasn't a decent way to burn cash like a lottery winner, why not send the Happy Mondays to Barbados to record an album? Maybe you'd prefer to keep it simple and run up production costs of over £400,000 recording an album, like New Order did with *Republic*?

In the end, although Factory was created with the best of intentions, the label struggled due to its ill-conceived principles. Sometimes this happens with an artistic project. Big dreams, cinematic visions and creativity that push boundaries are all wonderful; however, it's a business, and someone must make sure the innovation stays connected to reality, and must pay the bills and keep the spending in check. Mavericks like Tony Wilson and labels like Factory are defined by their fearless creative vision and by not being afraid to fail. The label found itself bankrupt in 1992. Months earlier it turned Oasis down for sounding 'too baggy'. So it goes.

PLAYLIST: MY TOP 5 ALBUMS

Joy Division: *Unknown Pleasures*
Durutti Column: *Another Setting*
A Certain Ratio: *I'd Like to See You Again*
Wake: *Here Comes Everybody*
Railway Children: *Reunion Wilderness*

FAST PRODUCT

Formed: Bob Last and Hilary Morrison

Influential: The Mekons, The Human League, Gang of Four

IF ECONOMISTS AND SCIENTISTS could formulate an equation to work out influence over lifespan, then Edinburgh's Fast Product would be off the scale. Bob Last formed the label in 1977 along with Hilary Morrison. Both had been roadies for the Rezillos, and Last became their manager.

Perhaps we should contextualise. I was 10 in 1977. Even then, as a pop lover, I could see through this whole punk thing. It was too gimmicky and would never last. Wrong. The term 'post-punk' would later be used for bands like XTC and Joy Division. Forget safety pins and zips. Get a second-hand raincoat, find a wall that looks like Warsaw, or a depressed-looking tree in the snow, and fake a Nordic winter scape and shoot the band poetically staring into the distance.

Punk was big in London and Manchester, but punks in Glasgow and Edinburgh had to be brave, and most were. They were in the minority and liked it that way. In the cinematic fog of memory, the late 1970s in Scotland were a picture of grime, dirt and tenement flats. The colours of your dreams were the dull blue and sick mustard of the electric trains that drove you to Glasgow or, if there was some money around, to Edinburgh for the day out. Your trip to Glasgow would throw up more grey people in denim, in dull shops and rows of beige and rust. The world was shot in Super 8, not Cinemascope. It was a vicious world of football hooliganism and even the ice cream men were declaring war on each other. There were rats the size of Rottweiler pups and the army showed up in Green Goddesses to cover striking firemen and put out chip-pan fires. Glasgow had the bare-faced effrontery even to ban punk shows. Any punks still around were courageous; I admired them so much. Our valiant local punk was Womble.

Meanwhile, at this point, somewhere else, indie know-it-alls were playing mind games with the London majors. People who understood about applying theory to marketing a product were disrupting the status quo. These cats knew how to agitate. Their turnout was a distinct dry DIY funk and punk-disco energy. Most importantly, they were making records that sounded great, or different, and the *NME* was reviewing them.

In 1978, when FAST01 was released, the top hits of the day were from movies. *Saturday Night Fever* and *Grease* provided nine number 1 singles over thirty-one weeks. We also had Gerry Rafferty's 'Baker Street', The Commodores' 'Three Times a Lady', Meatloaf's 'Two Out of Three Ain't Bad' and Rod Stewart's 'You're in My Heart'. The charts included Supertramp's 'The Logical Song' and The Knack's 'My Sharona'. Let's just say it was a confusing time musically.

Companies like Fast Product knew something. Meanwhile, over on Radio 1 at 10 p.m., we had John Peel sessions by Public Image Ltd and Bauhaus, and Spizzenergi singing 'Where's Captain Kirk?'. All this was happening at a time when some people, with a unique take on life, were processing music through the prism of art and film. Bob Last was given a Buzzcocks EP by his partner, Hilary Morrison. The *Spiral Scratch* EP has been elevated to mythical status because it was the first punk record to be released independently, away from London, on Manchester's New Hormones label. Last listened, but he was also working through the process. He could do this too.

Fast Product had the ear and eye, like the old-school talent scout who gave acts their break, seeing that initial spark, recognising something and releasing their records. In Fast Product's astonishingly short career, it released The Mekons, The Human League, Gang of Four and Joy Division.

The first time I held a record on Fast Product, it was the Leeds band Gang of Four's 'Damaged Goods'. It was bright red and orange. I remember seeing the words

'Fast Product' on the sleeve. This was later, around 1981. It belonged to one of my brother's friends who was cool, and uncannily that record and The Human League's 'Being Boiled' were sitting at the front of his eclectic record collection. I 'borrowed' both. As soon as the house was empty, I'd play along to Gang of Four on my drums.

Like Postcard later, Fast Product was run from a flat – number 2 Keir Street (down from the castle and close to Edinburgh University's Lauriston Campus) – but it was run much better. It was also a creative hub for bands. Its first release was The Mekons' 'Never Been in a Riot' (FAST 1), in January 1978.

Fast Product's last release was the Dead Kennedys, a move that spawned a fruitful and eventful career for Jello Biafra and his band. It was also Fast and Last who put their record out when those in the USA were dismissive of 'California Über Alles'. It must be irritating to talk about your influential short-lived label. Influence doesn't pay the bills.

There should be a plaque on the wall of the flat. In this case, I'd propose a disposable plaque made of rotten orange peel that will decay and rot just like their disposable pop music. Those who know, kind of knew about Fast Product, but it took a while for the wider UK music scene to realise just how special and influential its two-year existence would become.

Hilary Morrison approached Geoff Travis at Rough Trade about stocking The Mekons' single. He refused, based on their musical incompetence. Meanwhile, over at the offices of the *NME*, they were hailing it as Single of the Week and the record flew. After The Mekons came Sheffield band 2.3 with 'Where to Now?' Scars were the band everyone in Keir Street thought had it, and eventually, when Last watched them live, he agreed and released 'Horror Show/Adult-ery. They were considered the ones most likely to prosper.

Those running labels or record shops understood how pivotal the Edinburgh label was, but the vast swathe of the general public didn't quite realise its significance. Bob Last was an original thinker, one who influenced Tony Wilson at Factory, who was

> **FANORAK FACT**
>
> Bob Last sacked Martyn Ware from his band, The Human League, before masterminding their global domination.

of a similar bent in terms of worldview. Postmodern, Situationist and smart arse. Clever clogs. Last provided the template and format for Factory and influenced Tony Wilson.

While on the Rezillos tour, Last had met and liked the Salford-based band Warsaw, and he remained friends with them and almost signed Joy Division – Last and Morrison liked Curtis and the band, but not their new name. They also rejected The Cramps. The label used distinctive artwork to stand out. There was a concept here and it was context. How it was presented and its distinctive look were pivotal to the Fast product. Last had studied architecture but also worked as a tech and designer for a theatre group. He devised the record label as a conceptual arts project, and its first fanzine, *The Quality of Life*, was issued in a plastic bag with a rotten piece of orange peel (hence the orange peel plaque). This label was based on an aesthetic about the importance of artistic taste – the feel of the product, and the sound of the record.

Fast Product released eight singles, three split EPs, one album and two fanzines between 1978 and 1979. In 2015, the label featured in the film *Big Gold Dream*, about Fast, Postcard and the Scottish post-punk scene. But Fast's influence on Postcard, Factory and 4AD was significant. Later he would manage The Human League, ABC, Scritti Politti and Heaven 17. In 2011 he produced the film *The Illusionist*.

The major record companies initially ignored Fast Product but took notice when it was showing them in a bad light. If the music industry is about talent, songs, recording, design and distribution, here were these fly-by-nights in Scotland belittling conglomerates by doing their job far more effectively. Their DIY marketing was cheaper and they were applying a punk rock spirit and socialist ideology. Their method of communication spread quickly through underground fanzines and college radio. The cool music fans got that.

In 1981, Last signed the jagged, angular and gloriously pop Fire Engines and rereleased their album *Lubricate Your Living Room*, which also came in a plastic bag on Pop:Aural. Everyone decries the short time the label existed and how amazing it could all have been. However, Last actively encouraged bands who signed to Fast Product to move on if a major came in for them. All the myths still fly around – but in some ways, it was fated to be and the label's short-lived time was really what it was all about. They brought postmodernism to the mainstream without leaving their flat.

Writing in *The Guardian* in 2016, Dave Simpson sums up Fast Product's influence perfectly: 'It's hardly ever recognised that Fast Product created a blueprint for British independent labels – in everything from the aesthetics to the manifesto of taking on the major labels. Despite all of its wonderful achievements, it is rarely talked about these days.'

Mentions in despatches for the energy, menace and melody of The Scars and The Mekons. But it was always supposed to be quick and disposable. Job done.

PLAYLIST: MY TOP ALBUM

FAST 11: *The First Year Plan*

FATCAT RECORDS

Founders: David Cawley, Alexander Knight and Andy Martin

Influential: Sigur Rós, The Twilight Sad, Frightened Rabbit, Holiday Ghosts

FATCAT RECORDS WAS FORMED in Brighton by David Cawley and Alex Knight in 1997. They've barely looked back since and have released artists such as Sigur Rós, Múm, Animal Collective, Vashti Bunyan, Frightened Rabbit, We Were Promised Jetpacks, The Twilight Sad, and current bands like Holiday Ghosts.

Like many labels originating at this time, they cut their teeth in retail before evolving into a label. FatCat was a record store in Crawley, West Sussex, in 1989. Here, Knight and Cawley were joined by Andy Martin. The three had been friends growing up and loved acid house. They moved to a small, dimly lit, but perfectly formed basement in Covent Garden in 1990, carving out a niche by championing music from Detroit, Chicago and Berlin. They became something of house and techno specialists. Their shop was the go-to place for top DJs like Andrew Weatherall, Richie Hawtin and Aphex Twin. When the shop closed in 1997, they evolved into a label, eventually moving to Brighton in 2001. The Brighton base, beside the sea, seems to work wonders.

Instead of being a niche dance bolt-hole for elite aficionados, FatCat opened up to a broader base, covering genres such as psychedelic folk, electronica, experimental rock, post-punk and contemporary classical. When they hit it big with Sigur Rós, their fortunes changed. Knight, in an interview with Carhartt Radio in 2012, claimed: 'Sigur Rós albums *Ágætis byrjun* and *( )* both sold remarkably well and forced us to grow up very quickly as a label. From being almost a bedroom label, we were fully exposed to the real business of the wider record industry, both good and bad!'

Why has it worked for FatCat? There are the previously mentioned reasons: the label's broad base and strength in different areas, as well as an extensive roster; they seem to have a close bond with and firmly believe in their acts. With FatCat, it feels like they are involved in music because they can't imagine doing anything else. It seems like a real labour of love.

As we are finding out, the labels with longevity that continue to improve usually start with a simple intention: to release music they love, no matter what the genre. In FatCat's case, they felt the store had become too confined as a house music specialist.

If there is one constant throughout the label's acts, it's that they merge into different genres and are difficult to categorise – a nightmare for record shop workers but a creative boon for the label. My introduction to FatCat was via Twilight Sad. They do a mean delight of post-punk indie shoegazing. After being sent a demo, Alex Knight loved it enough to head to Glasgow to see them live, and at the band's third-ever gig, he signed them. Both The Twilight Sad and Frightened Rabbit were signed after Knight heard their demos.

When asked in the same interview with Carhartt to describe the essence of FatCat in one sentence, Knight said, 'Eclectic, forward-facing and a somewhat haphazard mishmash of conflicting styles and influences.' And that, dear reader, is the label in a nutshell.

PLAYLIST: MY TOP 5 ALBUMS

The Twilight Sad: *Fourteen Autumns and Fifteen Winters*
Sigur Rós: *Ágœtis byrjun*
Holiday Ghosts: *Absolute Reality*
Frightened Rabbit: *The Midnight Organ Fight*
TRAAMS: *Modern Dancing*

FONTANA

IN 1958, PHILIPS FORMED a subsidiary called Fontana and installed Jack Baverstock as the label's A&R manager. He had previously worked at *New Musical Express* and was instrumental in the introduction of the UK Top 20 record charts before working at labels Oriole and Embassy Records. Baverstock was given a blank canvas and brought in to build the label from scratch. He remained undaunted, structuring and planning out a label that consistently delivered hits throughout the 1960s.

Baverstock told David Griffiths of the *Record Mirror* that he put his success down to having worked at Embassy Records, a budget label that recorded covers of the hits of the day and then sold cheaply in Woolworths:

> I'd previously worked on a label specialising in making inexpensive cover versions of current hits. Every shilling counted. I had to make sure nothing was wasted. When I got to Fontana, I began looking for talent in all directions, but first I concentrated on building a strong catalogue to give the label a firm grounding. I recorded Irish folk music, and it sold well. Johnny Mathis did well for us too.

Fontana started out releasing acts on 78s, including Sinatra and Matt Monro, before moving towards a diverse portfolio. The original acts of the 1950s included Dusty Springfield as one of the Lana Sisters (along with Iris Long and Lynne Abrams). The label had a consistent run of hit singles across the 1960s.

Fontana generated cash by briefly licensing Motown Records, Columbia and Epic in the UK. In late 1969 and into 1970, Philips restructured and Fontana became Vertigo, housing prog rock bands before being resurrected to house UK bands in the 1980s.

The label, under the auspices of Baverstock, proved fruitful. He had an intuitive process, one that focused on unusual songs or artists who stuck out from the usual sound of the day. A case in point is 'Take Five' by Dave Brubeck. 'I just liked it,' Baverstock told David Griffiths, 'thought I'd put it out as a single and up it came.'

There's a peculiar and charming randomness, a broad musical canvas, to the 1960s era of Fontana, reminiscent of an antique fair or car boot sale, offering a piece of everything. Apart from Dave Brubeck, the label had Jane Birkin and Serge Gainsbourg's, 'Je T'aime ... Moi, Non Plus'. It also had five number 1 singles: 'Keep on Running' and 'Somebody Help Me' by The Spencer Davis Group (Chris Blackwell of Island licensed to Fontana), The Troggs' 'With A Girl Like You', Dave Dee, Dozy, Beaky, Mick & Tich with 'The Legend of Xanadu' and Manfred Mann's 'The Mighty Quinn'.

Fontana had mid-1960s psyche from Riverside, California's The Misunderstood with 'Children of the Son', Sooty and Sweep doing 'Sooty at the Organ' and Wayne Fontana's superb 'Game of Love'. The label certainly covered all bases, from Cleo Laine to Black Sabbath and from Nicky Hopkins to The Merseys. It even had Slade who, as Ambrose Slade, released *Beginnings* in 1969 on Fontana. It was a wonderfully eclectic home for music.

So what does Fontana mean to me? One band drew me to the label like no other: Harlem Jonns Reshuffle. I was obsessed with them and their eponymously titled album. I was fascinated with this soul review group who ripped it up musically, with covers by Solomon Burke, Clarence Carter and Willie Mitchell. They dared to rework Willie Mitchell's 'That Driving Beat', calling it 'Back Driving Beat'. It was a thumping, pounding beast of a version including a Hammond organ, a pumped-up Spencer Davis on speed and steroids with a great, driving brass section. Harlem Jonns are an unbelievable-sounding band and it would have been a treat to see them play live at Wigan Casino, where they were photographed on the record. This band epitomises Fontana for me, yet I found their album in a skip while walking home from the pub.

The evening started in our local, the Staging Post, Airdrie, on a Thursday during a time when the weekend lasted four nights. I was in a band, and my friend Mark used to be in bands and was now at Glasgow School of Art. We left an indie music night in Coatbridge's Club de France, skint, and walked home to Rochsoles via a village called Glenmavis, where we found a full skip including discarded bags of vinyl. We climbed in and instead of the usual detritus were amazed to find original Lovin' Spoonful albums on the Kama Sutra label, The Zombies' *Odessey and Oracle* original on CBS and then this Fontana album, *Harlem Jonns Reshuffle* (STL 5509). We managed to get the priceless records out of the skip without being arrested and hid them in nearby bushes, covered with polythene packaging also found in the skip, and we collected them the next day by car.

FANORAK FACT

One of Fontana's big hits was by husband and wife Serge Gainsbourg and Jane Birkin, 'Je T'aime ... Moi, Non Plus'. Birkin had previously been married to John Barry, who wrote 'Born Free'. That song was sung by Matt Monro, the singing bus driver with the golden voice and perfect baritone. Monro became famous after singing on a Peter Sellers comedy album.

I would eventually inherit them: Mark was having a mad clear-out and had got into Chopin and jazz. By then, 1960s pop was passé, so he gave them to me.

This might sound crazy if you aren't into vinyl finds, but it's difficult to explain the sheer thrill and excitement when you know you've found a batch of mint-condition, highly collectable, rare vinyl. There's a really intoxicating, exhilarating sensation, a ridiculous moment of satisfaction and self-approval in your ability to sniff out the truffle. Years of practice give you a head start, knowing every nook and cranny in a shop where you might find something, no matter where you are in the world. Most vinyl collectors chase 7in singles. I prefer albums. If you're looking for anything from the last fifty years, chances are it's now defunct as it's from a small independent. If there are any records left, they will only exist on 45.

Most of my music from this genre would be the deep funk and soul from Keb Darge's Deep Funk and Funk Spectrum series on

Barely Breaking Even, a label I wanted to include but no one else agreed. BBE kindly take all these wonderful soul nuggets and share them on various funk and soul compilations. If you see the BBE logo on anything, pick it up and buy it. You are never disappointed. Incidentally, I haven't sold any of those records; I listen to them. They are not an investment.

Fontana is Italian for fountain. It's obvious once you know. To me, the font of all things poetic and literal, and what it means to be a true artist, pretentious, complex and mercurial, is Scott Walker. He released most of his work on the parent label, Philips, but *Tilt* came out on Fontana. I loved Scott Walker for continually trying to reinvent himself and destroy his previous Scott. People refuse to recognise the achingly awkward beauty in the complexity of his work, even his record company: 'The record company asked me to change my approach,' explained Scott, speaking to the music website *God Is In The TV* in 2016. 'My approach is my approach; we parted.' One of the main reasons I respect him so much is his determination to kill off the smouldering pop idol, the heartthrob, Scott the torch singer of the 1960s. It's OK. You don't have to. We can have every facet of your career. *The Drift* (2006) is best listened to around people on the train with bad breath and the wrong teeth, shouting with much banality into their phones, 'I'm on the train!' No doubt they will be texting everyone to discuss the weirdo without the phone, listening to music by someone squealing in a warehouse who sounds as if he's having a nervous breakdown. Scott Walker was an artiste. (Born Noel Scott Engel in Hamilton, Ohio in 1940, he passed away in March 2019, aged 74, after suffering from cancer.)

Then there were The Pretty Things, one of the most underrated bands of the 1960s. They deserve to be mentioned with Small Faces, The Yardbirds and The Kinks. Bowie covered two of their songs on *Pin Ups*.

Fontana lay dormant from the mid-1970s until being relaunched in the 1980s, releasing work by Pere Ubu, The Teardrop Explodes and The Lilac Time, followed in the 1990s by The House of Love, Gorky's Zygotic Mynci, Ocean Colour Scene and James.

PLAYLIST: MY TOP 5 ALBUMS

Pere Ubu: *Cloudland*
The Pretty Things: *Emotions*
Harlem Jonns Reshuffle: *Harlem Jonns Reshuffle*
Scott Walker: *Tilt*
The Lilac Time: *Paradise Circus*

FOOD RECORDS

Founder: David Balfe (soon joined by Andy Ross)

Influential: Blur, Diesel Park West, Jesus Jones

ON 25 JANUARY 2022, it was announced that Andy Ross, the co-founder of Food Records, had died from complications following cancer treatment, just short of his 66th birthday. His death was met with a heartfelt outpouring of grief from bands, artists and label bosses. Blur's drummer, Dave Rowntree, wrote: 'Really sad to hear the passing of my friend and mentor Andy Ross. He was one of the good ones – generous, warm, and kind.' Alan McGee, whose label went head to head with Food, was unequivocal in his praise for Ross as both a music executive and a person: 'Gutted my friend Andy Ross passed last night. One of the all-time good guys in the music game ... Will miss him. RIP.'

Food was launched in 1984 by former Teardrop Explodes keyboard player, and founder of Zoo Records, David Balfe. Ross's route into the music business was interesting, if unconventional. While gaining a BA in History at Leicester University, he formed a band called Disco Zombies. He started in a record shop and had spells managing the bookmaker next door, but with an eye on securing a mortgage, he joined that great rock 'n' roll pantheon, the Inland Revenue.

Ross's friend from his university days and singer of the Disco Zombies, Dave Henderson, could see from the start that he had something. 'He launched the indie label South Circular Records with

FANORAK FACT

As a sarcastic and witty *Sounds* journalist, Andy Ross is credited with coining the term 'shoegazing'.

our single "Drums Over London" in 1978; his lyrics were way too clever for our own good,' Henderson explained when writing on his death in *The Guardian*. 'Andy was obsessed with music, always enthusiastic for something new, and could spot a tune from the briefest of listens.'

Henderson brought Ross to *Sounds*, where he wrote under the pen name Andy Hurt as a somewhat sarcastic, pun-loving music journalist. Both Balfe and Henderson recognised that Ross had a feel for the music scene, and was music-mad and knowledgeable about the industry, but his greatest attribute was his ear for a song. He left HMRC to join Balfe at Food Records, in Camden, in 1986.

In 1989, Ross's attuned ear picked up something from a demo sent by a band, then known as Seymour and led by art student Damon Albarn. It featured four songs, 'She's So High', 'Dizzy', 'Fried' and 'Long Legged'. Ross saw them at the Powerhaus in Islington and the Bull and Gate in Kentish Town in the winter of 1989. Blur signed with Food in March the following year and the band would go on to define the label with four albums.

Coming into the 1990s, among bands and critics Food Records was seen as something of an anomaly. Here was a label that was set up like an indie, had all the ethos and spirit of an indie, but was funded by EMI. Thanks to their ground-breaking deal with the major record label, Ross and Balfe found success with Blur, Diesel Park West, Idlewild, Jesus Jones, Dubstar and Shampoo.

While on an American tour, Blur became homesick and came close to calling it a day. Albarn started thinking of quintessential English music like early Syd Barrett-era Pink Floyd, Bowie, The Kinks and XTC. Their next two albums would be the antithesis of the prevailing US sound of grunge. *Modern Life Is Rubbish* could have killed them off completely yet became the catalyst for the game-changing *Park Life*.

It would be remiss to speak about Food Records and not mention the famous battle between Blur and Oasis, when in August 1995 they both released singles on the same day. 'Country House' and 'Roll With It' went head to head. Blur won it,

> **FANORAK FACT**
>
> Blur wrote 'Country House' about Dave Balfe.

reaching number 1 after selling 270,000 to their rivals' 220,000. Even the race was mired in controversy with Oasis claiming their barcodes were faulty.

It's difficult to quantify how important it was for both bands, their labels and the music industry. At the time I loved all this. It was, allegedly, the brainchild of Andy Ross, who told the *NME* in August 2019:

> Damon and I were sitting outside The Freemasons Arms, near the old EMI building, having this chat, and I said, 'Look, if we go the week after, we're Number Two. If we go the same week, we have a chance of maybe Number One.' So we looked at each other, Damon seemed up for it, and we thought, 'Well, let's go head-to-head, go for broke.' We perceived that we were picking up the gauntlet that they'd cast down.

Food was originally distributed via Rough Trade and would license bands via WEA Records. However, its close alignment with Parlophone saw the label bankrolled by EMI. Eventually, when tensions between Balfe and Blur had grown fraught, Balfe and his wife, who owned 75 per cent, left just before the release of *Park Life,* selling their shares in Food to EMI in 1994.

Ross took over as boss, signing The Supernaturals and Idlewild. He remained with Food until EMI/Parlophone gained full control of the company in 2000 when EMI became part of Parlophone.

> ## FANORAK FACT
>
> Andy Ross appeared on the BBC TV quiz show *Only Connect.*

PLAYLIST: MY TOP 5 ALBUMS

Blur: *Modern Life Is Rubbish*
Idlewild: *100 Broken Windows*
Jesus Jones: *Doubt*
Dubstar: *Disgraceful*
Blur: *Park Life*

GEFFEN RECORDS

Founder: David Geffen

Influential: John Lennon, Neil Young, Nirvana (DGC), Sonic Youth (DGC)

GEFFEN RECORDS IS ANOTHER label linked to my record shop days. My manager at Our Price was a tall chap called Matthew Cassan. Matt was a knowledgeable music man, with a discerning ear for indie, 1960s music, folk and pop songs, and an acutely keen eye for what would sell and what wouldn't. He would have made a great promoter or A&R guy. He'd arrived at an uncool Our Price as a disillusioned victim of a merger between W.H. Smith and Virgin.

Matt had a simple theory. Anything on Geffen was a guarantee of quality and we were always allowed to play it on the shop sound system. He trusted the label to deliver a quality artist. John Lennon, Aerosmith, Don Henley, Guns N' Roses or Lone Justice – whatever was played with the Geffen logo was rarely poor. It sounds trivial, but in a record shop, as with DJ-ing, there was a clear understanding that your job was to read and play the room. You had to quickly check the audience in front of you and show some taste. That's undoubtedly why many label bosses get a solid foundation and feel for the record industry, by starting, quite literally, on the shop floor.

David Geffen's journey has one of those classic New York rings to it, the type of story a Broadway hit is made of. It's the classic story of living the dream: the boy from Brooklyn making it way beyond New York and his wildest imagination, to his first love, Hollywood and the movies. In common with many creative people from Bowie to Morrissey, Geffen was driven towards fame and fortune through a fear of normality. His journey from relatively humble beginnings to becoming one of the richest and most successful men in the USA proved quite a ride and it started in the music industry.

He attended the University of Texas, in Austin, followed by Brooklyn College, and then, after moving to Los Angeles, he was at the University of California, but he left all three due to poor grades. After various jobs, one as an usher at the CBS TV studio, he was getting closer to showbiz, witnessing the stars, usually in rehearsal. From here, in 1963, he became a receptionist on a CBS show. At this point reports vary: he was sacked, some say for punching someone in the crowd who applauded when it was announced that JFK had been shot, others for telling a producer how to do his job. Someone involved in casting at CBS suggested his nature might see him better served by becoming an agent, so he did.

Geffen, now aged 21, blagged his way into a job in the mail room of the prestigious William Morris Talent Agency by using a fake UCLA degree. Here, he learned from the ground floor about the entertainment industry and how it worked, mainly by intercepting memos, eavesdropping on phone calls and talking on the phone.

After becoming a junior agent, he chose the music department as he'd noticed it was the quickest way to get promoted. At William Morris, Geffen was immediately cultivating contacts and searching for talent. In the evenings, he would be at gigs, checking bands and artists. His first break came with The Youngbloods, a Byrds and Buffalo Springfield-styled folk rock and pop band from Greenwich Village who looked and sounded great and should have broken through.

He signed them to RCA. Then he signed and managed Laura Nyro, who became a successful songwriter. Geffen and Nyro created a publishing company called Tuna Fish Music, which they would later sell for $4.5 million to CBS. Through Nyro, Geffen met artists Janis Joplin, Crosby, Stills, Nash & Young, and Joni Mitchell.

With his half of the money from selling to CBS, he formed Asylum Records in 1970 with business partner and William

FANORAK FACT

David Geffen attended the same school (New Utrecht High School in Brooklyn) as David Bowie's producer, Tony Visconti.

Morris Agency colleague Elliot Roberts. Asylum was formed because they had struggled to find a label that would sign their client, Jackson Browne.

In negotiations with Atlantic Records, Ahmet Ertegun refused to sign Brown. When Geffen said, 'You'll make a lot of money', Ertegun replied, 'You know what, David? I have a lot of money. Why don't you start a record company and then you'll have a lot of money?' Ertegun struck a deal: Atlantic would put up the initial funds and distribute Asylum Records, and the profit would be split fifty-fifty.

It was the troubled Judee Sill who was Asylum's first signing. Proficient on bass, flute and piano, Sill was classically trained with a heart-breaking voice, performing songs that were infused with JS Bach, baroque, folk, and country. She died in November 1979, of a drug overdose, in north Hollywood, in obscurity without even an obituary. The Eagles (Geffen managed Glenn Frey and encouraged him to form the Eagles), Linda Ronstadt, Tom Waits, Warren Zevon and J.D. Souther were distributed by Atlantic.

Geffen was now an agent, manager and record executive who, in the early 1970s, nurtured his artists, allowing them time to develop. The Eagles would eventually become a multimillion-selling album band. When Asylum was taken over by Warner Communications, it merged with Elektra to become Elektra/Asylum in 1973. Geffen remained with the label, bringing in Joni Mitchell and Bob Dylan.

By 1975 and now part of Warner Communications, he was offered the role of vice-president of Warner Bros. Pictures. Finally, he could fulfil his lifelong ambition of becoming an old-school movie mogul. Things didn't go to plan; he couldn't handle the slowness of the corporate structure and had a personality clash with the man he was being primed to replace, Ted Ashley. His contract stipulated that he wasn't allowed to take any Warner Bros. ideas elsewhere for the subsequent two years. With time to reflect and regroup, interrupted by a misdiagnosis of bladder cancer, Geffen considered his next move.

In 1980, he launched Geffen Records. He struck a deal with Warner Bros., which financed the project and paid for operational and distribution costs. Warner Bros. would handle the distribution in the

USA and Canada, while Epic Records took care of the rest of the world. This deal lasted until 1985, when Warner Bros. took the overseas territories. The contract gave Geffen and the various distributors a fifty-fifty split. Geffen's first signing was Donna Summer and he struck gold with her album *The Wanderer*, released in 1980.

With almost a decade having passed since The Beatles split, the rumour mill was in overdrive. The industry was buzzing. John Lennon was back in the studio recording. Record company executives were circling The Dakota, attempting to get to John Lennon. The release of *Shaved Fish* in 1975 meant his contractual obligations had been met. He was a free agent and not re-signing with EMI/Capitol. Geffen adopted a different tack. He knew the person to approach wasn't John but Yoko. She was managing the calls about the comeback album.

Most of the record industry alpha males behaved dismissively or rudely towards Yoko, asking her to put John on the phone. When they insisted on speaking to Lennon, he would signal to Yoko to kill the call. Geffen knew John was raw because of the treatment and criticism meted out to Yoko. Being respectful to Yoko would be the key to winning John over. The wooing needed to become more strategic.

Geffen had done his research on Yoko and understood she was superstitious about numbers and loved the colour white. So, Geffen decided to wear a white outfit to their first meeting. Luckily for him, his phone number, birthday and address – all his numbers – were excellent too. Lennon was nervous, as he had turned his back on the music industry. His 'Long Weekend' – the debauched equivalent of two gap years – meant he'd had his fill of hedonism and was ready to step back from the limelight for a quiet life, with Yoko, to raise Sean. David Geffen had been through a similar musical hiatus and was looking to add to the success of Donna Summer, so who better than a former Beatle to consolidate Geffen Records?

Geffen managed to secure the signature of John Lennon and Yoko Ono. *Double Fantasy* was released on 17 November 1980. The reviews and the sales were underwhelming. What should have been a comeback record became Lennon's farewell album. Tragically, he was killed three weeks later, murdered outside The Dakota building on 8 December 1980. The album sold in its millions, giving the label its first number 1 album and single.

The subsidiary, DGC (David Geffen Company), was created in 1990 to house alternative artists like Sonic Youth, Nirvana, Beck, Hole and Weezer. The profile and dynamic at DGC changed completely after Nirvana came from leftfield and exploded into the mainstream. They were signed to Sub Pop for the release of their first album, then signed to DGC, and released their era-defining album *Nevermind* in 1991. At the time, Nirvana's signing to DGC, an imprint of Geffen (which had been owned by MCA since 1990), was seen as selling out. Many contemporaries thought they would fail.

Nirvana were signed through the patronage of Sonic Youth. Kim Gordon and Thurston Moore of the band suggested to their management, Gold Mountain's Danny Goldberg and John Silva, that they should sign Nirvana. The band's momentum changed when drummer Dave Grohl joined. Nirvana had impressed Sonic Youth when they opened for them on a European tour. Solid rehearsal and constant live shows across 1991 were perfectly timed and captured the band at the peak of their form. Again, Sonic Youth convinced their A&R rep at DGC, Gary Gersh, to check them out. He loved them, spoke to Silva and Goldberg, and a deal was made. Nirvana were quickly in the studio recording with Butch Vig and had the quiet confidence of knowing they'd recorded and mixed songs that had exceeded even their expectations.

Kurt Cobain said on many occasions that he would have been content to reach the lofty heights of The Pixies or Sonic Youth in terms of sales and popularity. He wasn't to know that their music, full of energy and anger, a ferocious sonic blitzkrieg, a deliciously powerful concoction of The Beatles, Black Sabbath, The Pixies, Aerosmith, Scratch Acid and Cheap Trick, would change the game completely.

Nirvana were left of centre, oozing punk-rock angst yet with a mainstream sound that engulfed the airwaves. They pitched their wagon firmly to the independent scene. Nirvana steadfastly refused to be part of the prevailing sexist and clichéd music scene of the time and instead embraced

FANORAK FACT

Kurt Cobain wanted *Nevermind* to be called *Sheep*. The album was initially going to be split into a 'boy side' and a 'girl side'.

feminism. Many forget that they were initially based in Olympia, a hip college town, and Kurt's friends were feminists and part of the Riot Grrrl scene. Even in the video of 'Smells Like Teen Spirit', the cheerleaders were most certainly not stereotypical metal bimbos. Their songs were infused with pro-feminism – 'Molly', 'Breed', 'Rape Me', 'All Apologies' and 'Penny Royal Tea'. Kurt also added a bit of punk rock to it and liked to provoke, wearing dresses to get a reaction.

Their music was cool enough to be played on college radio and mainstream enough for MTV. They even had their DGC release emblazoned with the Sub Pop logo. Nirvana's *Nevermind* became one of the most influential and biggest-selling albums of all time, with over 30 million sales worldwide. It transcended its genre. Suddenly, the underground was mainstream.

On *In Utero*, the sound reflected the group at that point, particularly Kurt's inner turmoil. It was raw, emotional and fractured, with producer Steve Albini's trademark 'live, in the room, feel' presented as a dry, abrasive onslaught. Not only was it a reaction to the polished, radio-friendly *Nevermind*, but it accurately mapped where the band stood artistically, professionally and privately. It was another powerful album; one that has been slowly embraced and, over time, has been re-evaluated as possibly their best. It sold 15 million copies and, along with the posthumously released and critically acclaimed *Nirvana: MTV Unplugged in New York*, sells to this day.

Drug addiction and depression combined to see Cobain tragically take his own life in April 1994. Krist Novoselic and David Grohl have handled the death of Kurt Cobain with great grace and delicacy despite the morbid fixation around their friend's life and death. Kurt was a fan of John Lennon and The Beatles. The world will mourn the loss of both artists. They have left a fascinating legacy, one forever linked to the Geffen story.

Geffen are now part of Interscope Geffen A&M, a New York-based label, owned by Universal Music Group. After founding David Geffen Records, he co-founded Dreamworks, becoming a successful Broadway producer with the shows *Dreamgirls* and *Cats*. By October 2023, David Geffen had an estimated net worth of $9.1 billion. He has since returned from Hollywood to New York and appears to be exciting the city with his philanthropy.

PLAYLIST: MY TOP 5 ALBUMS

Beck: *Sea Change*
John Lennon and Yoko Ono: *Double Fantasy*
Sonic Youth: *Goo* **(DGC)**
Hole: *Celebrity Skin*
Nirvana: *Nevermind* **(DGC)**

HARVEST RECORDS

Founders: Malcolm Jones and Norman Smith

Influential: Deep Purple, Pink Floyd, ELO, The Move

HARVEST RECORDS IS FAMOUS for one reason. The Louvre is home to the *Mona Lisa*, Graceland home to Elvis: Harvest is home to Pink Floyd's *The Dark Side of the Moon*. The album's colossal popularity made the label famous, yet its impact wasn't entirely positive. There was much more to the label imprint than Pink Floyd.

Harvest was set up by EMI, in 1969, to house prog rock. EMI knew there was a market for this happening genre. Progressive rock evolved from psychedelic music, when musicians shunned the confines of the classic pop song structure, to go more experimental and freeform by throwing folk, jazz and classical into their particular bag.

Despite being regarded as an underground scene, prog rock was a thriving movement, yet its popularity remained under the radar. It was a clever move by EMI, though, and not without precedent. Majors like Philips and Decca had already formed Vertigo and Deram, respectively, for their more experimental acts; hence EMI's decision to set up Harvest.

Harvest's A&R staff were given a clear remit to find progressive bands – artists who were out there, who pushed the envelope and who created music you weren't going to hear on mainstream daytime radio. The acts needed freedom and time to develop and experiment. EMI gave Harvest staff their own unassuming world, in the incongruously modern structure of the EMI offices. They were tucked away in the corner, allowed to percolate, while benefiting from the corporate structure of EMI's global backing and distribution.

The plan worked. Left to its own devices, Harvest would focus on the more left-of-centre artists to create a diverse and eclectic roster. Its formula pointed towards the more challenging artists like The Third Ear Band and Shirley and Dolly Collins, but the books were balanced with big-selling acts: Pink Floyd, Syd Barrett, ELO, Deep Purple, Edgar Broughton Blues Band, Kevin Ayres, The Move and The Pretty Things.

Harvest was launched in 1969 with Deep Purple, a high-profile band, to set up the imprint. There was already a link to the band at EMI, as their first album had been released on Parlophone. The album, *The Book of Taliesyn*, had also been released in the USA (on the Tetragrammaton label), so Harvest had the UK release of the album.

The real challenge for EMI's Harvest was to compete against Island Records. Island was the label artists chose in the 1960s, one which embodied the essence of artistic freedom and creative cool. Island allowed artists to express themselves without placing pressure on them to deliver huge-selling albums, so Harvest took a similar approach.

As well as having a broad canvas and an intuitive approach, the branding was crucial — and successful. Harvest's product was designed to catch the eye of the casual record-buying fan. You were able to tell a Harvest artist by looking at the cover. Then, once you were inside, the vinyl itself had the distinct Harvest logo, created by internationally renowned artist and designer Roger Dean. The vinyl label was a distinct greenish-yellow colour, close to chartreuse.

By far the most influential and best-selling album on Harvest is Pink Floyd's *The Dark Side of the Moon*, released in 1973. The famous cover with a glass prism and spectrum, which found its way into record collections across the globe, was created and designed by an art group called Hipgnosis. They specialised in album sleeves. The actual concept for the album was designed by Storm Thorgerson and the artwork created by his associate, George Hardie. Special mention should be made, as they are often overlooked, of the work

FANORAK FACT

Dave Gilmour played drums on 'Octopus' by Syd Barrett on the album *Madcap Laughs*.

done by EMI engineers like Alan Parsons at Abbey Road, and the highly efficient quality of their studio work.

I used to borrow *The Dark Side of the Moon* from my brother's record collection to see what all the fuss was about. I was wary of prog rock. Pink Floyd's eighth album caught my attention, so it must have had something special. I liked the weird 7/4-time bass rhythm (apart from the guitar solo part, when it kicked into 4/4) of 'Money'. Roger Waters explained that it was his attempt at Booker T. & the M.G.'s, telling *Rolling Stone* magazine in 2003: 'I was a big Booker T fan. I had the *Green Onions* album when I was a teenager. In my previous band, we went through the Beatles and Beach Boys, on to all the Stax and soul stuff.'

My mistrust of prog was based on Yes and Genesis and public schoolboys banging big gongs, dressed as court jesters, farting around with an Edwardian fugue organ. I liked three-minute punk pop garage rock. Prog was self-indulgent music you couldn't dance to. It meant relentless guitar or keyboard solos, and beards – there were many beards. I understood the need for the musicians to show off. I didn't get the gnomes, wizards and overtures to Tolkien. Yet here was an album which, over time, would intrigue me and millions of others.

> **FANORAK FACT**
>
> Barry St John, who sings backing vocals on *The Dark Side of the Moon*, is a female session singer, real name Elizabeth Thompson, born in Glasgow, who worked with Elton John, Bryan Ferry and Squeeze.

Harvest released many notable albums, including ELO's first two, their debut *Electric Light Orchestra*, and follow-up, *ELO 2*. Then there were Syd Barrett's solo albums: *The Madcap Laughs* and the follow-up, *Barrett*, both released in 1970, provided the quintessential, if fragmented sound of English psychedelia. Barrett would later prove influential with groups like XTC and their psychedelic offshoot The Dukes of Stratosphere. His music would be covered by REM, The Flaming Lips and Smashing Pumpkins, as well as inspiring Alan McGee and his pal, Bobby Gillespie. Barrett's music would influence McGee's early label signings, Television Personalities, The

Pastels and early Primal Scream. Blur, in their formative, pre-Britpop era, loved Barrett's work.

When *The Dark Side of the Moon* became one of the biggest-selling albums of all time, the impact changed the label. Harvest suddenly moved from the periphery. The hippies running the experimental project were dragged kicking and screaming into the mainstream. Once accountants see how much a global smash accrues, they don't say 'Well done, take a holiday, buy a car, spend more.' They ask, 'Where's the next one?' The phenomenal sales of the album changed the perception of the label. Expectations changed and so did the artists the label signed from then on.

While Pink Floyd were busy recording *The Dark Side of the Moon*, the band's manager, Steve O'Rourke, was negotiating a deal away from Capitol (EMI-owned Capitol in the USA). They left, signing with Columbia Records reputedly for $1 million, a steal for Columbia.

Harvest's haphazard and arbitrary A&R policy would mean many of its signings were misplaced. It took risks with numerous bands, and many would not succeed. Let's accentuate the positive and say their obscurity gave record collectors some enviable rarities to hunt for – like Panama Limited Jug Band's eponymous album from September 1969. An original, in good condition, would cost almost £200.

By 1975, Harvest had become a heritage label. At the end of the 1970s and into the 1980s, the focus changed slightly when it signed The Saints and Wire. Thomas Dolby and Duran Duran were released on Harvest in the USA.

Capitol Musical Group announced in 2013 that it was going to revive Harvest. It would be based in the USA, in Los Angeles, with Piero Giramonti installed as general manager. In 2016, the company announced that Jacqueline Saturn, from Epic Records, would be co-general manager of Harvest Records, along with Giramonti. Harvest currently has bands such as Glass Animals, TV on the Radio, and The Libertines. Morrissey signed with the label in 2014, but this didn't last very long. He told Australian

FANORAK FACT

Cash from the sales of *The Dark Side of the Moon* were used to subsidise *Monty Python and the Holy Grail*.

news site News.com.au, in his usual undramatic manner: 'I couldn't go through a Harvest Records situation again – they almost killed me, and probably regret that they didn't.' All of this proves that the label is back and relevant.

PLAYLIST: MY TOP 5 ALBUMS

Syd Barrett: *Barrett*
Deep Purple: *Fireball*
The Pretty Things: *Parachute*
Electric Light Orchestra: *Electric Light Orchestra*
Pink Floyd: *The Dark Side of the Moon*

HOMESTEAD RECORDS

Founder: Barry Tenenbaum

Influential: Sonic Youth, Dinosaur Jr.

HOMESTEAD RECORDS HAS ALWAYS intrigued me. Anyone involved in bands around the late 1980s would have loved to sign to Homestead. But we were different; indie kudos beats major label cash. We were young and foolish, and history has proved we were desperately ill-informed. When I worked in record shops, Homestead was an anomaly. It always came up as part of the Dutch East India Company. It had a brilliant roster of acts that I loved. However, there was always a reason why the same bands packed up and left Homestead; its owner, Barry Tenenbaum, was notorious for refusing to pay his artists.

The young Barry Tenenbaum was mad for The Beatles. His entry into the music industry started as a teenager when he realised he could buy their records more cheaply from the UK and sell them for a profit from his Long Island home. He set up an extensive mail-order company called Lord Sitar Records, which did well. Tenenbaum used to act older, posh and English when he answered the phone. His activities spread to a broader selection from more UK labels and Tenenbaum upped scale and started to distribute to record stores.

In 1980, an amendment to the Copyright Act (1976) banned the importing of products already owned by US labels and everything changed. Tenenbaum, who by then had built up an impressive distribution network which he called Dutch East India Trading, moved to license bands. In 1983, Homestead was set up to release the punk and new wave acts coming through. The buyer at Dutch East, Sam Berger, came in to manage the label.

The label would prove crucial to post-punk US music in the late 1980s. Homestead housed alternative artists like Sonic Youth, Green River, Big Black, Screaming Trees, Giant Sand, Daniel Johnson, Dinosaur Jr., Sebadoh, Nick Cave and the Bad Seeds, and Einstürzende Neubauten. At the time they were the embodiment of a cool US label, yet its former acts, when interviewed, often accused the company of mismanagement and ripping people off.

One of the more notable early releases was by a Chicago-based group, Big Black, led by Steve Albini. He went on to produce Nirvana, The Pixies and PJ Harvey. Albini remained reluctant to hand over the rights of his music, suggesting Big Black only license their albums to Homestead.

Berger left in 1984 and was replaced by Gerard Cosloy, who had dropped out of the University of Massachusetts-Amherst, worked in a record store and knew about music. He published a hip underground magazine called *Conflict*, which somehow made him eminently qualified to come in as label manager. Cosloy remained in charge for the next six years, during which time he learned that four people had said 'no' to the role before he took it. Cosloy was left to sign bands and do the promo for radio and the press, but he was learning on the hoof.

Cosloy, however, had a great instinct for talent and, allied with his extensive connections via the magazine *Conflict*, attracted the best bands from cities across the country. He picked up Sonic Youth, Swans, My Dad is Dead, Green River, Beat Happening and Screaming Trees. There were bands from the emerging scene in New Zealand: The Chills, The Verlaines and Tall Dwarfs.

All of this was done on the cheap, though. It was mainly Cosloy and a handful of low-paid staff and interns running things. Bands found it difficult to track Cosloy down, and if they did, the business side was always vague, and money seldom forthcoming. When bands complained about the lack of recording and promotional budget, they needed to speak to the untouchable Tenenbaum. Cosloy had the eye and ear for a great band, but the business side was slipping. Another magazine editor, Craig Marks, came in to help and signed Giant Sand.

Tenenbaum remained in charge of the finances and was by now being portrayed as some kind of Scrooge figure. In 1986 Sonic Youth went to SST. Some would suggest that was out of the frying pan and into the fire. Then Dinosaur Jr. followed them.

Tenenbaum's treatment of Homestead artists had forced both Cosloy and Marks to quit in January 1990. Labels like Sub Pop were heavily leveraged and perilously close to financial meltdown, but at least they were paying their talent. Then Nirvana hit big. Homestead was left behind, unable to fund any serious recording time, or advertising and promotion. Sub Pop was able to thrive and push its acts; it was attracting talent and selling product.

Ken Katkin, a college DJ from Princeton, then took over but everything remained low-budget. He was still at the beck and call of Tenenbaum's old-school (and illegal) financial approach. To this end, he deliberately started signing bands with an indie sensibility, knowing they wouldn't sell, so he would be saved the embarrassment of not being able to pay them while at least providing a platform from which they might move on.

Katkin left in 1992 because of Tenenbaum's behaviour. In his two-year stint in charge, Tenenbaum refused to pay any artist or send out royalty statements. Katkin took Tenenbaum to court for not paying his final wage. *Magnet* magazine published Katkin's account in August 2006:

'The last time I saw Barry was in court,' says Katkin. 'I sued him, because he [swindled] me out of my last paycheck. I took him to small-claims court in Nassau County, and he showed up and actually tried to argue that he didn't have to pay me my last paycheck.'

Next to take over as Homestead's manager would be Steven Joerg, who had worked at Bar/None Records and changed the outlook by bringing in avant-garde jazz bands and artists like saxophonist David S. Ware. Despite his best efforts to improve the label, however, Joerg ultimately left to form his own jazz label, AUM Fidelity.

Homestead eventually stopped releasing records but Dutch East India continued to distribute until 2003. While the legacy should have been a wonderful back catalogue of great music, it is now a litany of hatred, litigation and unpaid earnings, and sadly, it all points to one man, Barry Tenenbaum. The moral of the story is simple: this is not how to run a record label.

PLAYLIST: MY TOP 5 ALBUMS

Daniel Johnson: *Continued Story /Hi, How Are You?*
Sebadoh: *III*
Dinosaur: *Dinosaur*
Big Black: *Atomizer*
Sonic Youth: *Bad Moon Rising*

HUT RECORDS

Founder: Dave Boyd

Influential: Smashing Pumpkins, Moose, Revolver

HUT RECORDS WAS A peculiar yet potent force at a strange time in the British music scene. Formed in 1990 as a wholly owned imprint of Virgin Records, it was created to provide independent distribution for the bands Moose and Revolver. This way, Hut would be judged as an indie label, so its acts could make a far more considerable dent in the UK Indie Chart. The label became home to some great bands and was perfectly marketed at the more discernible and loyal independent music fan.

County Antrim-born Dave Boyd managed the operation. He had worked at Rough Trade in the late 1980s and by 1990 was put in charge of distribution at Hut Records. Within two years, he had taken full control of the entire label. When Boyd was 16 his family had emigrated to New Zealand. A lover of motorbikes, he had started in a local bike shop, serving his apprenticeship as a mechanic. The capricious nature of music seems to favour zigzag wanderers. Boyd was also a keen photographer, and when the music scene in New Zealand took off, he was there, taking shots of bands. He left the bike shop, became a freelance photographer and worked in a local record store.

He then moved to London and began working at Virgin as a retail assistant. Around then, New Zealand bands he was close friends with started to take off in the UK – bands like The Chills who were on Flying Nun. When they were in London, they slept on the floor of his Clapham Junction flat. Roger Shepherd who owned Flying Nun contacted Rough Trade from New Zealand, recommending Boyd as he knew and understood the Kiwi scene. He then joined Rough Trade, initially looking after Flying Nun but also a variety of different labels and dance acts, and was placed in charge of international exports.

The upshot of all this was that Boyd knew his business back to front, upside down; every facet from artist to pressing, from artwork to distribution, from the marketing budget to the customer. He knew the business literally from top to bottom, from the bands recording the album to the fan buying the record.

He was then approached about a role coming up at Virgin Records – more of a marketing than an A&R role – because he knew the indie scene. He accepted the job, but once settled in, he didn't like how it was being run. He asked to speak to his boss and suggested that, if the label was going to work, he would have to do it his way; if not, he was leaving. He had to love the bands, do the A&R and be able to sign the bands he wanted to work with. Unbelievably, his boss agreed and let him get on with it.

So he was given complete control with Hut and allowed to manage the label. Boyd knew he needed to expand quickly. To do this, he wanted to license the Chicago-based alternative rock band, Smashing Pumpkins. When the band released *Gish*, he was adamant Hut could do a better job promoting it than Caroline's UK arm. So he licensed Gish from Caroline (USA), now Caroline Records, and got to work.

This album became one of my favourites from this era. I was the drummer in a band called Captain America. We toured with Nirvana in 1991. At the end of the tour, we played an in-store gig to promote a new EP, at Rough Trade in Covent Garden. Our pay was to pick two records each. I chose a Velvet Crush LP and Smashing Pumpkins' *Gish*. I knew the drums would sound great because the producer was Butch Vig, who had produced *Nevermind* for Nirvana. Record shop experience told me the Caroline Records version was a more expensive US import!

The first band Boyd officially signed to Hut were The Auteurs, whose album *New Wave* was nominated for a Mercury Prize in 1993. Then came The Verve, who eventually made a major breakthrough in 1997, with *Urban Hymns*. When asked in an *Irish News* interview in 2016 about his proudest moment, Boyd was unequivocal: '*Urban*

Hymns. It has to be: 14 weeks at Number 1, 13 million albums sold and their first Number 1 single with "The Drugs Don't Work"!'

Boyd had a great business sense and charm but also stood up for his bands and remained loyal to them. In its brief life, Hut launched the careers of The Verve, Placebo, The Auteurs, Gomez, McAlmont & Butler, Embrace and David Gray.

Hut was closed down in a round of cutbacks. Boyd would become head of A&R at Virgin, spotting and signing The Chemical Brothers, Massive Attack, the Spice Girls and later, famously, signing Bowie and The Rolling Stones.

PLAYLIST: MY TOP 5 ALBUMS

The Smashing Pumpkins: *Gish*
The Auteurs: *The Upper Classes*
Revolver: *Cold Water Flat*
Placebo: *Without You I'm Nothing*
Gomez: *Bring It On*

IMMEDIATE RECORDS

Founders: Andrew Oldham and Tony Calder

Influential: Small Faces, The Nice, P.P. Arnold

WHEN RAYMOND CARVER, the brilliant short-story writer, was asked for advice on the genre, he famously said, 'Get in, get out, don't linger.' Carver might have been describing the fast life, glorious musical output and spectacular rise and fall of Immediate Records.

Immediate was founded by Rolling Stones manager Andrew Loog Oldham and impresario Tony Calder in 1965 with the slogan 'Happy to Be a Part of the Industry of Human Happiness'. Andrew Oldham also appointed a 21-year-old Jimmy Page as house producer and A&R man. The label became a high-profile independent with acts like Small Faces, John Mayall, P.P. Arnold, The Nice and Chris Farlowe.

Immediate, as a label, was far from having the best business model, yet in less than five years it encapsulated every inch of what pop music should be about – explosive, excessive, controversial, entertaining and short-lived. Its existence was brief but intense and it left a significant roster of artists to flourish, chiefly Small Faces. The bands and artists were a fresh rejuvenation of R&B which slowly evolved into a rich tapestry of psychedelia. The label presided over and presented us with electrifying and vivid music of an exacting standard.

Where did it all go wrong with Immediate, then? Well, the cracks start to show when you look in more detail. It's generally the same charge sheet: over-indulgence, decadence and bad business practice, combining to

> **FANORAK FACT**
>
> Keith Richards conducted the Aranbee Pop Symphony Orchestra.

force the label to fold by 1970. Immediate should be curated under the section marked 'Chaotic'. It was a financial train wreck; however, with Oldham and Calder at the helm, it was seldom boring.

Their style was more about being movers and shakers than about business. Oldham was inspired more by the public relations and promotional side. He was born in London in 1944 – it couldn't have been in any other city or year. He was ambitious and learned his trade at night, working in Soho at the 2Is coffee bar, then later at jazz hotspots, The Flamingo and Ronnie Scott's. By day he worked as a window dresser on King's Road, in Bazaar, a hip boutique run by Mary Quant. Music, jazz, image, fashion, nightlife and style. It all connects. He was tailor-made for PR. He did Bob Dylan's press during his first UK visit and they hit it off. Oldham freelanced with press work for Brian Epstein and helped promote 'Love Me Do'. Through this he teamed up with Tony Calder, a Decca press officer and DJ. They formed a PR company called Image. The obsession from the off was about publicity and becoming famous by whipping up a frenzy. Manipulating the media was the aim, and fame the game. Oldham's role models were Phil Spector and Berry Gordy, whose Motown label was the template. The aim with Immediate was to create a cool roster of acts.

Just like Phil Spector, Andrew Loog Oldham would be in charge of a label by the age of 21. When he managed The Rolling Stones, he would appear on stage in TV performances with them. He was the same age as the groups he managed and was prone to behaving as if he were part of the group.

Oldham spearheaded the attack, casting The Rolling Stones in the role of the nation's bad boys by creating their rebellious image. It was an ingenious plan: he deliberately made them the opposite of everything The Beatles represented. Oldham and Calder worked out that if The Beatles were clean, poppy and family-friendly, and parents approved of them, The Rolling Stones would be dirty, R&B bad boys, who scared the living daylights out of parents and the authorities.

They would bring The Rolling Stones into the mainstream by striking fear in suburbia. Oldham baited parents, famously asking:

'Would you let your daughter marry a Rolling Stone?' They delighted in winding up the establishment, and if the band wasn't being talked about in the newspapers, Oldham would make up stories. 'To hell with those who don't understand' was another famous line coined to ensure The Stones were being talked about.

There's nothing wrong with going down the PR route. Many bigger and better labels have done it before and many will do it again. Oldham and Calder brought the same sense of purpose to their label. PR helps establish bands by simply gathering momentum and raising profile by any means necessary. Any publicity is the order of the day. Oldham and Calder were smart, though, and among the madness they emerged with a label that produced some of the finest exponents of British R&B, soul and rock in this era.

My first introduction to the Immediate label was with Small Faces' *Ogdens' Nut Gone Flake*. The band had been on a psychedelic high, coming off the hit single 'Itchycoo Park' in 1967. When the album came out in 1968, it was received as one of the better concept albums of the era, along with The Beatles' *Sgt. Pepper's Lonely Hearts Club Band* and The Pretty Things' *SF Sorrow*. With Kenney Jones' thundering drum performance on 'Rene' and the powering guitar of Steve Marriot on 'Song of a Baker', *Ogdens' Nut Gone Flake* would, over time, influence bands like The Jam. Its energy and quirkiness would also prove influential on many Britpop-era bands, especially Blur on *Parklife* and Ocean Colour Scene.

FANORAK FACT

Nico made her debut on Immediate with 'I'm Not Saying'. It bombed and she eventually found fame with The Velvet Underground in New York.

Small Faces merge soul, beat pop and psychedelia on *Ogden's Nut Gone Flake*. Steve Marriot was considered one of the most authentic white soul voices of the 1960s. He happened to be backed by Kenney Jones, Ian McLagan and Ronnie Lane, who were heavily influenced by the sound and feel of Atlantic, Stax and R&B. However, the album's charm lies in its quirkiness, somewhere between a love-a-duck-Cockney-knees-up and a serious pop and soul outfit.

Immediate's approach defined the clichéd pantomime villain style of running a label. It exercised complete control over the A&R and talent spotting, production and promotion. The trouble with Immediate was that it also copied the old-school Svengali types by not paying their artists royalties. Oldham wasn't even subtle about the mismanagement. The bands wanted fame and he wanted to make money. He candidly admitted to avoiding paying artists and being in it solely for the money. He explained in a TV interview how he rigged the charts by bribing Stones fans to buy records from chart return shops to gain chart positions.

Both Oldham and Calder were schooled in the old-style ways of the music business and knew how the game worked. There was one purported 'money in a paper bag' deal with Don Arden. Oldham wanted Small Faces. Their manager, Don Arden, had them pinned down to a brutal contract. To free up Small Faces from their contract, Oldham allegedly gave Arden £25,000 in a brown paper bag.

Arden had Small Faces playing three gigs a night. Immediate placed fewer demands on them. While it allowed them time to work in the studio, though, Immediate didn't get around to giving the band what they were due financially. In the days before the minimum wage, most bands were treated like slaves.

The label wasn't without great musical highlights. Its first hit single was with the Jagger and Richards composition 'Out of Time', performed by Chris Farlowe. Peter Frampton's supergroup Humble Pie released three LPs on the label and were huge in the USA. Immediate also had hits with Amen Corner's 'If Paradise Is Half as Nice' and, in May 1967, with P.P. Arnold's 'The First Cut Is the Deepest'.

Oldham and Calder split in 1970, owing over £1 million. Record labels should always be placed in a historical context. Oldham and Calder were expected to play their part. They managed to lord it up with the best of them and they delivered, showing up for work in limos just as office staff in their opulent New Oxford Street were leaving to go home. Profligate to the last, they ignored the governance required to run a business properly as they headed off to the next party. Immediate's ruthless ambition was focused on the wrong areas.

FANORAK FACT

Stanley Unwin's gobbledegook on *Ogdens' Nut Gone Flake* was meant for Spike Milligan, who turned it down.

The label had so many great bands, yet it was haemorrhaging money. It was doing the artistic equivalent of the KLF decades before they decided to burn a million quid.

Immediate could have made a serious impact in the music industry if they had held on to both Rod Stewart and Fleetwood Mac, who were both allowed to slip through their fingers. Stewart had a one-off release with 'Little Miss Understood'. Fleetwood Mac released 'Man of the World'. Yet both were allowed to move on.

It's difficult to look at the Immediate story without asking if perhaps Oldham had missed his true calling. Instead of working in the music industry, maybe he should have been the boss of an advertising agency. He was skilled at marketing a product, raising the profile and selling the message. Ultimately, though, the problem appears to have been quite simple. Oldham and Calder were too busy focusing on entertaining and having a good time. More emphasis on the day-to-day running of the business, looking after the artists and paying people what they were owed might have given them a longer shelf life. However, over half a century later, we're still talking about the label and its music, and Oldham is now regarded as one of the key figures of the 1960s music industry.

In the end, it was only fitting the party had to come to an end. The bill? £1 million of debt and, no doubt, quite a party. Today, Chrysalis Music owns BMG Rights Management and controls the catalogue in the UK, with Charly Records owning rights worldwide. If you have to buy one album that captures the spirit of Immediate, try Small Faces' *Greatest Hits: The Immediate Years 1967–1969*. It contains fantastic mono mixes of the singles.

PLAYLIST: MY TOP 5 ALBUMS

Small Faces: *Autumn Stone*
Humble Pie: *As Safe as Yesterday Is*
Amen Corner: *Greatest Hits*
Small Faces: *Greatest Hits: The Immediate Years 1967–1969*
P.P. Arnold: *The First Lady of Immediate*

IMPULSE! RECORDS

Founder: Creed Taylor

Influential: John Coltrane

SHARP, CLEVER BRANDING. GREAT-SOUNDING music. The new wave of jazz is on Impulse!

Here we have yet another example of the classic jazz label earning its reputation based on its artists and how they were presented. These American jazz labels knew how to brand and promote their business properly. Alongside Blue Note and Verve, Impulse! is perhaps best viewed as the hip, more avant-garde kid on the block, and the youngest of the three. It may also be considered the label with the richest parents, the vast entertainment corporation ABC-Paramount, which allowed Impulse! to sign the top talent of the day, while rarely flexing any of its corporate muscle by interfering in Impulse's creative decisions.

Impulse! Records was set up in 1960 by producer Creed Taylor. ABC-Paramount wanted to form a jazz wing, so it brought in Taylor from Bethlehem Records, a lucrative jazz label, where he was the in-house producer and A&R manager. Impulse! Records was able to afford wonderful gatefold sleeves and what would become its world-renowned design, the orange and black branding of its album covers.

This was quite a sublime piece of marketing. No other labels had used orange, so it was easily identifiable in a record shop or record collection. Every part was exactly as it should be: stylish design, exceptional presentation, a great logo and elegant photography. Then you get inside, to the vinyl itself, with its distinctive label logo. The design statement means nothing if the music doesn't match the presentation. The sound was one of improvisation and invention.

Impulse! Records went beyond music; this was a celebration of an innovative art form being raised to a higher plane.

The label was set for success with sympathetic tastemakers such as Creed Taylor in charge and high-quality mastering from eminently sublime engineer Rudy Van Gelder, who captured the sound. Again, let's repeat: Impulse! Records did incredibly obvious and simple things, brilliantly.

Along with having a great eye for talent and an ear for a tune, Taylor was acutely aware he had to attract the attention of record buyers to the product. The cover design was pivotal. If Blue Note transported you to a smoky basement in Greenwich Village in the late 1950s, when jazz and sin were king, Impulse! sleeves were simple, clean and bold; the artist was the star, with their face on the front.

Creed Taylor brought designer Robert Flynn from the advertising agency Viceroy. They worked together on most of the ABC-Paramount output. Flynn was responsible for the distinctive look, layout and typography, designing most of the Impulse! covers in the 1960s. Impulse! used characteristic brooding images and typographical modernism. Designer Fran Scott joined from ABC and came up with the distinctive black and orange spine. Designer Margo Guryan created the logo by inverting the lowercase Sans Serif 'i' into an exclamation mark.

All of their work appeared as a glossy, laminated, gatefold sleeve. Taylor came up with the perfect marketing tagline: 'The new wave of jazz is on Impulse!' It was a design statement that matched the ambition of signing John Coltrane and his movement towards the burgeoning free jazz scene. You knew you were looking at the latest Impulse! Records release.

Taylor realised that with the lucrative backing of ABC-Paramount came the pressure of having a hit, and quickly. Ray Charles was already signed to the parent company and wanted to release a jazz record, so it seemed perfectly natural he'd bring out *Genius + Soul = Jazz*, on Impulse!

> **FANORAK FACT**
>
> When he was at Verve, Creed Taylor introduced the US audience to bossa nova, producing Stan Getz/João Gilberto's version of 'The Girl from Ipanema'.

It sold over 150,000 copies. With heavy rotation and continual airplay, shops were soon out of stock, and when they contacted the distributor, it was also out of supply. No one could find the must-have record of the day. Buzz created: jazz fans are talking and everyone wants what they can't have.

When Impulse! bought out John Coltrane's contract at Atlantic in April 1961, the industry was beginning to take notice. Again, it's about the funding. Impulse! signed John Coltrane because the parent company could afford to pay him. Coltrane was given a $10,000 advance for the first year with a two-year option, which would double the advance. He announced his arrival with his Impulse! debut, *Africa/Brass*.

Impulse! would go on to release over twenty albums with John Coltrane before the saxophonist's premature death of liver cancer in 1967. Metro-Goldwyn-Mayer, which the previous December had bought Norman Granz's Verve Records (see Verve) from under the nose of Sinatra, was interested. By the summer of 1961, Creed Taylor had been enticed to join MGM.

His successor as label boss would be Bob Thiele. By 1961, Thiele was a bona fide music industry veteran: an avid jazz buff and DJ, who formed a fourteen-piece swing band that played across New York. In 1939, he started a magazine called *Jazz* (in 1962 at Impulse! he relaunched his magazine). He formed Signature Records with artists like Lester Young, Earl Hines and Coleman Hawkins. Signature sank and, four years later, Thiele joined Decca/Coral. He took over Coral and produced Buddy Holly and Jackie Wilson. In 1959, Thiele produced an album for Dot Records of Jack Kerouac reading his poetry. Dot Records deemed the Kerouac recital obscene and recalled the album. Thiele resigned, formed a company with Steve Allen, and released it on his new label, Hanover Signature. So, by the time he was approached by Impulse!, he had experience in every aspect required to run a label properly.

FANORAK FACT

Thiele co-wrote Louis Armstrong's 'What a Wonderful World' with George David Weiss. Thiele used the pseudonym George Douglas, named after his two favourite uncles, George and Douglas.

Over the next decade, Bob Thiele worked with, guided and produced top artists including Duke Ellington, Count Basie, Charles Mingus, Coleman Hawkins, Alice Coltrane, Archie Shepp, and Earl Hines. However, Thiele will be remembered for his close working relationship with the label's star signing, John Coltrane, and his most important work, *A Love Supreme*, in 1965, an album that would define the label.

Coltrane's masterpiece was recorded in one session. It is one of the most revered and sanctified albums of all time. By 1970, it had sold half a million copies. These are sizeable sales figures for what was then considered a niche market. To put the sales figures into perspective, a Coltrane album would usually expect to sell around 30,000.

Bob Thiele's era, 1961–69, coincided with renowned engineer Rudy Van Gelder at his New Jersey studio in Englewood Cliffs. This fruitful association underpinned the label's best work. The project was about building up the label over the long term. Along with big names, he would sign emerging talent, allowing them to develop. If artists were given the time to make albums and build a career, they would make inroads, selling more each time, over a prolonged period.

Bob Thiele had a clear understanding of the mindset of the jazz market and how fans loved obscurity. A small, yet loyal, fan base was a good long-term investment. While remaining sympathetic to the real jazz aficionados, he was unafraid of bringing stars together, knowing big-name collaborations were popular. This is what separated him from Creed Taylor. Thiele's was a more pragmatic approach, moving away from Taylor's vision of the purist, cool, jazz label. He wasn't scared of popularising Impulse! He teamed up Duke Ellington with both Coleman Hawkins and John Coltrane, and signed Dizzy Gillespie and Sonny Rollins for one-off albums as these big-selling projects balanced the books.

The death of Impulse!'s biggest asset in 1967 shook the label to its core, but the cracks were beginning to show as early as 1965, due to friction and differences of opinion between Thiele and ABC-Paramount's new boss, Larry Newton. The power of the civil rights movement and social unrest made it particularly uncomfortable at times for the bosses at the parent company. They were growing fearful of the powerful radical voices among the intelligent, articulate and angry African Americans on their roster. BPM wasn't beats per minute; it was the Black Power movement. They would have preferred their artists to stop being so political and concentrate on their music. The music itself was also changing, as it always should, reflecting the era, edging and meandering away from jazz towards more psychedelic influences.

Since the 1970s, Impulse! has kept changing parent owner, currently existing as a reissue label within the Universal Music Group. The label became inactive in the 1970s. The 1980s saw various signs of life with sporadic releases from McCoy Tyner, Michael Brecker, Henry Butler, Diana Krall and Alice Coltrane.

While Blue Note prospered by balancing its back catalogue with more recent stars Norah Jones and Gregory Porter, jazz fans were wondering why Impulse!, with its outstanding innovative back catalogue containing Coltrane's work, wasn't fully operational. Thankfully, someone at Universal Music Group was thinking the same and relaunched Impulse! Interestingly, the new label will be based in Paris and Blue Note will deal with US distribution.

PLAYLIST: MY TOP 5 ALBUMS

John Coltrane: *A Love Supreme*
Charles Mingus: *Mingus Plays Piano*
Elvis Jones and Richard White: *Heavy Sounds*
McCoy Tyner Trio: *Reaching Fourth*
Pharaoh Sanders Quartet: *The Creator Has a Master Plan*

IRS

Influential: REM, The Go-Gos, The Cramps

IRS WAS ONE OF those labels whose bands played live, constantly. If you liked a band on its roster, you would be guaranteed they'd be playing a town or city near you within weeks. The label is known for two things: for being founded by Miles Copeland III, whose father was involved in the formation of the Central Intelligence Agency, and for being the label of rock band REM.

Stewart Copeland, born in Virginia, was the drummer in The Police. His brother Ian was a tour manager, promoter and head of a talent agency called Frontier Booking International. He was born in Rif Dimashq, near Damascus, Syria. (He died in 2006, of melanoma.) A third brother, Miles Copeland III, was born in London, formed IRS, and managed The Police and Sting. Their collective backstory is underpinned by the link to their father being involved in forming the CIA. The brothers were raised mostly overseas, which may have given them a broader outlook, some urbanity, as they went where their father served. He was the boss of the Middle East bureau in Lebanon for a while. The other part of the label's story is the Athens-based college rock band, REM. They began their long, distinguished career on IRS before finding worldwide acclaim.

For those interested in the history of pop and its movers and shakers, the Svengali types always enthral and beguile. Miles Copeland has been a significant player and master of many skills: producer of bands like Renaissance and Wishbone Ash, as well as a manager, agent and record company owner. He originally gained traction in the music industry in 1977 as manager and agent for Squeeze, Chelsea, The Fall and Alternative TV, before forming Deptford Fun City Records, Step Forward Records and Illegal Records.

When he began managing his brother Stewart's band, The Police, the impetus changed. The band formed in London, in January 1977, when it seemed anyone with any proficiency was getting a deal. Perhaps they were too proficient or too new wave. Struggling to secure The Police a recording contract, he decided to do it himself, launching Illegal Records with the May 1977 release of The Police's 'Fall Out' backed with 'Nothing Achieving'. It sold out its initial pressing, going on to move nearly 70,000 copies.

Copeland approached A&M Records, pitching an option on the song 'Roxanne'. A&M liked what he was doing and the fact that Copeland requested a low advance against a higher royalty, and a deal was agreed. In a low-risk gamble, A&M would simply manufacture and distribute while Copeland would market and promote. The Police were older, had been around the music industry for a while and knew that if they recorded in budget studios, used cheap hotels and toured in a van, a low advance against a high royalty meant they would be earning big if they were successful.

Meanwhile, A&M knew Copeland was a master of promotion. He was high profile, loved working in the music industry and had a touch of the megalomaniac about him. Shyness came hard. Bravado and self-assurance were the order of the day and came with the territory. In an attempt to impress A&M for an album deal, Miles called in his brother Ian from the US booking agency. He had the band do a US tour in a rented van before they even had an album released. A&M was impressed and signed them.

The Police found fame and fortune with Copeland at the helm. A prolific run of albums between 1978 and 1983, *Outlandos D'Amour*, *Reggatta De Blanc*, *Zenyatta Mondatta*, *Ghost in the Machine* and *Synchronicity*, yielded five number 1 singles in the UK: 'Message in a Bottle', 'Walking on the Moon', 'Don't Stand So Close to Me', 'Every Little Thing She Does Is Magic' and 'Every Breath You Take'; the last of these also reached number 1 in the USA. The band's achievements allowed Miles to focus on his new project, IRS. Copeland kept adding to his record companies, publishing companies and management agreements. When it came to naming his next company, it felt appropriate, with the family in-joke of government names, to call his label IRS (which also stood for Internal Revenue Service in the USA).

IRS was originally launched to find a foothold for Copeland's UK acts in the US market. Jerry Moss (the 'M' of A&M) liked Copeland's style and exuberance and, obviously impressed by his initial success with The Police, agreed to the idea of International Record Syndicate (IRS) in the USA in 1979. Yet it was a brave move by A&M as the label didn't have the structure in place. At first, it was more of an indie conglomerate with major label backing. IRS launched in 1979 with a compilation by The Buzzcocks, an album called *Singles Going Steady*.

Being around the record industry in the UK during punk, Copeland knew the power of controversy and how it helped raise both the artist's and the label's profile. He signed the Dead Kennedys and planned to release *Fresh Fruit for Rotten Vegetables* on Christmas Day. A&M bosses were wary of another high-profile Sex Pistols-style backlash. Copeland formed another label, Faulty Products, and released the Dead Kennedys through that label.

When Miles Copeland saw how great a job A&M's college radio promoter, Jay Boberg, was doing in promoting The Police and showcasing many of the other acts on his label, he decided to make him president of the company. He stayed there until the label was sold in 1994.

IRS would be indebted to The Go-Gos. They hit platinum with *Beauty and the Beat* in 1981. The 1960s produced a plethora of great garage-punk girl groups and the previous few years had seen more all-girl bands, yet at this point, record labels wouldn't sign them. They weren't subtle about it either. The Go-Gos were a live sensation, a major pull at college gigs, yet couldn't get a deal anywhere. Miles Copeland signed them to IRS despite the major labels ignoring them.

For me though, IRS is inextricably linked with the rock band REM. The band released its first five albums on the label before signing to Warner Bros. in 1988. On IRS, REM released an album every year from

FANORAK FACT

Peter Buck claims that the title for 'Life's Rich Pageant' came from a Peter Sellers line delivered by Inspector Clouseau in *A Shot in the Dark*.

1983 to 1987, from *Murmur* to *Document*. They started out when I was beginning to find myself musically, around the age of 16 or 17. It's the time when you start to make your mind up: books, films, art, and especially records, come with you. Their albums shaped my musical life. I stood by them through thick and thin.

My first experience with the band was *Murmur* and the song 'Radio Free Europe'. I saw them overreach and play shows to half-empty halls of confused drunks. I saw them packing out Glasgow Barrowlands in 1989, joyously playing three encores including a cover of Suicide's 'Ghost Rider'. I was also secretly happy when their second LP, *Reckoning*, received critical acclaim though not too much fame, as it meant they would remain accessible, retain cult status and be my band.

My faith in them didn't diminish when they changed producers from Mitch Easter and Don Dixon to Joe Boyd, and unlike most fans I was supportive of the incongruity of *Fables of the Reconstruction*. They received poor reviews for the album, which was recorded in England. They were unhappy with the weather and the food and, at this point, came close to splitting. You can hear that frustration in some of the songs too. But I remained loyal and even enjoyed some of the album because of its unsettling strangeness.

By their fourth album, *Life's Rich Pageant*, their producer, Don Geham, who had just won a Grammy for his work with John Mellencamp, had forced Stipe to sing more clearly, pushed the band out of their comfort zone and given Bill Berry a killer drum sound with a searing, thunderous snare. The record had a gorgeous, natural sound. They also made inroads when 'Fall on Me' reached number 5 on the *Billboard* Mainstream Rock Chart. It was a significant breakthrough. You could hear what Michael Stipe was singing. What was happening here? The band sounded happy again. The weather was no doubt hotter, the sun shining, the food and the mood vastly improved as the band worked in Belmont, Indiana.

Stipe had previously explained that the lyrics were deliberately obscure as he was 'insanely shy' about revealing them and self-conscious about his vocal delivery. I loved the opener, 'Begin the Begin' and the cover of The Clique's 'Superman'. I've listened to the song so often that I know the clicks and snaps of the plastic within the grooves before the song even starts. I loved the fifth IRS studio album *Document,* but by then I knew I was losing them to the world.

IRS also released a compilation album of REM rarities, outtakes, covers and B-sides, called *Dead Letter Office*, in 1987. When REM signed with Warner Bros., IRS released a greatest hits album called *Eponymous* in 1988.

Over the years, IRS issued a great assortment of other talent: The Cramps, Henry Badowski, Wazmo Nariz and Brian James, Let's Active, The Alarm, Oingo Boingo, Alternative TV, Fine Young Cannibals, Timbuk 3, The Bangles and Wall of Voodoo. The label itself is now defunct. It stayed with A&M for distribution until moving to MCA in 1985. It then left MCA in 1990 to become part of EMI before leaving in 1996. EMI revived the label in 2012 but shut operations down again in 2015.

Mitch Easter of Let's Active, and an REM producer, summed up IRS brilliantly:

> The philosophy of IRS was sort of cool. You could almost say 'crass', or even 'smart', of just messing around with these little bands that had a punk sensibility and being like, 'We'll give you a little bit of money to make an album', which sort of fit the times.

PLAYLIST: MY TOP 5 ALBUMS

The Go-Gos: *Beauty and the Beat*
REM: *Life's Rich Pageant*
The Cramps: *Psychedelic Jungle*
REM: *Reckoning*
Let's Active: *Every Dog Has Its Day*

ISLAND RECORDS

Founders: Chris Blackwell, Graeme Goodall

Influential: U2, Bob Marley, Grace Jones, Nick Drake, Roxy Music

CHRIS BLACKWELL HAD OTHER options before deciding a career in music was for him. He had an idyllic childhood, growing up in Jamaica. Errol Flynn and Noel Coward were family friends. Flynn was the first person Blackwell ever saw wearing water skis. Initially, Blackwell started working in the film industry. He worked for James Bond producer Harry Saltzman as a production assistant and location scout on *Dr No* (he introduced Saltzman to Laughing Waters, which sounds like a blues-playing comedian, but is the beach made famous by Ursula Andress in the memorable scene when she emerges from the sea).

While working in Jamaica in 1959, Blackwell was inspired to get into the music business. He released records by Laurel Aitken, Jackie Edwards and Owen Gray under the Jamaican blues and ska label, R&B Records. As Blackwell explained in an interview with *The Independent* in 2009, while discussing the label's fiftieth year, his first Island Records release was of a blind jazz band pianist named Lance Hayward. 'When I recorded Lance Hayward at the Half Moon in 1959 at Federal Records Studio in Kingston, I had no inkling what path this had set me on.'

The Jamaican music scene in the late 1950s and 1960s involved big old speakers and sound systems playing the latest sounds from the USA. Blackwell saw a marketplace for sourcing and selling these records, mostly US imports, to a captive and eager audience in Jamaica, at a higher price.

Island Records was founded in Kingston, Jamaica from an extremely small office in 1959. The company was named after the Alec Waugh novel, *Island in the Sun*. It started thanks, in the main, to the expanding Jamaican community in London and Birmingham. In June 1948, the *Empire Windrush* brought 492 Caribbean passengers to Tilbury docks, mostly men who had left their families behind. When the families eventually joined, the West Indian population in the UK rose to 172,000 by 1961. Here we had a lot of homesick souls, missing the music of their homeland. Island Records flourished by exporting reggae music to the UK.

In 1962, Blackwell moved to London to be closer to his target audience. He drove around Jamaican communities in London and Birmingham, selling imports to record shops from his Mini Clubman. He avoided radio stations as they would rarely play his Island Record artists. When the label took off, Blackwell broadened the acts on the label's roster with Elmore James (blues), Lee Dorsey (R&B) and John Martyn (folk-jazz). By 1967, Island had created Trojan Records, a spin-off label specifically for reggae acts (see Trojan).

FANORAK FACT

Jamaican-born Chris Blackwell became so effective at providing the UK with reggae music that the UK government invited him to relocate to provide reggae for the country's growing Jamaican population. He also owns Ian Fleming's old house 'Goldeneye'.

With Bob Marley, Blackwell deliberately tweaked the reggae sound to make it more appealing to UK and US markets. He also did a minor piece of rebranding with Marley, moulding him into something of a heroic, Che Guevara revolutionary. It worked; Blackwell brought reggae to the world. Island Records was responsible for taking a roots-based niche and transforming it into an international genre.

Initially, Blackwell's fledgling Island Records label focused on licensing master tapes. In 1963, he found a recording of Millie Small's cover of Barbie Gaye's 'My Boy Lollipop'. He knew it was a hit. He produced it and in 1964 was proved right. He had licensed the song to Fontana because he immediately understood that it was going to be a smash and too big for Island to handle. The song would go on to sell 6 million copies worldwide. Supply and distribution are among the first issues an independent label faces when it has a hit single. The pressing plants need to be paid to manufacture the records quickly to satisfy demand, and independents generally struggle with cash flow. Licensing to Fontana was an astute move.

While chaperoning the 15-year-old Millie around TV studios and radio stations, Blackwell met The Spencer Davis Group and decided to move into rock music. Island had been distributed via Fontana/Philips. With the capital from 'Keep on Running', it was able to build up the label, signing Fairport Convention and Free, and their success would bring further artists: King Crimson, Roxy Music and Traffic. In the 1970s, Island would launch the career of Cat Stevens, and in March 1980, it signed U2.

Most people associate Island Records with Bob Marley and U2. For me, the band that encapsulated the essence of the label was Sparks, with 'This Town Ain't Big Enough for Both of Us', which reached number 2 in May 1974.

This song (along with 'Ticket to Ride' and 'His Latest Flame') was most responsible for shaping my understanding of the concept of pop music as an 8-year-old. The information on the vinyl, the label artwork, the island, the palm tree. The writer was Ron Mael and the producer was Muff Winwood. The B-side was 'Barbecutie'. They were on the Island label. There were other labels. If your song sold the most over the week, you would reach number 1 and appear on *Top of the Pops*.

'This Town Ain't Big Enough for Both of Us' still sounds strange, even today, never mind in 1974, and it captures what made Island Records unique. Labels are defined by their artists. Strong identity: quality music. Then there was another hero, drummer Dinky Diamond on *Top of the Pops* playing that Premier kit. Island instinctively signed original and unique bands because Blackwell was adventurous, entrepreneurial and a natural risk-taker. So he would surround himself with like-minded, shrewd A&R teams, schooled in the label's philosophy. They were people willing to take a chance on more left-of-centre artists, not only Sparks, Fairport Convention and Roxy Music, but also Amy Winehouse, Grace Jones, Julian Cope, Jethro Tull, Kid Creole and the Coconuts, and Marianne Faithful.

Let's take two random Island artists. Imagine hearing Tom Waits and Nick Drake demos for the first time. You'd be interested, and certainly want to put them aside and listen again; they had a certain charm. While you hesitated, Island Records would have signed them.

Blackwell has said on many occasions that Island didn't have hit singles; it looked for longevity and album sales. He worked with artists he believed in, so there was an instinctive balance between the creative, artistic side of the deal and the business side. This wasn't always a successful approach, but it showed commitment to the acts. The label was prepared to spend if the artist deserved it. The rationale was simple: if bands are allowed to develop, they will eventually become accomplished and sell.

Entrepreneurial spirit and an affection for music will only take you so far. Once you've signed the specifically eclectic artist, there's a subtle requirement to promote and build interest and sell their product.

In 1980, U2 were signed to the label, in the ladies' toilet (better light) of the Lyceum theatre, by Nick Stewart. The group became so gargantuan that in 1986, when Island faced bankruptcy, U2 bailed out their record company. Blackwell had fallen into difficulty funding a film and distribution company. There might have been some shrewd business behind the deal ironed out to save the label, though U2 may also have remembered Blackwell's unstinting loyalty when most bosses would have dropped them based on their second album, *October*.

While they recorded *The Joshua Tree*, the band were informed Island couldn't pay them the $5 million they were owed. U2 reportedly did a deal with Chris Blackwell where, in return for the loan, they would waive their royalties for a 10 per cent stake in the company and full ownership of their master tapes. In 1989, Island Records was bought by PolyGram and the band reputedly made $30 million. After Blackwell sold Island to PolyGram, he remained CEO of Island Entertainment until 1997.

FANORAK FACT

Sparks used to be called Halfnelson and released an album of the same name in 1972, produced by Todd Rundgren. It contained two Mankey brothers, Earle and Jim.

Pop historians consider the label's peak to be from 1967 to around 1987; the period from The Spencer Davies Group and the psychedelic pop of Traffic to the stadium rock of U2's *The Joshua Tree*. During this period the label had been independent and was able to take risks on artists. However, according to the BBC4 documentary *Keep on Running: 50 Years of Island Records*, U2 became so massive that the label came to mirror a vast corporation, more concerned with logistics and dealing with sales targets, staff and overheads rather than looking for diverse and innovative bands to add to the roster.

In the 1990s, Island would be back, with Pulp, P.J. Harvey, Tricky, DJ Shadow and Portishead. The star who shone most for the label in the 2000s was Amy Winehouse. Her debut, *Frank*, in 2003, heralded a star, a bona fide 100 per cent jazz soul voice, full of emotion, strength and vulnerability. She sounded like Sarah Vaughan, Billie Holiday and Lauryn Hill, skimming across jazz, soul and R&B. Her second album, 2007's *Back to Black*, containing the single 'Rehab', won five Grammy Awards. Success in both the UK and USA accelerated her erratic behaviour, and over the next four years, she became classic tabloid fodder. Tragically, most, apart from Amy herself, could see it coming; she was found dead in July 2011, aged 27.

In recent years, Island has relied upon Keane, The Feeling and Jake Bugg, a far cry from the diverse range of artists that once made it such a cool and vibrant label. Times change. The label exists within the structure of the Universal Music Group.

PLAYLIST: MY TOP 5 ALBUMS

Grace Jones: *Nightclubbing*
Amy Winehouse: *Back to Black*
Sparks: *Kimono My House*
U2: *Boy*
P.J. Harvey: *The Hope Six Demolition Project*

KILL ROCK STARS

Founder: Slim Moon

Influential: Bikini Kill, Slater-Kinney, Deerhoof, Elliot Smith

KILL ROCK STARS IS one of my favourite labels. I think Bikini Kill's 'Rebel Girl' is a wonderful song. Deerhoof's experimental rock gets me, as does their drummer, Greg Saunier. I get the label's left-wing attitude, its feminism, its all-women staff (since 2006), its anti-war stance, though most of all, I respect its music and independent spirit.

Two defining factors come into play to make Kill Rock Stars stand out from the crowd: location and timing. Location is crucial. Know your geography. It's central to the label's approach and can be a key factor in any label's longevity. The Portland/Olympia Pacific Northwest base of Kill Rock Stars has worked well for the label. It provided an identity that fed into its independent ethos and artistic freedom. Here we have the liberal sensitivities of the collegiate and young educated audience, a creative hub where expression is encouraged, giving artists a certain confidence. This allowed bands like Sleater-Kinney with their erudite, smart, sharp feminism to forge ahead. Kill Rock Stars would also be clever enough to know the hard work was done decades before, by strong women like Sister Rosetta Tharpe, Loretta Lynn and Nina Simone.

In Portland, Oregon, in the year 1991, an indie music fan called Slim Moon formed a label with a profoundly simple intention. He was frustrated that his friends in bands were unable to get deals, so he formed a label to release them. He was also a fan of spoken-word singles, something unusual and quirky at the time.

The label is now based between Olympia – a cool, hip, college town – and Portland, which gave us The Kingsmen and the old familiar tried-and-tested template with 'Louis Louis'. It has always had an inventive music scene: The Wipers, Sleater-Kinney, Blitzen Trapper, The Shins, The Dandy Warhols and the punk venue The Satyricon, now gone, where Kurt met Courtney. Portland also gave us the sketch show *Portlandia,* which brilliantly aimed at the city's politics and anti-establishment attitudes. *The Guardian* even named Portland the most vibrant music scene in the USA in 2013, so it must be cool.

Olympia, the state capital of only 40,000, is an hour south of Seattle. A thriving college town, it is home to Evergreen State College. The college allows students to build their own coursework, and this flexibility and approach has encouraged more creative artists, musicians and filmmakers. Olympia is also home to one of the best college radio stations, KAOS, famed for its strict 80 per cent independent music playlist policy.

So, this attitude and creative liberalism go a long way to making the Northwest appear an interesting, happening region. Both Portland and Olympia share a particularly supportive and encouraging approach to music and performing arts, which makes it a haven for creative people.

Timing, on the other hand, could also be filed under luck – for example, a label being lucky enough to sign a band at a game-changing moment in popular culture: Parlophone with the Beatles just ahead of Beatlemania, Virgin with punk and the Sex Pistols, Creation with Britpop and Oasis. A label can be fortunate to find itself in the perfect place and time for a genre's peak.

> ### FANORAK FACT
>
> *The Simpsons* creator Matt Groening attended Evergreen State College, as did producer Steve Fisk, Sub Pop's Bruce Pavitt and Michael Roberts who played Cosmo Kramer in *Seinfeld*.

Kill Rock Stars was formed in 1991 just as the Pacific Northwest's underground scene erupted to the sound of grunge. What made this genre different? Well, it wasn't New York- or Los Angeles-based for a start (it was location). KRS released an album with their friends on it, made it available, and it sold. It provided an alternative to the alternative. Its grunge was more for people who enjoyed reading well-structured fiction and loved fresh-roasted ethical coffee. It was less angst and more literate indie rock.

I have always been fascinated with the geographical connection between a particular place and a particular sound. Kill Rock Stars has found its identity and a wholly independent sensibility and credibility because of its base. In 1991, a celebrated music festival was held at the Capitol Theatre in Olympia, for six days, called the International Underground Convention. It was organised by Calvin Johnson of K Records, Beat Happening and currently Dub Narcotic Sound System. This was viewed as a seminal moment, inspiring many people already in bands, or those watching, to form one. It was perfectly acceptable to get creative and do something you wanted to do.

When Nirvana broke through, the rules changed. It became more challenging for labels to champion independent creativity. If they were effective at their job, finding bands, getting their music out there, selling and making money, the majors tracked them down, calls would be made and vast trucks containing ridiculous amounts of cash would be theirs. It's difficult to remain wholly independent when your life can be changed forever. Thankfully, not every record label wants to become part of a multibillion conglomerate.

What makes KRS special? Well, like most well-run businesses, it does the simple things well. The technology may have changed in the music industry, but the key elements and principles are the same. It's about production, manufacturing, distribution, marketing and promotion. The great labels do those well. With Kill Rock Stars, we have a label understanding the balance from an indie perspective, in terms of taste and sensibility, while maintaining a professional approach. It is also there to enable bands, not spoon-feed them. The bands have to work in partnership with the label.

After some success with spoken-word singles, the label moved to produce compilation albums. Its first major release in 1991 was a compilation album featuring bands Bikini Kill, the Melvins, Nirvana and Elliot Smith. It made further waves when the Riot Grrrl feminist punk of Sleater-Kinney and Bikini Kill took off. Whether it's Kinski's *Conflict Free Diamonds*, The Thermals' *Never*

FANORAK FACT

The name Kill Rock Stars came from a painting by Slim Moon when he was going through a short-lived phase as an artist.

Listen to Me or Slumber Party's *Psychedelicate*, it's always interesting and never boring.

In 2006, Kill Rock Stars hit big with the irrepressible force of nature Beth Ditto and Gossip. Anyone who has heard 'Standing in the Way of Control' live will know how Gossip have been a crucial voice for their generation, kicking down many barriers for the LGBTQ+ community.

In her book *Against Interpretation*, the American essayist and intellectual Susan Sontag, also known as 'The Dark Lady of American Letters', suggested that critics spend so much time analysing art they can't ever enjoy it. Music is the same. People spend too much time poring over genres instead of letting it go and letting it flow. Trying to pigeonhole the eclecticism that exists in a well-run label defeats the purpose, taking away from the enjoyment.

TV producer Phil Redmond, who created *Grange Hill*, *Brookside* and *Hollyoaks*, has shared a funny anecdote about a discussion on genres that he'd had with then Channel 4 Head of Nations and Regions, Stuart Cosgrove. Cosgrove had recently quit after twenty years, going on to write *Detroit 67: The Year That Changed Soul*, *Young Soul Rebel: A Personal History of Northern Soul*, *Memphis 68: The Tragedy of Southern Soul* and *Hey America!* (all published by Polygon). Cosgrove asked, 'Who watches TV by genre? Oh, tonight I might watch a bit of religion, followed by some factual, then some drama.'

Equally, with music, we don't get home to our record collection and think, 'Tonight, I'll open with some gospel, then Algerian dance, then some punk, jump over to R&B, back to Lebanese folk music, then some Moroccan jazz, finishing with a 1960s psychedelic box set.' We grab what catches our eye. The sensible approach, with a record company, is to accept a broad roster and not get overly concerned about niche or genre.

Kill Rock Stars eventually looked away from the Pacific Northwest, signing bands from elsewhere. It prefers bands that cultivate a scene, knowing they will connect and spread the word. Now it could be anywhere geographically, so if you're in a band in Brighton, Chicago or Sydney, expect a call.

Slim Moon left the label in 2006, taking on an A&R role at Nonesuch Records then Rykodisc. In between spells working at his wife's management company, he also co-founded the Portland Folk Festival.

In 2014, he left music to become a minister at the First Unitarian Church in Portland. When Moon left the label, his wife, Portia Sabin, took over. Kill Rock Stars is now one of the few female-run record companies in the USA. Its commitment to spoken-word releases continues today, with a run scheduled by the area's best stand-up comedians. The best of the comedy can be found on Cameron Esposito's *Same Sex Symbol* and in Amy Miller's quietly ferocious style on her *Solid Gold* album.

PLAYLIST: MY TOP 5 ALBUMS

Kill Rock Stars: *Kill Rock Stars*
Bikini Kill: *Pussy Whipped*
Sleater-Kinney: *One Beat*
Matrimony: *Kitty Finger*
Deerhoof: *The Tears and Music of Love*

MERGE RECORDS

Founders: Laura Ballance and Mac McCaughan

Influential: Superchunk, Spoon, Magnetic Fields, Arcade Fire

MERGE WAS FORMED IN 1989 in Durham, North Carolina by Laura Ballance and Mac McCaughan. Like many US indie labels from this era, the label was created with the express intention of releasing the founders' or their friends' music. They wanted to curate a musical legacy for the future, so from Ballance's home, they began to release singles; it was grassroots, word of mouth, and the process was slow and organic. Yet they would prove adept at it. Within a few years, they had formed one of the most successful independent labels in the USA, and it continues to be one of the most implausible stories in the US independent music industry. Merge managed to outthink and outflank the majors by reaching the top of the *Billboard* charts with Arcade Fire.

While on a road trip, Ballance and McCaughan dropped by the offices of Sub Pop in Seattle. This is when their idea crystallised. Seeing a regional label focus on local bands like Mudhoney and Nirvana was a moment. Ballance explained to David Chiu in *Forbes Magazine*:

> It kind of pushed us over the edge into this idea that, 'We live in this place where there's all these people who are in bands. There are lots of awesome bands around and they come and go. Wouldn't it be cool if we could just put out seven-inches or something to document what's happening in our little scene?' I didn't think that we'd be doing it this long.

Like Sub Pop and Kill Rock Stars, geography and base were key. Merge Records formed in Durham (home to Duke University and North

Carolina Central University) and is now based in Raleigh, the state capital of North Carolina, the city of oaks and neighbour to Chapel Hill (University of North Carolina). It's a vibrant, creative area full of students, bars, venues and bands.

Highly respected within the US music scene, Mac McCaughan is rightly considered the real deal. And unlike contemporaries running established indie labels, he practised what he preached, delivering melodic punk with an indie twist with his band, Superchunk. They released their debut album in September 1990, and by 1993, their popularity and the area's alternative-rock scene threatened to nudge Chapel Hill and Durham into becoming the next Seattle. From Superchunk tours, Merge started to meet and release other friends' work. Bands like Lambchop would eventually go on to release fifteen albums with the label.

Merge's roster, with Fruit Bats, Bob Mould, Magnetic Fields, Neutral Milk Hotel, She & Him, The Mountain Goats, Hiss Golden Messenger, Imperial Teen, Teenage Fanclub and Spoon, makes it one of the labels indie music fans adore. You can see how its business model worked. The approach was simple: the label was for artists they loved. McCaughan, speaking in 2015, told NPR: 'We've always run the label like music fans.' He continued, 'And our customer base is music fans. We started a label, and we run a label counting on there being people like us.' However, having to be 100 per cent convinced with an artist can also prove disadvantageous. It means Merge's approach eliminates any punts. The history of popular music is full of A&R people acting on instinct when no one else can see it. In not risk taking, Merge would be missing out.

In the same NPR interview, McCaughan suggested that as a kid he had a feeling, universal to music fans. 'Growing up and looking at my dad's record collection, I didn't know how stuff got from music being played by the Rolling Stones to music on a record in my dad's living room.' That sums up the thought process of many young music fans, bedazzled by how it all connects.

Like many other eventual label bosses, he spent time at the coal seam, working in Schoolkids Records in nearby Chapel Hill. Meanwhile, Laura Ballance did the accounts, packaging and dealing with the logistics, while attending university and holding down two jobs.

Their game plan – working with bands they are into – sounds over-simplistic but it has proven a winning approach. Like most fledgling independent labels with the same ethos, they just kept slowly improving by limiting their mistakes. In an article by Michael Azerrad in Columbia University's alumni magazine, McCaughan claimed that majoring in history helped his mindset: 'I learned how to think critically at Columbia,' he said. 'I use that every day.'

Merge remains low-key, and has been based in the same offices since 2001, jammed between a hair salon and a furniture store in a now gentrified and up-and-coming Durham. The premises were acquired after the success of Magnetic Fields and Neutral Milk Hotel.

There's business acumen there too. With its band, Superchunk, Merge had a manufacturing distribution deal with Touch & Go, which allowed it to start making albums. This raised both the label and the band's profile. Before this, the band had signed with Matador Records for their first two albums. In between their two Matador albums *No Pocky for Kitty* and *On the Mouth*, they released a compilation on Merge called *Tossing Seeds (89–91)*. The label started to take off with Superchunk albums *Foolish* (1994) and *This Is Where the Strings Come In* (1995), then in the late 1990s with Neutral Milk Hotel, The Magnetic Fields, Spoon and Arcade Fire. In 2001, Spoon were picked up after the band had been discarded by Elektra – the relationship worked; they are still on Merge.

It was Canadian band Arcade Fire who would prove the label's game-changers, becoming one of the biggest bands in the 2000s with the albums *Funeral*, *Neon Bible*, *The Suburbs* and *Reflektor*. It was McCaughan's friend and Arcade Fire's original drummer Howard Bilerman who alerted Merge to the Montreal band. By their third album, *The Suburbs*, they had achieved a different level globally, reaching number 1 on *Billboard* and winning Grammy Awards.

Merge has even behaved responsibly with its prosperity. It's given proceeds of releases to organisations such as the Southern Poverty Law Center. Merge has backed and sponsored various local artistic projects, Durham's Full Frame Documentary Film Festival and Duke

University's Nasher Museum, as well as improving local buildings and investing in businesses around its offices.

Currently, Merge has a mixture of experienced artists like Teenage Fanclub, Bob Mould and Redd Kross, and new artists like Waxahatchee, Titus Andronicus and Torres. The label started locally and is now global. Its founders' expectations remained realistic and they took small steps. It was 1994 before Merge hired its first employee. They refused moves to big city music industry hubs, New York or Los Angeles, and remained in North Carolina where they now have sixteen employees. Sometimes good intentions can work. In the same Columbia University magazine interview with Azerrad, McCaughan underlined his ethos and approach. 'When people ask, "How do you decide which artists you want to work with?" the answer has always been: artists that we like,' McCaughan said. 'There are no criteria beyond that.'

PLAYLIST: MY TOP 5 ALBUMS

Superchunk: *Foolish*
Neutral Milk Hotel: *In the Aeroplane Over the Sea*
Magnetic Fields: *69 Love Songs*
Hiss Golden Messenger: *Heart Like a Levee*
Spoon: *Ga Ga Ga Ga Ga*

MOTOWN

Founder: Berry Gordy Jr

Influential: The Temptations, The Four Tops, Marvin Gaye, The Supremes

This is a brief overview of Motown. There would eventually be around seventeen labels under the 'Motown' umbrella. My focus is mainly on the first imprint, Tamla Records, founded on 7 June 1958, Motown Records, set up around the same time, and then just Motown, the famous one. I've referred to any and all of these as 'Motown'.

BERRY GORDY'S BIGGEST INSPIRATION as a youngster was Joseph Louis Barrow. He wasn't a singer. He was a hero to most African-American kids: Joe Louis, 'The Brown Bomber', the heavyweight champion of the world. Gordy left school at 16 to become a boxer. The featherweight would prove promising, though any poetry in motion and emerging songwriting talent would be placed on hold. In common with the formative years of many label bosses, Gordy had a few twists and turns before becoming a musical heavyweight.

Gordy served in the army in the Korean War. His first musical venture proved disastrous. He opened a jazz record store at a time when the workers in Detroit wanted to hear the blues. A colossal error in judgement led him to bankruptcy. It also found the now-married father of three in the more arduous location of Detroit's Ford Lincoln-Mercury automobile plant. But even on duty at the car plant, he continued to hone his songwriting. Realising it was all or nothing, he quit his job and his wife threw him out. At this point, he wrote the song 'To Be Loved', which became a hit in 1957 for Jackie Wilson.

(He also co-wrote 'Reet Petite'.) Most importantly, Gordy proved to himself that he could do this.

In a conversation with his friend, Smokey Robinson, the singer was complaining about his frustrations at not getting a break with The Miracles. Gordy told Robinson to go home and listen to the radio. To listen carefully to what was being played, process it, break it down and learn from it. To focus on the lyrics, the shape and the hook of the music being played on the radio.

This is where The Silhouettes' 'Get a Job' becomes a crucial song in the Motown story. It was a hit in 1957, reaching number 1 and seldom off the radio. Robinson had been doing what Berry told him ... listening. He wrote a reprise called 'Got a Job'. Berry loved it, thought it was clever, recorded it, took it to New York and sold it to End Records, where it became a hit for The Miracles. When Gordy showed Robinson the cheque for $3.18, Smokey said: 'If that's all you can make, you'd be better forming your own record company.' Thus, Motown would be formed.

Gordy discovered Marv Johnson, singing at a fair, and convinced him to sign with his fledgling label. He produced and co-wrote his first single, 'Come to Me' (T 101), for Tamla, recorded in February and released in May 1959. It became a local hit across the Midwest, but Gordy wasn't able to distribute the song nationally, so he sold the rights to United Artists. Already possessing a great ear for a hit, Gordy knew it had the potential to be a nationwide crossover. Leasing it to United Artists, to be distributed nationally, he needed $800 to secure his end of the deal, and to quickly set up an imprint for regional release. So Gordy borrowed $800, a considerable sum in the late 1950s, from his family to start up a record label. They reluctantly agreed to help. The label would be called Tamla Records. By the end of the

FANORAK FACT

One of the secrets to getting the Motown sound was created by the chief engineer, Mike McClain, who had a pocket-sized radio built on the studio wall. Any recordings were played through the radio to make sure records had the high-end treble and sharpness to cut through. If it didn't work on the wall radio, it wouldn't work on a car radio.

year, the song had started to become a hit, reaching number 30 on the *Billboard* charts and number 6 on the R&B charts.

Motown Records released the Miracles' 'Bad Girl', written by Berry Gordy Jr and Smokey Robinson. Again, it was the same approach – it was released regionally on Motown Records and nationally by Chess Records. It was the only song the band would release on Motown Records; in future, they issued via Tamla Records.

Learning from their previous releases, particularly 'Got a Job', Gordy and Robinson realised they would never make money unless Motown went national by itself. They had to do their distribution. The label's first breakthrough song would be 'Money (That's What I Want)' by Barrett Strong, co-written by Berry Gordy. It reached number 2 on the *Billboard* R&B chart.

The label would do many things; it chimed and resonated through its astounding music, the sound of blues and gospel blended into glorious pop. It would, through the popularity of Black artists, help the civil rights movement, as their broad crossover success suppressed racial tensions.

Gordy's experience at the automobile plant would prove fruitful. It was here that he learned about assembling, manufacturing, teamwork and production – he would bring the same process to his label, writing, producing, manufacturing, selling and churning out hits like cars. Events moved quickly; Gordy bought a property in Detroit, converted the garage into a recording studio, and with a console, the kitchen became the nerve centre and control room.

As the 1960s dawned, 1961 saw Smokey Robinson and the Miracles have the label's first million-selling 45 with 'Shop Around'. The Marvelettes had the label's first number 1 single with 'Please Mr Postman'. Then they signed The Temptations and The Supremes – acts who, over the coming years, would release era-defining classics, making the label a driving force, a pulsating back beat and soundtrack to the decade.

Motown (and its subsidiaries like Tamla) produced hit after hit: 'Dancing in the Street', 'Baby Love', 'My Girl', 'Stop in the Name of Love', 'Reach Out (I'll Be There)', 'Tears of a Clown', 'Nowhere to Run', 'The Tracks of My Tears' and 'Uptight, Everything Is Alright'. The music cut across all factions of society. In 1969, Motown signed

The Jackson 5. The Temptations would close the 1960s with the watershed, psychedelic classic album *Cloud Nine*.

When it looked like the label might have peaked, the 1970s arguably brought some of its best-loved and most popular albums, including Marvin Gaye's *What's Going On*, in 1971 (Tamla). In 1972, Gordy moved operations to Los Angeles and Stevie Wonder's *Talking Book* (Tamla) was released. He would go on to release *Innervisions* in 1973, and *Songs in the Key of Life* in 1976.

The label produced music so unique that it became known as the 'Motown Sound'. This was engineered pop, gospel, soul and blues with driving bass lines, tambourines, car horns, bicycle chains, and distinctive rolling drum beats augmented with hand claps and foot stomps. The music was tight and hit with a punch, thanks to the experienced backing musicians and vocal groups. If anyone asks you to drum in a 'Motown style', it's easy: don't hit any crash cymbals in the drum patterns. There's a reason for this. The songs would be recorded in one room and the sound of the crash cymbals would bleed into the other mics in the tiny room. So drummers had to learn to improvise with high tom fills, rarely using any swishing crash cymbals.

As one of the most high-profile African American record labels, Tamla Motown's very existence did more for social reform than any politician has ever done. Before Motown was on the scene, there were only two other Black-owned labels in the USA: Duke Records in Houston and Vee-Jay Records in Chicago. They were gospel and R&B labels – Vee-Jay was the first to release The Beatles in the States. There had also been Black Swan, a short-lived Harlem label, mostly jazz, in 1921. The trouble, though, was getting sales, as distribution and radio play were in the hands of whites. The Motown label transcended the musical sphere and broke down racial prejudice. This was the sound of a confident Black

FANORAK FACT

An early vocal backing group on several Berry Gordy-produced songs, The Rayber Voices, included Brian Holland, Robert Bateman and Raynoma Liles. The name Rayber is made up of the 'Ray' from Raynoma and the 'Ber' from Berry. Raynoma would become his second wife.

America; one of strong, successful entertainers, songwriters and producers who changed perceptions.

As with all the best labels, many components and factors came together at once: the identity, the geography, the sound and the great songwriters like Smokey Robinson, as well as Eddie Holland, Lamont Dozier and Brian Holland (Holland-Dozier-Holland). It worked with the Funk Brothers, accomplished session men who were paid by the day. Songs were written, recorded, produced and released quickly, just like on the production line Berry Gordy had stood and watched, and learned from. Now his commodity wasn't cars, it was music.

Uncomplicated. Band. Songwriters. Songs with a simple formula: beginning, middle and end – short stories about happiness or heartache. The house band played and then it was recorded. Keep on keeping it simple. Motown was famous for having quality control meetings every Friday where songs would be pitched. The young stars who signed would have lessons in deportment, stage presence and dance moves.

In the end, despite everything, the approach, the brand identity, Motown was about the wonderful songs and music produced by incredibly talented people. People like Smokey Robinson and the Miracles, The Temptations, Gladys Knight and the Pips, Martha Reeves and the Vandellas, The Four Tops, Stevie Wonder, The Supremes, Marvin Gaye and The Jackson 5.

By the 1980s, Motown seemed more about Hollywood glamour, with artists like Diana Ross, who played Billie Holiday in *Lady Sings the Blues*. It would also prove fruitful for Rick James and Lionel Richie. By 1988, after almost thirty years in the business, Berry Gordy sold the label to MCA, which would go on to sell to PolyGram, which in turn was bought by Universal.

Motown was part of the Universal Music Group until 2011 (Universal Motown and Universal Motown Republic Group). From 2011 to 2014, it was part of the Island Def Jam Music Group. Universal Music Group then announced the dissolution of Island Def Jam, and Motown moved to Los Angeles as part of the Capitol Music Group.

FANORAK FACT

The name of Tamla Records came from *Tammy*, a Debbie Reynolds movie popular at the time.

The fiscal moves, mergers and takeovers can't overshadow a label that became a force for social change. Its music, style and attitude helped break down barriers in a dangerously divided, racially segregated society. Motown scored over 200 number 1 hit singles worldwide. They are best encapsulated in Berry Gordy's Motown Records, Tamla (T 54176) release, written by Motown writers Whitfield and Strong, produced by Norman Whitfield in Hitsville USA (Studio A): the near perfection of Marvin Gaye, singing 'I Heard It Through the Grapevine'.

PLAYLIST: MY TOP 5 ALBUMS

Marvin Gaye: *What's Going On*
Smokey Robinson and the Miracles: *Goin' to a Go-Go*
The Temptations: *The Sky's the Limit*
Gladys Knight and the Pips: *Nitty Gritty*
Stevie Wonder: *Innervisions*

MUTE RECORDS

Founder: Daniel Miller

Influential: Depeche Mode, Nick Cave and the Bad Seeds, Moby, Richard Hawley

I'M ALWAYS CAPTIVATED BY the journey taken by those inspired to start a label. With Daniel Miller, the founder of Mute, it began when he was watching a guest lecturer during his three-year course in film and TV at Guildford Art School. The man in question was a poet and sound artist, Ron Geesin.

Geesin had recently worked with Pink Floyd and brought along a synthesizer, an EMS SYNTH A, the portable version of what Brian Eno played in Roxy Music. Miller was both inspired and mesmerised. He eventually bought a Korg 700s and, with a love of German bands like Can, Neu! and Kraftwerk, made music in his bedroom.

Inspired by J.G. Ballard's *Crash*, Miller wrote 'Warm Leatherette', releasing it under the name The Normal. He considered doing 500 singles. This was 1977. Creative optimism was everywhere.

After collecting some test pressings, Miller found shops that would order some. The pressing plant was in East London; the first place he came to was a cool shop called Small Wonder, which ordered ten copies. He then headed to the Rough Trade shop where Geoff Travis and his business partner Richard Scott had a listen, loved it and offered him a distribution deal. When they asked how many copies Miller was considering pressing, and the answer came back as 500, they said they needed at least 2,000.

The record took off. One of the big three influential music papers of the time, *Sounds* (the others were *Melody Maker* and *NME*) reviewed it as 'single of the century'. More great reviews followed. However, when the influential Radio 1 DJ John Peel gave the record his seal of approval and heavy airplay, 'Warm Leatherette' went on to sell over 30,000 copies. Miller's life changed. It would be redefined by this song. This critically acclaimed debut eventually allowed him to form and run his own record label. Setting up Mute, Miller had the willingness and determination to have a go, unafraid of the consequences of failure.

Miller had placed his name and address on every copy of his single sold, so started receiving fan mail, letters and demos. He loved one tape in particular, by Fad Gadget, real name Frank Tovey (1956–2002), an avant-garde performer and pioneer of electronic music. Miller decided to release it. In 1978, Mute's second single was Fad Gadget's 'Back to Nature'. While the first single may have been a lucky break, the sales of his second confirmed Daniel Miller as a record label boss.

The first album on the label was Deutsch-Amerikanische Freundschaft's *Die Kleinen und die Bösen*. DAF were a modernist synth pop punk duo. They were entertaining, hedonistic and difficult to place musically, but great to dance to on your own when the house was empty. Most label bosses, though, naturally gravitate towards a particular artist on their label, like a favourite child. For Miller, this would be Depeche Mode. While promoting his second album, Fad Gadget was playing at a pub called The Bridge House in Canning Town. Miller noticed this young-looking support band, wearing questionable, homemade, New Romantic clothes. Their gear consisted of three keyboards balanced on top of beer crates. However, from the first song, they blew his mind. Each song was better than the previous one.

Most of the material from the same gig would become the basis of their debut album. When Miller tried to speak to them, they shrugged him off, saying they were supporting someone else the following week: if he wanted to see them again, he should come along. This time he took a few trusted allies, who agreed that Miller had to sign Depeche Mode. Miller offered them a deal and put out their first single, 'Dreaming of Me', in 1981. He would also have a hand in co-producing their first five albums, and at this point, he was thought by the band as something of an unofficial member.

Depeche Mode's debut single, taken from the album *Speak and Spell*, reached number 57 in April 1981, and the band followed it up with a remarkable run of hits between 1981 and 1985: 'New Life' (number 11), 'Just Can't Get Enough' (number 8), 'See You' (number 6), 'Everything Counts' (number 6) and 'People are People' (number 4), to name a few. Despite Vince Clarke leaving and Martin L. Gore taking over writing credits, Depeche Mode exceeded even the band's expectations. By the 1990s, they would be playing in vast arenas in the USA and crossing over to alternative rock audiences. Inventive MTV videos and songs such as 'Personal Jesus' (number 13) and 'Enjoy the Silence' (number 6) cemented their reputation.

Capturing the essence of the label is difficult. Mute, as it should, has been defined by Daniel Miller's tastes. He had a strong affinity with every act he signed. Mute's legacy is one of clever contradiction. An outline sketch highlights the first tranche of bands: The Normal, Fad Gadget, DAF and Silicon Teens. They were followed by the unbelievable pop music of Depeche Mode, Yazoo, The Assembly (Dave Clarke and Feargal Sharkey) and Erasure. Later, you would also have Einstürzende Neubauten, who eschewed the classic beat combo for their sonic scrap yard art. In 1983, the highly influential, post-punk Birthday Party left 4AD to sign with Mute. They would split and Nick Cave and the Bad Seeds would start a long and fruitful career with the label. Mute would house acts like Laibach and Nitzer Ebb. There would be various collaborations and the securing of the back catalogue of Throbbing Gristle, Cabaret Voltaire and Richard E. Kirk. Then came imprints like Blast First and Novamute, which featured artists such as Sonic Youth and Richie Hawtin.

We then have the label's next chapter, with Goldfrapp, Moby and Liars, selling to EMI and the final section of the story, when the label was back as an independent again, with the release of New Order, Can (*The Lost Tapes* on Spoon Records and Mute reissuing the classic *Tago Mago*), Kraftwerk and The Residents.

You can make sense of anything if you pore over it enough: Picasso, Joyce's *Ulysses*, even Captain Beefheart. Perhaps the branding or the common thread is incoherence, randomness, the idea of the outsider, a label pushing the envelope. This diverse range of artists is what binds the label and makes Mute special. It's like an avant-garde jigsaw where the pieces aren't supposed to fit, yet somehow make sense. Post-industrial music or electropunk, classic post-punk and pop all meshed together, and all underpinned by the remarkably consistent Nick Cave and the global reach of Depeche Mode.

Label highlights? Again it's purely about music with a personal connection. Nick Cave is probably one of my favourite artists. I've seen him in his many guises, as a solo artist, with the Bad Seeds, and with Grinderman, and have enjoyed his collective work. From *Tender Prey* and *Henry's Dream* to *Abattoir Blues / Lyre of Orpheus*, to *Dig, Lazarus, Dig!!!* and *Push the Sky Away*, I haven't been let down by any album he's done.

Former Longpigs and Pulp guitarist Richard Hawley's third album, the Mercury-nominated *Coles Corner*, confirmed him as something of the country-tinged crooner with an ear for a song (in the Lee Hazelwood, Fred Neil songbook), and the texture, space and orchestration of Scott Walker. All the good stuff, for tasteful punk, grunge and indie kids to grow old with.

You regularly hear the term 'influential' used when you discuss record labels and bands. In the case of Mute Records, the term is merited. Mute has been a significant creative force because of its wide-ranging impact, from punk/DIY with Fad Gadget, Robert Rental, DAF and Silicon Teens, to pop with Depeche Mode, Yazoo and Erasure. Meanwhile, the label was dark and avant-garde with Smegma from Los Angeles and even had a Satanist, as you do, Boyd Rice, banging out seminal experimental noise as NON. It had post-punk with the Birthday Party and Einstürzende Neubauten. Miller explains how it all makes sense to him in the notes of *Mute Audio Documents 1978–1984*. 'It all fits together in my head, but almost every time we sign a band, whether it was the Birthday Party or Erasure, people would say that's a bit weird for Mute.'

In the end, a label can have its identity, sound and bands, its unique flavour and taste.

The owners who guide the ship tend to show loyalty. Some label owners, like Simon Reynolds at Bella Union and Laurence Bell at Domino, favour the long game: if you are patient enough, it can work. In the same way, Miller has resolutely stuck by his artists.

EMI bought Mute in 2002 and Daniel Miller was given a role as executive chairman. However, in 2010, Miller and Mute left EMI to become independent again, kind of. The parting, unusually for the record industry, was an amicable and mutual one. However, the current trend towards conglomerate ownership due to EU regulations made the deal complex. Miller started a brand-new company. He licensed the label name and brand, Mute, from EMI. Universal bought EMI, and then BMG bought Mute from Universal as part of an EU divestment (all in accordance with EU regulations). BMG currently owns the Mute catalogue, name and trademark, and the licence agreement has been transferred to BMG Music Rights, though of course where all this lands in a post-Brexit UK is anyone's guess.

PLAYLIST: MY TOP 5 ALBUMS
Nick Cave and the Bad Seeds: *Dig, Lazarus, Dig!!!*
Depeche Mode: *Speak and Spell*
Richard Hawley: *Coles Corner*
Nick Cave and the Bad Seeds: *Push the Sky Away*
Goldfrapp: *Black Cherry*

OHR

Founders: Rolf-Ulrich Kaiser and Peter Meisel

Influential: Tangerine Dream, Guru Guru and Ash Ra Tempel

'IT BEGAN OUT OF nothing, was given a joke name, and became the pop influence *du jour*: krautrock, kosmische musik, elektronische musik, or whatever you wish to call German experimental rock from the 1970s'. Thus wrote *Guardian* music journalist and author Jon Savage, in March 2010.

Chief among this movement was the record label Ohr (German for 'Ear'), an enormously influential and pioneering jazz, electronic, experimental and rock label, based in Berlin. It was formed by producer Rolf-Ulrich Kaiser and the founder of Hansa Records/Metronome, Peter Meisel.

The label's output would have a broad influence, especially the minimalist motorik beat – a 4/4 rhythm associated with bands like Neu! and the Krautrock movement. Here we had groups like Faust, Can, Organisation and Amon Düül II, cognisant of a trippy, avant-garde Pink Floyd, Frank Zappa and The Velvet Underground.

Most people have an introduction, an 'in', leading them to a certain band or genre. My way to Ohr, the home of Krautrock, was the music of Ash Ra Tempel and came via the recommendation of Julian Cope. His description of their 1973 album *Join Inn* intrigued me somewhat, especially mentions of their space rock and psychedelic feel. In one review, Cope waxed lyrical about the drummer Klaus Schulze. With regard to Schulze's playing on *Join Inn*, Cope remarked:

> *Join Inn* saw the return of Klaus Schulze, who is the one person to hugely influence the whole sound of their first album. Playing drums

as egolessly as it is possible, and yet creating a rumbling thunderstorm of sound. Also on their first album he used synthesizers/keyboards to create a cosmic vibe never before heard on record.

The album has two songs, one on each side. Like some other cat once familiar with Berlin would say, it's a moonage daydream.

Sometimes words like 'influential' and 'experimental' can be overused and scare people off. Don't be. Ohr was formed by experienced producers and music business people. In terms of the label's actual set-up, we have the familiar template: a defined genre, the classic label name and the idea of the ear; it's simple but great. Then we have producers and experienced music industry people at the helm. We have the image, marketing and artwork. The first five releases on Ohr used the artwork of Mainz-based artist Reinhard Hippen, famed for using dismembered toy doll parts in his work. So we now have a distinct sound, brand and genre.

Like many other labels that encouraged and fostered collaboration, Ohr soon faced a mountain of legal Spiegel. Rolf-Ulrich Kaiser moved to set up two different labels. First, there was Pilz, used for more folk-sounding artists, then his space-rock label Kosmische Kuriere (later Kosmische Musik). Both became subject to litigation.

Ohr's most famous band were Tangerine Dream. Their debut album, *Electronic Meditation*, featured Edgar Froese, Conrad Schnitzler and Klaus Schulze, and was recorded as the band improvised during rehearsals. Their spaced-out riffs sounded like Pink Floyd, and that was enough for Ohr – a deal was offered. Ohr also had Embryo, Guru Guru and Ash Ra Tempel.

Considering its short existence, Ohr was nevertheless highly productive. The first Ohr album was released in April 1970 and the final one, recorded in 1973, came out in early 1974. Ohr only existed for four years, but in that small period it released an unbelievable thirty-three albums, four of which were double LPs, and there were also twelve singles. After that, Ohr, Kosmische Kuriere/Musik and Pilz faced legal challenges from their own artists, which led to the seizure of the three labels.

Any label that is worthy of discussion some fifty years later usually encapsulates the spirit of that age. The social backdrop of the time and the desire for expression were crucial. Coming into the new decade, Europe had been awash with political activists and student riots. People had the social and creative freedom their parents never had. Stockhausen was the man, the avant-garde – his music was perhaps best described as The Clangers on a night out with the Daleks, on acid. Thinking and playing outside the box was the order of the day, and artistic freedom was cherished.

I make no apologies for including this short-lived but incredibly productive label.

PLAYLIST: MY TOP 5 ALBUMS

Tangerine Dream: *Electronic Meditation*
Ash Ra Tempel: *Join Inn*
Klaus Schulze: *Irrlicht*
Birth Control: *Operation*
Embryo: *Opal*

PARLOPHONE

Founder: Carl Lindström

Influential: The Beatles, Kraftwerk, Bowie, Pink Floyd, Blur

IN COMMON WITH MANY recording companies at the turn of the nineteenth into the twentieth century, Parlophone's history is a confusing and convoluted one. The Carl Lindström Company, founded in Germany in 1896, owned several record companies including Odeon and Parlophone (founded as Parlophon). Odeon had operations in India, Africa and South America, and succeeded by assimilating and recording whatever music was popular in each region. Odeon is famous for being the first company to use both sides of a vinyl record. It made inroads when it formed OKeh Records in the USA, named after the initials of Otto K.E. Heinemann who managed the label. Heinemann made it big in the USA by mining a hitherto untapped seam of 'race' music – what we now call the blues.

OKeh was formed in 1916, breaking big with Mamie Smith in 1920. This was a significant moment in popular music history. It was the first recording of a Black blues singer. In 1920, Mamie Smith cut 'That Thing Called Love' and 'You Can't Keep a Good Man Down' with Perry Bradford. Bradford, a Black songwriter and bandleader, had trouble convincing the label's musical director, Fred Hagar, to record the song. Hagar had been threatened with a boycott if he proceeded with a Black singer who was backed by white musicians. He did, and Mamie Smith went on to have smash hits with two songs written by Perry Bradford, 'Crazy Blues' and 'It's Right Here for You' (If You Don't Get It 'Taint No Fault of Mine)'. Both sold millions and opened up the African American audience.

The UK offshoot, Parlophone Records, was set up in 1923. By 1926, though, it had been acquired by the Columbia Gramophone Company, which eventually merged with the Gramophone Company, becoming EMI. In the 1930s and 1940s, Parlophone was considered a jazz label and introduced US names like Louis Armstrong and Duke Ellington to the UK.

In the 1950s, Parlophone licensed influential acts from cool New York/Los Angeles label, Bethlehem Records. Gus Wildi's great jazz label had a large and varied roster of artists including Charlie Mingus, Howard McGhee, Nina Simone, Mel Tormé, Billy Eckstine, Art Blakey, Dexter Gordon and Duke Ellington. It also had top producer Creed Taylor, harnessing the sound of both East Coast bop and West Coast jazz. The Bethlehem acts gave Parlophone kudos and credibility, though as far as EMI was concerned, insufficient income was being generated.

In 1950, George Martin joined EMI as an assistant to the Parlophone label manager, Oscar Preuss. When Preuss resigned in 1955, Martin was promoted to boss. At this point, Parlophone was considered EMI's poor relation, a largely ignored label save among jazz enthusiasts and fans of comedy records. Martin's early hits would be novelty records like 'Hole in the Ground' by Bernard Cribbins, *The Goons* and *Beyond The Fringe* with Peter Cook, Dudley Moore, Jonathan Miller and Alan Bennett.

However, Martin, as well as being a great musician (he was an accomplished oboe player), was forward-thinking and keen to experiment. He had even recorded and released a dance record, in 1962, called 'Time Beat' under the pseudonym Ray Cathode. Perhaps he was frustrated and needed a project, a band that matched his ambition. He was desperate to work with musicians instead of another comedy project.

In many subsequent interviews, George Martin admitted he was keen to find a tight, efficient backing group behind a named lead singing star. He was jealous of Norrie Paramor's success with Cliff Richard and

> **FANORAK FACT**
>
> Many people think the Parlophone logo is a UK pound sterling sign. It is the German letter 'L' for Lindström, the original founder.

the Shadows. Martin knew it would be a lucrative move if Parlophone could find a matinee-idol crooner, supported by a talented, proficient, popular, beat combo band.

By the end of the 1950s, as rock 'n' roll became more polished and mainstream, Parlophone had its first number 1 hit with Adam Faith's 'What Do You Want' (with more than a passing nod to the pizzicato string style of Buddy Holly's 'It Doesn't Matter Anymore'), making a star out of Faith.

A manager from Liverpool, Brian Epstein, had been in London, trying to push his band, The Beatles. Martin heard on the grapevine that Epstein was actively promoting his band and knew they had failed an audition with Decca. He agreed to meet with Epstein on 13 February 1962 to listen to the Decca tapes, famously describing them as 'unpromising'. However, he believed they had something different, an interesting sound, and he heard authenticity and power in the rock 'n' roll vocals of Lennon and McCartney.

After a further meeting, in May 1962, Martin agreed to offer a basic industry-standard deal. The offer of a contract was dependent on an audition tape. Martin wouldn't sign the contract until he'd heard what he always referred to as a recording test. If he was happy with them, he would sign the deal. The Beatles would receive a penny for each record sold. Martin viewed it as a nothing-to-lose punt, later conceding that he had almost taken pity on Epstein for his lack of luck with the band. The drummer aside, he recognised a vibrancy in the band members that fitted the shape of a great backing band for the handsome crooner. That they wrote their own songs was a bonus.

Martin believed their original compositions weren't strong enough. He also convinced them they must substantially improve and needed significant changes in equipment to make it as professional musicians. After the debriefing, Martin asked if there was anything the band didn't like. This is when George Harrison famously quipped, 'Your tie, for one.' As well as breaking the ice, it sealed the band's fate. Martin loved their personalities and charm, and knew he could work with them. However, he had major misgivings about drummer Pete Best; he would have to be replaced.

In September 1962, The Beatles returned with Ringo Starr as their new drummer. Martin wanted to release Mitch Murray's 'How Do You

Do It?' The band reluctantly performed and recorded it, but refused to release it as their first single. The song had already been turned down by Adam Faith and Brian Poole. Martin knew it was a hit and fitted with both 'Love Me Do' and the original (slower) version of 'Please Please Me'.

Unimpressed with Ringo's performance on 'Love Me Do', he brought in an experienced session drummer, Andy White, to re-record it the following week. 'Love Me Do' reached number 17 and Martin moved quickly to record a follow-up. 'Please Please Me' was originally written by John and presented to Martin in the style of Roy Orbison's 'Only the Lonely'. In November 1962 – at George's insistence – they sped up the song and recorded an up-tempo version. Martin famously announced over the studio speakers, 'Gentlemen, you have just made your first number-one record.'

With the vital change to 'Please Please Me', Martin transformed the band's career. Here was a band that stood out from the crowd. The *NME*'s Keith Fordyce was positive, summing up what it must have been like to hear the band at this point. On 11 January 1963 he wrote: 'This vocal and instrumental quartet has turned out a really enjoyable platter, full of beat, vigour and vitality – and what's more, it's different. I can't think of any other group currently recording in this style.'

It would create a sea change like no other in the history of music. Parlophone released nine Beatles albums between 1963 and 1967. The label transformed from a comedy department jazz imprint irrelevance into a world-famous name.

After The Beatles made Parlophone hip, Epstein's other NEMS artists (named after North End Music Store, NEMS Enterprises was Epstein's management company), Cilla Black, Billy J. Kramer, The Fourmost and, from Manchester, The Hollies, were signed. However, in 1973 the label became dormant when EMI phased out its antiquated labels for the revamped EMI label.

You'd assume The Beatles were always there, everyone's favourite, yet their popularity has waxed and waned. When I started getting into The Beatles, they were at their least popular. After punk and new wave and into the 1980s, bands dismissed The Beatles as has-been hippies and sneered at anyone who showed any kind of reverence towards the band. However, they, along with The Rolling Stones and The Kinks, grabbed me.

I've been fortunate to be surrounded by tasteful friends and music fans who have always nudged me in the right direction. My introduction to The Beatles started with a cassette a friend gave me with *Revolver* on one side and *Rubber Soul* on the other. We always shared and discussed The Beatles and followed the same journey; you start with the big hits like 'Ticket to Ride' and inevitably find your way to 'Sexy Sadie' and 'Bungalow Bill'. You soon tune into songs like 'Rain' with backwards guitar loops and the opener on *Revolver*, 'Tomorrow Never Knows', which had five loops faded up and down at once, with every available hand in the studio put to full use. In effect, 'Tomorrow Never Knows' deconstructed the concept of 'song' as we knew it, redefined the musical landscape and paved the way for the remainder of the band's career, committed to studio experimentation.

My other defining Beatles moment occurred when I found an album called *A Collection of Beatles Oldies* in Paddy's Market, off Glasgow's Saltmarket, for 99p. When anyone asks the obvious question, 'What's your favourite Beatles album?', I usually shock everyone by saying *A Collection of Beatles Oldies*. I played it thousands of times and one of my favourite songs wasn't even a Beatles number. It was Lennon's version of Larry Williams's 'Bad Boy'.

The band's popularity started to lift again by the 1990s, helped by the release of *Live at the BBC* in 1994, the *Anthology* series and the reissue and remarketing of the band's work on CD. By 2005, the compilation of the band's number 1 songs, *1*, had sold 25 million copies. They were on Apple (see Apple) by then and not Parlophone. The public had changed its mind on The Beatles and loved them again.

The label was revived in 1980. Parlophone will forever be synonymous with

FANORAK FACT

The Beatles' appearance on *Thank Your Lucky Stars*, in January 1963, coincided with one of the worst British winters on record. People were snowed in, and the resulting TV ratings helped fire the public's imagination and propel The Beatles up the charts.

The Beatles and the Merseybeat bands. But over the following decades, at various times, the label was also home to names like David Bowie, Pink Floyd and Kate Bush. It continued to keep its finger on the pulse through the 1990s and beyond, with Blur and Radiohead, and in 2000, the label launched the multimillion-selling Coldplay. By 2017 they had racked up twenty-two Top 40 hits. Their 114-date world tour, *A Head Full of Dreams*, became the third biggest-selling tour in history and grossed $523 million in ticket sales.

In February 2013, Warner Music Group bought Parlophone Label Group for $765 million. With artists like Richard Hawley, David Guetta, Two Door Cinema Club and Gorillaz, Parlophone has been able to diversify, assimilate, evolve and survive, despite being the label defined by the phenomenal achievements of The Beatles.

PLAYLIST: MY TOP 5 ALBUMS

The Beatles: *A Collection of Beatles Oldies*
The Beatles: *Revolver*
Deep Purple: *Shades of Deep Purple*
John Lennon: *Plastic Ono Band*
The Aerovons: *Resurrection*

PHILADELPHIA INTERNATIONAL RECORDS

Founders: Kenneth Gamble and Leon Huff

Influential: The O'Jays, MFSB, Harold Melvin and the Blue Notes

PHILADELPHIA INTERNATIONAL RECORDS HAIL from a time when record labels sounded more like an airport or hotel chain. My initial attraction to the label wasn't the cool grooves or epic sounds. No, I loved the colours of the label's logo. So what, I'm shallow. The colours were a pale yellowish-orange and red like the Kodak film boxes. I also remember the word 'Philadelphia'. It was a common phrase around our house at the time, a dig at someone able to win an argument or wriggle their way out of anything: 'You'd need a Philadelphia lawyer to beat them.' Philadelphia sounded like the height of exotica and bookish intelligentsia. What did Philadelphia have to do with lawyers, a record label and cheesecake?

The label was formed in 1971 by renowned songwriters and producers Kenneth Gamble and Leon Huff with the express intention of going head-to-head with Motown. Between the lyrical skill of Gamble and the musical ear of Huff, they had enough clout and respect to approach majors for backing and distribution because of their songwriting reputation. They came close, yet couldn't agree a deal with Atlantic, which considered their asking price too high, so Gamble and Huff approached Clive Davis at CBS, who agreed to back and distribute their releases. By the time they had funding in place, they were ready to start their fledgling label.

Before launching Philadelphia International Records, Gamble and Huff earned their first hit in 1967 with The Soul Survivors' 'Expressway to Your Heart'. In 1968, for their own Gamble Records, they produced (and wrote) the brilliant Top 10 hit single, 'Cowboys to Girls' for Philadelphia's The Intruders. They were invited to work for Atlantic Records and had hits with Dusty Springfield, Archie Bell and the Drells, The Sweet Inspirations and Wilson Pickett. At Mercury, they had hits with Jerry Butler and Dee Dee Warwick.

So, having served their time, they knew what they wanted, and Philadelphia International Records would go on to exceed expectations by cultivating a local sound that became global. Like Sub Pop with Seattle, Factory with Manchester and Postcard with Glasgow, again we keep saying it, geography is crucial in cultivating a sound and a scene. Motown was Detroit, Stax was Memphis and Philadelphia International Records was, you guessed it, Philadelphia. It became one of the hippest Black music labels of all time and was instrumental in giving us the Philly Sound, or TSOP – The Sound of Philadelphia.

What defines the Philly sound? Cascading strings, the influence of soul, jazz and gospel. The steady hand and distinct sound of a team of producers and a family of diverse and talented session musicians. There's the arrangement too. It's also about the distinctive use of the groove on the hi-hats; it's always about the hi-hats. It's about the drumming – it's the sound of a shuffle – positive and upbeat. It's the point in music when the upstroke Motown beat merges with the laid-back funky groove of the Memphis sound, then gives birth to funk and opens up to disco.

Another distinguishing factor in the sound of Philadelphia International Records was the use of the voice. There was something raw and real amid the polished sound. As great soul music should be, it's the authentic sound of controlled rage and anger. However, instead of a struggle, there's a strut. There's a groove with attitude. At the heart of it, along with every

FANORAK FACT

Ironically, Gamble and Huff won the first Ahmet Ertegun award at the Rock 'n' Roll Hall of Fame Awards. At the start of Philadelphia International Records, Ertegun refused to back or distribute the label.

hit, in songs like 'The Love I Lost' by Harold Melvin and the Blue Notes and 'Love Train' by The O'Jays, there's a longing, a melancholy in the lyric, which counter-balances the positivity and energy of the beat.

Philadelphia International was forward-thinking. Gamble and Huff knew the sleek, radio-friendly texture that worked for FM radio. They also had bass players who would DI (direct input) playing directly into the mixing desk. Years of producing hits meant they knew where to place the voice, positioning it carefully, taking aim and ensuring it was ready to break your heart.

Like many labels with a top production team, Philadelphia had the crucial studio base, Sigma Sound Studios. This helped establish the Philly sound. The studio had a warmth, captured brilliantly by great mic technique and overspill. It had a network of talented studio musicians, accomplished session men and women, arrangers, writers and producers, who helped create the songs that defined the sound. Under the brilliant title of MFSB, standing for Mother, Father, Sister, Brother, or the less spiritual Mother F*****g Sons of Bitches – based on their musical prowess, not their belligerent attitude – they were the thumping heartbeat of the label's output.

MFSB were a crew of well over thirty people, primarily with Earl Young on drums, Ronnie Baker on bass and a roster of guitarists including Bobby Eli, Norman Harris (arranger too), T.J. Tindall and Roland Timbers. With vibes as in vibraphone from Vince Montana, co-owner Leon Huff would be on keys with strings by Don Renaldo. It was a phenomenal group of supremely skilled and superbly versatile musicians who would bring the sound required for the session. They knew how to play pop, bebop, jazz and soul. They would feel their way through each song and bring a unique interpretation to each session. They played with bands like The Delfonics, The O'Jays and The Three Degrees, and on the hits 'If You Don't Know Me By Now', 'Me and Mrs Jones', 'Back Stabbers' and 'When Will I See You Again'. They released eight albums under the mantle of MFSB. Their song 'TSOP (The Sound of Philadelphia)' became the theme for the TV show *Soul Train*.

The founder, owner and engineer at Sigma Sound Studio, Joe Tarsia, knew the room. (Tarsia died in November 2022. The wonderful *New York Times* obituary by Bill Friskics-Warren is a must-read.) He famously characterised the sound – the lavish strings and gospel – as 'Black music in a tuxedo'. 'If I made a contribution, it was that Philadelphia had a unique sound,' Tarsia told the *Philadelphia Inquirer* in 2018. 'You could tell a record that came from Philly if you heard it on the radio.'

Tarsia and the label's other house engineers were years ahead of their time. They gave their artists a sheen and an original sound. It was a modern, clean sound, yet this was the late 1960s and early 1970s. Gamble and Huff would be joined by masters of song arrangement, Thom Bell and Bobby Martin, to add their touch.

In 1976, Gamble and Huff produced the first of two Jacksons albums. The Jackson 5 had a distinct sound, moulded at Motown, now given the full Philly treatment. It was rumoured that their dad, Joe, had managed to negotiate a royalty rate with CBS that was nearly ten times better than their previous deal. The Jacksons were signed to Epic, which was part of CBS, who also distributed Philadelphia International Records.

There was pressure on Gamble and Huff with the albums *The Jacksons* (recorded June–October and released November 1976) and *Goin' Places* (recorded December 1976–August 1977 and released October 1977). This was a pivotal moment for The Jacksons. The albums relaunched the band, signalling a change in direction that would move them on towards the next phase of their career. Both records are magnificent. Subtle strings, great vocals, change of scene, fresh sound, smooth and upbeat: the Philly groove. Despite being on Epic, the two albums and the single releases (one, from *The Jacksons*, called 'Enjoy Yourself' went multi-platinum) have the Philadelphia International Records logo on the albums too.

Gamble and Huff's hit ratio was based on a tried-and-tested formula, followed by many before them. They had a highly respected studio base, an in-house band of top studio musicians and arrangers, and a geographical stronghold. They then created their distinct studio sound, using a talent pool that delivered polished R&B, with a plaintive vocal and a narrative of love, loss or regret, all wrapped up in an upbeat groove. The formula not only delivered hit records; these were all-time classics.

If I had to pick two songs that represent the spirit and sound of Philadelphia International Records, the first would be The O'Jays 'Back Stabbers', with its orchestral flourishes, seminal Latin groove and melodramatic lyrics. Then I would choose the Kenny Gamble and Leon Huff-penned 'When Will I See You Again' by The Three Degrees. In this song, we have an upbeat sophisticated groove and vocal arrangement that gave a worldwide hit with a histrionic song about love and longing – and someone having a fling.

Sony Music Entertainment now own the back catalogue. However, there was a feeling of loss when the building that housed Philadelphia International Records, in South Philadelphia's Broad and Spruce Street, was demolished in 2015. In 2010 the building was badly damaged by a fire, started deliberately. No one was hurt. The building was a tourist attraction and the bottom floor was a shop that sold merchandise; it was a physical reminder of the label's existence. The developers who bought it plan to build a hotel. Before Philadelphia International Records owned the building, it housed Cameo-Parkway, another great label and ironically where Gamble and Huff first met doing session work and where Joe Tarsia started out. The place may be gone, but the Philly sound, like the ones we love, lives on in our hearts, minds and record collections.

PLAYLIST: MY TOP 5 ALBUMS

MFSB: *Love Is the Message*
The O'Jays: *Ship Ahoy*
Various Artists: *The Sound of Philadelphia 73*
Tramps: *Disco Champs*
Harold Melvin and the Blue Notes: *Black & Blue*

PHILLES RECORDS

Founders: Phil Spector and Lester Sill

Influential: The Crystals, The Ronettes, Darlene Love, Ike and Tina Turner, The Righteous Brothers

IF YOU LOVE GLORIOUS pop music that reflects an era and believe it's best served within a backdrop of melodrama, exuberance, energy and great songs, then Philles Records has to be the textbook record label. The music sounds extraordinary. We've heard it so many times before, but when you listen again, it remains magical. This didn't happen by accident. It was sculpted, thought through and created by hard work. The environment and platform were set up with a formula and template to produce hits. The songs were carved, recorded and produced with invention by the colourful, demanding and egomaniacal Harvey Philip Spector.

With Philles, we must discuss the darkness and rage that would later come to define Spector, who died from complications of Covid-19 in January 2021, aged 81. Spector was a hugely influential and groundbreaking record producer. His lavish, thunderous music was often referred to as the 'Wall of Sound' and defined the 1960s. However, he was sentenced to life in prison for the murder of a woman at his home. Our focus here will be on the marvellous symphonies he produced and presented to us, yet it's impossible to separate the two. What made Spector special also made him terrifying. Throughout his life – one that reads like a novel – themes of fragility, insecurity, confusion and violence played their part in defining Phil Spector's story. His nature and personality are intertwined with his music, his life and therefore his label.

Phil Spector formed Philles in 1961 with Lester Sill. The name was created by joining Phil and Les. However, Spector's story precedes this: he was the producer and co-founder of The Teddy Bears in 1958. Showing maturity way beyond his years, Spector had his first hit single when he was in high school with The Teddy Bears and the song 'To Know Him Is to Love Him'.

For a while, after the early hits, Spector flitted between New York and Los Angeles, and it's fascinating to learn that after the second and third Teddy Bears' singles flopped, he was, for someone so committed to music, at a crossroads. In a change of direction, he enrolled at UCLA to learn about court procedure, working briefly as a part-time court stenographer. His mother was French and over the years Spector had become moderately fluent. Spector claimed to have used his French linguistic ability with his stenographic skills and headed back to New York for a job at the United Nations. When he arrived in New York without a place to stay, he headed for the offices of writers and producers Leiber and Stoller in the Brill Building, sleeping on their couch, then decided not to show up for his job at the UN.

Spector became increasingly impatient. He wanted to produce records. Ambitious to make it big in Los Angeles, he approached Lester Sill and Lee Hazlewood and convinced them to mentor him. They knew Spector had the necessary ear, vision and talent, so they spoke to Leiber and Stoller and arranged for them to take him under their wing. So Sill sent Phil back to New York to work with Leiber and Stoller. (They owed Sill: he had mentored Leiber and Stoller when they were launching their careers.) It proved a fruitful apprenticeship; Spector co-wrote 'Spanish Harlem' and played guitar on The Drifters' hit 'On Broadway'. With Leiber and Stoller, he also learned about arrangement,

FANORAK FACT

Annette Kleinbard, who was in The Teddy Bears with Spector, famously claimed Elvis as her first lover. She was nearly killed in a car accident in 1960 and suffered severe facial injuries. After the accident, she changed her name to Carol Connors and co-wrote the theme to *Rocky* along with Bill Conti and Ayn Robbins.

structure, dynamic, subtle use of strings, more nuanced orchestration, Latin rhythms and the use of backing groups.

Spector's career accelerated as a freelance producer, generating hit after hit including Gene Pitney's 'Every Breath I Take' and Curtis Lee's 'Pretty Little Angel Eyes'. It was at this point that Spector teamed up with Lester Sill to form Philles Records, in late 1961, moving out of New York and heading back to Los Angeles, working out of Gold Star Recording Studios. Having garnered advice from Sill, Hazelwood, Leiber and Stoller, on songwriting, production, A&R and promotion, Spector now had the tools required to reshape the sound and structure of popular music. He was ready to unleash what he called his 'Wagnerian approach to rock 'n' roll: little symphonies for the kids'. Speaking to London's *Evening Standard* in 1964, he explained: 'The records are built like a Wagner opera. They start simply and they end with dynamic force, meaning and purpose. It's in the mind, I dreamed it up. It's like art movies.'

Philles would start with the launch of a Brooklyn girl group called The Crystals. They scored with 'There's No Other (Like My Baby)', 'Uptown' and 'He Hit Me (And It Felt Like a Kiss)' followed in 1962 with the million-selling 'He's a Rebel'. By the age of 21, Spector would be a millionaire. He used the royalties from 'He's a Rebel' and bought Lester Sill out, gaining full ownership of Philles. Ownership meant control and the chance to develop and build his Wall of Sound with top session men like Glen Campbell and Hal Blaine. This would revolutionise the music scene and the art of producing records. The approach was quite simple: why have one guitar when you can have six? Double up and overdub, and forget one drum kit; let's have three and castanets and percussion. Strings? Yes. Orchestration? You got it, baby. You want choirs? Let's have a choir …

Within three years, the label had scored twenty consecutive smash hits, including the follow-ups from The Crystals, 'Da Doo Ron Ron' and 'Then He Kissed Me'. Hits followed, too, from The Ronettes with 'Be My Baby', 'Baby I Love You', 'The Best Part of

> **FANORAK FACT**
>
> Brian Wilson's favourite single was 'Be My Baby'. He considered Ellie Greenwich 'the greatest melody writer of all time'.

Breaking Up' and 'Walking in the Rain'. In 1963, Spector hit gold with his Christmas album, featuring Darlene Love's 'Christmas (Baby Please Come Home)' and the Ronettes' 'Santa Claus Is Coming to Town', now a Christmas favourite. The following year, The Righteous Brothers' 'You've Lost That Lovin' Feeling' sold over 2 million copies for Philles Records.

Spector had become a musical superstar, one of the biggest and most influential names in rock 'n' roll. Controversial and renowned for his temper, notoriety and work rate, he was, in 1964, famously interviewed by Tom Wolfe who hailed him, 'the first tycoon of teen'.

Genius brings its burden. Throughout his career, Phil Spector was considered an eccentric, tortured, sad but gifted artist and producer. There had always been that darkness. That sense of paranoia and depression. His fortunes most certainly turned in 1966, with the bad reception given to Ike and Tina Turner's 'River Deep – Mountain High'. Despite the quality of the recording, it was always rumoured (again this could be Spector's paranoia) that the music industry had conspired and decided to go cold on the single's release in response to Spector's rampaging ego. Ike Turner always believed the song was the victim of racial politics, with white radio stations refusing to play the record because his name was on it. The issue was most likely based on marketing. The song was produced like a pop record yet had R&B vocals. Pop fans thought it was R&B, and R&B fans assumed it was pop.

This was undoubtedly a major catalyst for Spector's disenchantment with the music scene at the time. Spector considered 'River Deep – Mountain High' his best work. It failed to score a hit in the USA, reaching only number 88 in the *Billboard* 100 (it did chart well in the UK, peaking at number 3, thanks to Rolling Stones' manager Andrew Loog Oldham's championing of the song).

'River Deep – Mountain High' was written by Spector and then husband and wife team Jeff Barry and Ellie Greenwich. The trio also wrote the timeless pop classics 'And Then He Kissed Me', 'Da Doo Ron Ron', 'Baby I Love You', 'I Can Hear Music', 'Chapel of Love' and 'Be My Baby'. But the

FANORAK FACT

Joe Meek killed his landlady, then himself, Buddy Holly's plane crashed, killing the pop genius, and Phil Spector shot and killed Lana Clarkson, all on 3 February.

negative reaction to 'River Deep – Mountain High' affected Spector's confidence and he started to become more reclusive. His life started to dismantle.

From this point, in 1966, the wheels came off at Philles. Spector stopped, turned his back on any serious work and took to repeatedly watching *Citizen Kane* and listening to Wagner's *Der Ring des Nibelungen* (The Ring Cycle). It's said *Der Ring* is the quintessence of operatic indulgence and excess, so maybe it's not too surprising Spector loved it so much.

In 1969, Spector was brought in to produce The Beatles' *Let It Be*. He and John hit it off, and he was invited to co-produce *Imagine*. He also worked with George Harrison on *All Things Must Pass*. Thanks to his work on this album, Harrison invited Spector to work on *The Concert for Bangladesh*. Spector also produced John and Yoko's *Some Time in New York City*.

With Philles Records, Spector changed how recorded music sounded. The label ran for only six years, but in this short time, Spector helped to redesign the musical terrain. Philles released twelve LPs from 1961 to 1967, though it was primarily a label best known for its prolific singles output. The Philles back catalogue is now run by Universal Music Group.

FANORAK FACT

When 'River Deep – Mountain High' co-writer Ellie Greenwich heard the acetate of the song, she yanked it off the turntable and threw it against the wall, inadvertently creating her own version of the wall of sound.

PLAYLIST: MY TOP 5 ALBUMS

Phil Spector: *A Christmas Gift for You*
The Crystals: *He's a Rebel*
The Righteous Brothers: *Just Once in My Life*
The Ronettes: *Presenting the Fabulous Ronettes*
Various: *Philles Records Presents Today's Hits*

POLYDOR RECORDS

Founders: Founded as German Polyphon-Musikwerke in 1913. It evolved from the popular music arm of Deutsche Grammophon, formed in Germany in 1946. The British subsidiary, Polydor, was started in 1954.

Influential: Cream, Jimi Hendrix, The Who, The Jam

POLYDOR RECORDS WAS AN important label, which over the years had a plethora of great artists across every genre. Its hit average is high and has been repeated over decades. Yet it is often overlooked by music fans and critics alike. Maybe it's because the label did its job so well. Shame on them for running their business properly, how uncool are they? While other labels sought out the white heat of chaos and unpredictability, Polydor worked with a cold, calculated consistency and ruthless efficiency. It's the music business. Artists have to be sold and companies benefit from effective infrastructure. Polydor had one of the best global distribution networks. Maybe its efficient business practice made the label appear bland and unexciting. But Polydor knew how to find talent, market and sell – and did it well.

There's also the perception that Polydor was an easy-listening label, one of international 'light' entertainers like Bert Kaempfert, Kurt Edelhagen, James Last and the Kessler Twins. It was successful in this field; the easy-listening sector was a vast and lucrative market. Polydor was the safe label that delivered hits with The New Seekers, Level 42 and Take That.

If I were defending Polydor in court, facing a charge of not being rock 'n' roll enough, I'd suggest that a smart team of talent scouts and deal makers brought you The Who, Jimi Hendrix and Cream. You try going for a drink or a night out with Keith Moon, Mitch Mitchell and

Ginger Baker in their prime. They also brought you James Brown's *Payback*, a landmark funk masterpiece. Polydor currently marshals the back catalogue of those shy, retiring, angelic cherubs, The Rolling Stones. People ignore Polydor because of snobbery. They'd prefer to talk about labels where it went wrong, where volatility and melodrama were the order of the day.

Witnessed collectively, we see a pattern emerge among most labels. There's a moment, an inciting incident that changes their fortunes. One such moment proved significant in the history of popular music. In August 1961, at Bert Kaempfert's recommendation, German Polydor released Tony Sheridan and the Beat Boys' 'My Bonnie'. It passed most people by at the time. However, the Beat Boys, Sheridan's backing group, were The Beatles. Sheridan was impressed with the band after seeing them on their three-month residency at Hamburg's Top Ten Club.

When a music fan called Raymond Jones went into Brian Epstein's Liverpool store, NEMS, asking if he had a song called 'My Bonnie', Epstein learned that the band performing on it, The Beatles, were causing quite a stir in the Cavern Club at lunchtime. He connected the two and became curious to see what the fuss was about. So Polydor, arguably, kicked off Beatlemania too.

Another reason for the lack of fanfare and high-profile business moves, especially in the 1960s, may have been Polydor's unique A&R approach. Unlike other labels, Polydor negotiated production deals with big-name managers and entrepreneurs of the day. In effect, it was producing and distributing the acts. Its vast experience in selling its classical and easy-listening

FANORAK FACT

Giorgio Gomelsky (who died on 13 January 2016) was responsible for calling Eric Clapton 'Slowhand'. I understood it as a compliment to his assured and self-confident style of playing: if you're accomplished, you don't need to rush it. It turns out that it was a clever play on words, alongside the 'Clap' of his name. Clapton preferred light-gauged strings and broke them constantly, and because he took so long to change, the audience would vent their frustration with a slow hand clap.

catalogue worldwide made it the perfect label because it had the size, reach and wherewithal to get product out there. Polydor was keen to edge towards the rock and pop market and cultivate relationships.

When Chris Stamp and Kit Lambert weren't ready to release Jimi Hendrix on their fledgling label, Track Records, they approached Polydor, who released 'Hey Joe' in December 1966. When Track became an operational imprint, it brought Hendrix, The Who, Thunderclap Newman and The Crazy World of Arthur Brown, all on Track Records, under the wing of Polydor for its substantial distribution network.

Polydor's approach of sealing deals with managers was proving fruitful. One such manager, Giorgio Gomelsky, rose to fame while the owner of the Crawdaddy Club. He briefly managed The Rolling Stones before managing The Yardbirds. He brought Brian Auger and Julie Driscoll to Polydor. Later, Robert Stigwood brought Cream and The Bee Gees, and suddenly people were treating Polydor as a serious player. Its approach, highly unusual at the time, has subsequently become the norm.

My first personal vinyl 'find' with links to Polydor came around 1975. It involved burned-out cars and gangsters. It was the 1970s, and kids were allowed to go off on their own for hours, 4- and 5-mile hikes, meandering, climbing trees and doing their thing. We were in a scrapyard, playing 'The Sweeney' in an old Ford Cortina, when I found a carrier bag of records under the passenger seat. One of them was a Bee Gees single called 'New York Mining Disaster 1941'. The title intrigued me; it sounded strange for a pop song. It also said something on the sleeve about them being the new Beatles. When home, I carefully cleaned the record, played and loved it. I couldn't stop listening to it. It was such a sad record and lyrically, for a 9-year-old, quite emotional. Later, I was told that a mining disaster had occurred not far from where I found the record, close to Greengairs, at Stanrigg.

Another example of Polydor's astute business savviness was its soul subsidiary, Mojo Records, which produced a wonderful output in three years with single releases from Tami Lynn, Doris Troy and The Fascinations. Polydor bosses effectively brought in John Abbey and Bob Kilburn, of *Blues and Soul* magazine, as A&R consultants. Their job was to find, seek out and release artists. Abbey had worked closely with Contempo International, licensing imports from Stax and

Atlantic. Their secret was classic older US reissues deliberately aimed at the Northern Soul scene and funk. They started with Tami Lynn's 'I'm Gonna Run Away from You', which reached number 4 in the UK charts in 1971, and charted again on its reissue in 1975. They also released James Brown, and Kool and the Gang.

Polydor continued to thrive with its American soul and R&B tie-ins and licensing of acts like James Brown. With Stax and Atlantic, it also brought in Aretha Franklin and Otis Redding. With the blues and folk of Rory Gallagher, John Mayall and Fairport Convention, it managed to maintain strong sales across many genres.

Then, for Polydor, there was the gift which kept on giving, especially around Christmas time: Slade. Following this, a Scandinavian band who won the Eurovision Song Contest in 1974 gave Polydor one of its most consistent sellers, Abba's *Gold*. And don't dare forget The Rubettes. With links to Robert Stigwood, Polydor would be central to getting those red cow RSO albums into your home during *Saturday Night Fever* mania. The Jam released their first single 'In the City' in April 1977, before releasing six albums between 1977 and 1982.

The 1980s saw Level 42 sell millions with their jazz pop-funk fusion. Polydor also had a run of form with The Wonderstuff and The Style Council. The 1990s would find Shed Seven, Cast, Lighthouse Family and Boyzone selling consistently across the world.

Polydor has something of a symbiotic relationship with Universal's Interscope Geffen and A&M label: they distribute UK Polydor acts in the USA. With Polydor returning the favour in the UK, it means that Polydor distributes and releases a vast number of high-profile names including Lady Gaga, Eminem and Will.i.am. It also deals with Nirvana's back catalogue.

The label continues to focus on its broad pop- and rock-based policy. The same label that released Motörhead, Dexys Midnight Runners, Sham 69 and Siouxsie and the Banshees currently has Ellie Goulding, Miley Cyrus, The Klaxons, Haim, Lana del

> **FANORAK FACT**
>
> Crawdaddy was originally called the BRRB club. Gomelsky changed the name to the Crawdaddy because The Rolling Stones' residency finished with an extended rendition of Bo Diddley's 'Crawdad'.

Rey and Kaiser Chiefs. Its indie imprint, Fiction, has Ian Brown, Snow Patrol, Crystal Castles and The Maccabees. This variety, via its various pop and indie labels, has helped Polydor command a place within the fickle mainstream.

The story of Polydor is one of disciplined business practice and consistency. It has always had a clear determination and a knack for knowing what makes a pop act sell, whether it's Take That, Girls Aloud and The Saturdays, or its album bands, The Bee Gees, The Jam, The 1975, Elbow and Snow Patrol.

Throughout its history, from Abba to neoclassical metal-playing Yngwie Malmsteen, Polydor has always been about diversity and sellable product. It has survived with a broad roster of popular acts. From Kaempfert to The Rolling Stones, it has kept going because of its smart and expansive vision and its clear understanding of how to run a business.

PLAYLIST: MY TOP 5 ALBUMS

Siouxsie and the Banshees: *The Scream*
Jimi Hendrix Experience: *Smash Hits*
The Jam: *Setting Sons*
Cream: *Best of Cream*
Slade: *Original Soundtrack from the Film Flame*

POSTCARD RECORDS

Founder: Alan Horne

Influential: Orange Juice, Aztec Camera, Joseph K, The Go-Betweens

ALAN HORNE FORMED POSTCARD in Glasgow in 1979 with two objectives: to launch Orange Juice's debut single, 'Falling and Laughing', and to compete with Edinburgh's Fast Product. While there may have been many falling, others, indeed, were laughing – but no one was buying. Neither the band's single in the shops nor the label's ethos. Horne's approach was the by now familiar 'mover and shaker' technique, like Andrew Loog Oldham with The Rolling Stones. If they couldn't get someone's attention, they would bludgeon them into submission. Horne was young too, the same age as the band, and as a music fan, he fancied himself as the pushy, opinionated manager and overseer.

Horne and Edwyn Collins of Orange Juice knew they had to get closer to the action, so they took their records and attitude to London, driving down in their ancient Austin Maxi. They would chase record company staff, music journalists and DJs down the street. Finally, their fortunes changed when Horne got to influential Radio 1 DJ, John Peel. After waiting for hours outside the BBC, Horne seized his chance, telling him: 'All those Manchester and Liverpool bands you play. It's all a nice bore. You need to wise up, old man. Forget all that Bunnymen and Teardrops shit. This is the future. Get wise to it now or you're going to look really stupid.' John Peel did play 'Falling and Laughing', though not before mentioning he'd been set about by a 'horrible, truculent youth from Scotland' who'd given him the record.

Postcard perfectly reflected the nature of pop music. It was the full bloom, the thrill of the glorious summer, the heartache of love and loss. For most Scottish post-punk bands, all roads lead to New York and The Velvet Underground. No mention of bands and The Velvet Underground can pass without dusting down the ubiquitous Brian Eno quote: 'The first Velvet Underground album only sold 10,000 copies but everyone who bought it formed a band.' We would be discussing Sony Postcard or Universal Postcard now if those inspired by the label had transferred into sales.

The label's look was kitsch – it had to be. The drumming cat image was acquired in Paddy's Market (see Parlophone), a now-closed second-hand street market where it was possible to find assorted bric-a-brac, from clothes and vinyl records to golf clubs and cookers. Postcard was branded somewhat cheekily – and with a fair dollop of sarcasm – as 'The Sound of Young Scotland', with a passing nod to Motown's 'The Sound of Young America'.

There was something deeper, though. It was also the sound of young Scotland finding and falling in love with its record collection and sifting through its 45s. Each piece of vinyl was a classic record from The Velvet Underground (yes again, it's important), Buffalo Springfield, The Byrds, The Lovin' Spoonful, The Buzzcocks, The Voidoids, Pere Ubu, Subway Sect, Chic, Television and Talking Heads. The flotsam and jetsam of each of those artists would form the blueprint of the label.

What evolved were Postcard bands: Orange Juice, Joseph K, Aztec Camera and The Go-Betweens. It was also the sound, for the most part, of playing high treble, clean guitars in a fast, funky Talking Heads disco style, which accidentally spawned the jangly pop sound.

The look and fashion of the label made its bands stand out. It was a backdrop to something unusual in Scotland, and especially in Glasgow: optimism and positivity. The equivalent of a Jehovah's Witness knocking on your door and waking you out of a deep sleep, while hungover on a Sunday morning. It penetrated, damaged and torched your soul. This was the dawning of a brave, innovative time when everything seemed possible, kind of: this was a milieu of self-confident and assertive creativity. It was short-lived.

In 1979, it wasn't only bands who wanted to be independent; the country did too. Scotland was having a referendum. Politically, the country was changing and so were the creative and artistic possibilities. Bill Forsyth was making films, first-class films too, with ordinary Scottish people, real people, with a story. There was a self-belief, a renewed assurance, and the music reflected that optimism and excitement.

However, this was also an era of Cold War indie rock; if Joy Division were a depressing yet required cold winter shower in an unheated bedsit, Postcard came after the thaw and offered pop as comforting as central heating and a fresh tartan duvet. It presented foppish fringes, suede boots and 1970s disco Chic guitars. What wasn't there to love? Legends were being made, though we didn't know it at the time. This wasn't an easy time to be bright and breezy, to get literal and figurative. Metaphors weren't mixed; they were taken out and subjected to GBH. Thinking you were a dandy in a charity shop suit made you assume you were something special. To do it wasn't composing a song; it was writing a suicide note.

Independence, both musical and political, has a narrative repeated so often it becomes a nostalgia fest. There's a warm haze of romanticism surrounding Postcard. There wasn't too much enlightenment, excitement or forward thinking at its bands' gigs. Scotland, or at least Glasgow, wasn't yet broadminded enough, struggling to get past the strangeness and illogicality of a quiffed crooner in plastic schoolboy sandals or a Davy Crocket hat. Those present reacted by shouting 'poofs!' throughout most early Orange Juice gigs. However, the clever people sensed Alan Horne was getting the reaction he craved.

Postcard's reputation was purely about Horne. He was one of those guys, in any social group, who would be the arbiter of taste in every conversation. The one who is full of controversial ideas, who shapes opinion and continually annoys and pushes everyone's buttons. Every scene where pals get together and form a band has a guy like this: someone who wrote the book of rock 'n' roll, knows everything, yet rarely has the musical ability to pick up a guitar. They can quote lyrics, name the line-ups and tell you who produced every Scott Walker album. They will play classic soul records and know every 1960s psychedelic band. Sometimes, though, being abrasive and scratchy can work and, in this case, thanks to Horne, Postcard did have an impact, shaking up the industry, all from Postcard HQ – Horne's flàt in West Princes Street.

Labels are often built on a perfect balance of myth and reality. Postcard's initial run lasted less than two years and produced eleven singles (none of the four Orange Juice singles sold over 2,000 copies) and one album (Joseph K's *The Only Fun in Town*). The party ended in 1981 when Orange Juice signed with Polydor. (In 1992 Postcard was reformed and released albums and retrospectives until 1995.)

The myths? Take your pick ... There's a vast and farfetched nearly-not-quite-could-have-been collection of yarns to choose from. Postcard nearly signed Sheena Easton and Bowie's son Zowie. It failed to lure a strung-out Nico to record a song. It came close to licensing and then decided not to release 'Oh, Superman', by Laurie Anderson. It turned down Altered Images, who eventually had six Top 40 hits. Oh, and don't forget Barry White being approached to produce Aztec Camera.

There's no doubt an element of truth in these claims. Postcard whipped up a story to attract publicity. It understood how to play the music press and how the process worked. Remember, this was long before social media. The downside? Amid the showbiz excitement, it wasn't run by great businessmen. Horne gained notoriety by stuffing the label's paperwork in his sock drawer.

The label's influence and legacy far exceeded its brief existence. The Bluebells were friends, part of the inner sanctum and expected to be the next big Postcard band. They had recorded 'Everybody's Somebody's Fool', intending to release it on the label. Events took over as they garnered publicity from high-profile front covers in the music press, early *Whistle Test* appearances, prestigious support slots

FANORAK FACT

Orange Juice started after Edwyn Collins responded to an ad in a fanzine, *Ripped and Torn*, which read: 'New York group forming in Bearsden'. It was placed by original singer Steven Daly, who was in a band called The Nu-Sonics. Daly became the drummer.

with Haircut 100 and Elvis Costello, and signed to London Records. Some of their early Postcard demos appeared on later compilations.

Bands like The Pastels and Shop Assistants would be inspired by the punk rock DIY approach and stripped-back sound; Belle and Sebastian, Franz Ferdinand and Teenage Fanclub by the melody; and The Delgados and Mogwai would be inspired to start their own labels. If Postcard was able to set up a label from a tenement in Glasgow and – initially at least – refuse to go to London, then so could they. The Delgados formed Chemikal Underground and Mogwai set up Rock Action.

The music remains fresh and vibrant. Postcard released singles, now an artefact in many an ageing uncle's record collection. Future generations will ask, 'Who were Orange Juice?' It will always happen, every five or ten years, because second-hand suits, a cool haircut, suede boots, jangly guitars with no reverb and great songs are cyclical. It's so quirky and cool and – wait, it's from 1979? What was Postcard? The drumming cat? And the beat goes on.

Postcard, in its own way, took something that appeared unattainable and made it seem possible. For kids my age – I would have been 12 or 13 at the time – who would go on to form bands aged 16 or 17, it changed the way of doing business. It was now a realistic concept to gig, save up, record a demo in a studio and make a record. Postcard provided tangible evidence it was possible. You do the 7in sleeve artwork, get the label to influential people and hope they will play it on the radio. It sounds so simple in hindsight, yet until then, getting to London was the tried-and-tested route, with many obstacles along the way.

Until then, bands recorded demos and played continuously, hoping their live performances would get some press or create a buzz; that a deaf DJ would play it by mistake on the radio or a record company would randomly check out a gig and offer a deal. My abiding memory of going into studios in my teens was seeing bitter old guys in crap bands well past it in their mid-twenties, with amazing gear and flight cases emblazoned with a clichéd name. It was whispered in hushed tones that they'd had a deal with RCA and been dumped. The cool guys mocked them, but I always thought, 'A wage, decent studio time, some big support slots, a year on the lash and a Ludwig drum kit with flight cases? Where do I sign?'

Horne used chutzpah, cheek and insolence and took Postcard a surprisingly long way. If it existed now, with social media, Postcard would excel in running the label and promoting bands like an advertising or PR company. Hipsters, operating with those buzzwords 'smart', 'energetic' and 'agile', would come up with crazy ways to catch your attention. Thankfully, we knew them when they made glorious-sounding pop records. Better still, timeless pop ages well – listen again and tell me I'm wrong.

PLAYLIST: MY TOP ALBUM

Josef K: *The Only Fun in Town**

---

* We're purists. Postcard 1979–81 only released one album. It would be two if you included the recorded though unreleased Josef K album *Sorry for Laughing*. There are a few white-label pressings in circulation. When the label was revived in 1992, it focused on reissues. Our principal concern is the cult status and impact of the original label, born in 1979, which died in 1981. Domino re-released all four of the Polydor albums as well as a compilation album, *The Glasgow School* (2005), and *Coals to Newcastle* (2010), a comprehensive six-CD compilation.

RCA

Founders: David Sarnoff and Owen Daniel Young

Influential: Elvis Presley, David Bowie, Iggy Pop, Lou Reed

RCA IS LIKE *DOCTOR WHO* – each generation has their favourite Doctor and most music fans have their favourite era on this illustrious label. I grew up in the 1970s. My favourite era was associated with the orange RCA label, started in 1968, synonymous with what we'd best describe as 'Bowie-era RCA'. There was also the green label of the 1970s, and then the black at the end of the 1970s and 1980s. Another favourite is the classic 1956 black Elvis-era RCA label – during his first year on the label, Elvis sold 12.5 million singles and 2.75 million albums.

If record labels stand or fall by the artists they showcase, then RCA should be acclaimed. The problem with RCA – in keeping with Polydor – is that it is rarely mentioned in glowing terms in the same breath as Warner Bros., CBS, Atlantic or Capitol, yet it deserves to be. Not only did RCA sign Elvis from Sun Records, it also signed Bowie, giving him a platform to weave his wondrously captivating spell at his peak, from *Hunky Dory* in 1971 to *Scary Monsters (and Super Creeps)* in 1980. RCA also gave us *The Sound of Music* ...

The company was formed in 1919 as the Radio Corporation of America, a subsidiary of General Electric, by David Sarnoff and Owen Daniel Young. The RCA we know and love – the phonograph part of the business – started in 1929, when RCA bought the Victor Talking Machine Company, becoming RCA Victor. This was when the label and the Jack Russell dog 'Nipper' were trademarked.

RCA Victor was originally intended as a label for jazz, blues and musicals. Yet today, RCA Records continues to have global reach and impact as part of Sony Music Entertainment and comprised of RCA Records, RCA Victor, Chess Club Records and Space & Time Records.

RCA pioneered the first 45rpm record in 1949. The single became the industry standard for pop records. Radio stations played the single and punters could buy it. Most of the older record labels, such as RCA, started out researching electronics. In this case, it was radio receivers, and then later, RCA was the first to produce TV sets. These companies were in the business of mass-scale communications. Again, for many labels, the music operations started as a by-product, something to sell with their gramophones. Then someone realised there was money to be made.

RCA went into business physically mastering and pressing for others on a contract basis. So, there wasn't only a focus on manufacturing its own artists; it also manufactured for third-party labels. This part of the business was called RCA Custom, and it prospered by pressing for local record labels across most of the USA from the 1950s onwards. The RCA plant used in each production would be lettered into the dead wax of the vinyl, called the run-out groove.

In 1950, Columbia changed the game completely when it produced the first album. RCA was quick to follow its lead, bringing out a series of vinyl LPs. This coincided with one of the biggest moves in musical history. RCA bought out Elvis Presley's contract with Sun Records for an unheard-of $35,000 (plus $5,000 to pay royalties that Sun owed Presley, in 1955). The biggest star in rock 'n' roll had his first gold record, 'Heartbreak Hotel', recorded in January 1956.

RCA's roster over the decades, from Elvis to Justin Timberlake, from Bowie to Britney, has always had a clear and defined focus on popular music artists who are entertainers. It also had a clutch of top artists, the hardy perennials who continued to sell, such as Lou Reed, Iggy Pop, Donna Summer, Harry Nilsson and Diana Ross.

The label's understanding of populist entertainment saw it embracing the official soundtrack album *The Sound of Music* (RCA Victor) in 1965, which reached number 1 and stayed on the charts for seventy weeks. It was the top-selling album in the UK in three of the following four years, and the seventh biggest-selling album of all time (not to be confused with the 1959 Broadway version).

The wonderful thing about Bowie's work on RCA in the 1970s is that anyone, on any given day, could pick and choose favourite Bowie songs for any number of reasons. Being a drummer who loves glorious pop harmonies might sway my choices. What follows is only a random snapshot, a pop Polaroid, thinking off the top of my head, in no order, of various favourite moments. It would be another list if I had to choose tomorrow.

In the first of the 'Berlin trilogy', *Low* (1977), Bowie is rattled from rehab, yet 'Sound and Vision' has clarity and a sense of purpose. It has a minute-and-a-half intro before the vocals begin, in a three-minute song. They say if something's good, don't mess around with it. Bowie loved the start; I think it's genius.

In *Station to Station* (1976), we have the coke-fuelled craziness. Amid the chaos emerges the inspirational 'Golden Years'. *Diamond Dogs* (1974) has the bubblegum of Mud, The Sweet and T-Rex on 'Rebel Rebel'. Then we're whizzed off to Philadelphia to Gamble and Huff's Sigma Sounds for the groove of *Young Americans* (1975). Blue-eyed soul rarely sounded better; listen to 'Young Americans' and 'Fame'.

The drumming on 'Black Country Rock' on *The Man Who Sold the World* (1970) is dynamite, as is Bowie's East Riding beat-king, Woody Woodmansey, who takes control. His playing reminds me of Blue Cheer's drummer Paul Whaley, one of my favourites, a vastly underappreciated drummer who puts Ginger, Mitch, Keith and Bonzo to shame with flourishes of tumultuous power – yet, despite his wondrous groove map, returns as and when required, at the start of each phrase, to serve the song. Woodmansey wonderfully underplays it.

FANORAK FACT

In 1956, Colonel Parker secured a deal for $50,000 for RCA artist Elvis Presley to perform three times, on *The Ed Sullivan Show*. His first performance, on 9 September 1956, attracted an audience of 60 million, over 80 per cent of the total TV audience. Sullivan had been in a car accident and was unable to host the show. It was hosted by actor Charles Laughton. (Elvis was filmed in full shot; it wasn't until the third performance that he was filmed from the waist up.)

The Rise and Fall of Ziggy Stardust and the Spiders from Mars (1972) brings the silly yet gloriously infectious middle-eight of track three: 'Moonage Daydream'. The next track is out of this world: the flawless pop perfection of 'Starman'. Again, it's the ease of the drumming, filled with subtle triplets as Woody does Whaley, again. Bowie is at his brilliant best, bursting with interplanetary pop melody. Mick Ronson's glorious guitar hook at the outro sure adds candy. It's hard to ignore *Ziggy*'s opening salvo, the wondrously moody 'Five Years'.

With *Aladdin Sane* (1973) it's the rifferama drama of 'The Jean Genie': it's Christmas and there's magic in the air and *Top of the Pops* is to be forever treasured. I fear we may have overplayed this impromptu and entirely random tribute. Legends such as Bowie are ever present as you write a book about the importance of their music to this record label and/or that record collection. Forever treasured. I'm sorry, I don't do 'Bowie RIP sad-emojis' to mark the passing of a great artist. (If you're reading this, the editor loves Bowie too.)

No matter what era or album you select from the vast archive of 'Bowie-era RCA', the work, like any great piece of art, is underpinned by the artist's back story and where he's at during each moment of his life. We humans send a text, email or maybe a postcard to let others know where and how we are. Extraordinary artists of the calibre of Bowie give you an album.

Listened to collectively in autumn 2016, the albums – and, indeed, his life – are presented like a storyboard for a movie or a novel. It has a beginning, middle and end. It has a remarkable plot with rebirth and reinvention, and by the end, as he publicly peels off each layer of the mask, we see it was all an act, an invention, a creation from a unique and special artist.

Lou Reed brought his discerningly tasteful muse to the label; a considerable body of work, some sixteen studio and live albums. The highlight is the album *Transformer* (produced by David Bowie and Mick Ronson; okay, enough already). Reed's 1972 masterpiece contains 'Walk on the Wild Side', 'Satellite of Love' and 'Vicious'. There's also Iggy Pop's solo debut, *The Idiot*, released in March 1977, then *Lust For Life* in the same year, in August ... both produced by (whispers) David Bowie.

Other label highlights (without Bowie) include Harry Nilsson's *Nilsson Schmilsson* and *Pandemonium Shadow Show*. There's also Elvis Presley's debut with 'Blue Suede Shoes', 'Tutti Frutti' and 'Blue Moon'. My personal favourites include The Sweet – popular, entertaining, glam rock and pop – with 'Blockbuster', 'Ballroom Blitz', 'Wig Wam Bam' and 'Teenage Rampage'. Thanks, Nicky Chin and Mike Chapman. Honourable mentions go to bop double bass legend Charlie Mingus, Alicia Keys, and Dave Grohl's post-Nirvana beat combo, Foo Fighters.

Over a century later, RCA continues to thrive. For the modern era, the label in the UK exists as an outlet for artists Bring Me the Horizon, Kodaline, Everything Everything, Olly Murs and Paloma Faith. The US branch can call upon a top trio of popular entertainers, Justin Timberlake, Beyoncé and Miley Cyrus, to keep things flourishing ... For most pop fans, RCA will be the label that gave us Elvis and David Bowie at their prolific best.

PLAYLIST: MY TOP 5 ALBUMS

Lou Reed: *Transformer*
Nilsson: *Nilsson Schmilsson*
Iggy Pop: *The Idiot*
David Bowie: *The Rise and Fall of Ziggy Stardust and the Spiders from Mars*
Elvis Presley: *Elvis Presley*

REPRISE

Founder: Frank Sinatra

Influential: Frank Sinatra, Neil Young, The Kinks, Gram Parsons

AS HE APPROACHED THE end of his contract with Capitol, Frank Sinatra had grown exasperated. Such was his sheer enormity, vision, power and ego that, when he grew sick of Capitol Records, he formed his own label, Reprise, in 1960. According to Nancy Sinatra, it cost her father $200,000 to set the label up.

At this point, he was one of the most famous stars of all time, yet felt tethered and bound. He made a few demands. He wanted creative control and artistic independence. He also felt, in principle, that artists should own their master tapes. The master tapes became the stumbling block in negotiations with Capitol boss, Alan Livingston. Full ownership of the master tapes. Simple. This made negotiations fraught and inevitably led to the end of a long and, at its peak, lucrative association.

Before setting up Reprise, Sinatra had approached Norman Granz, intending to buy Verve Records (see Verve). Sinatra assumed he and Granz had shaken on a deal. As both Sinatra and Granz shared the same lawyer, Mickey Rudin, there was a conflict of interest. Rudin stayed with Sinatra; Granz and Verve got new lawyers, but Rudin kept stalling on a deal.

FANORAK FACT

Scooby Doo's name was inspired by a Frank Sinatra song, 'Strangers in the Night', a song Sinatra hated. In an ad lib, Sinatra sings, 'Dooby-dooby-do ...'. The animator who created Scooby-Doo, Iwao Takamoto, was inspired by the line.

Granz bumped into MGM chairman Arnold Maxin at an airport and chatted about the sale of Verve. Granz explained it was close, though Rudin was trying his patience and they had yet to close the deal. Maxin wished Granz luck and added, almost as an aside, that if the deal fell through, he should keep MGM in mind; it would be interested.

Sinatra thought it was Granz who was being difficult, but it was his lawyer, Rudin, who was procrastinating. Granz remembered the meeting with Maxin at the airport and sold Verve to MGM for $3.1 million. Sinatra always thought Granz had done the unthinkable and reneged on a gentleman's agreement.

Having failed to get Verve, Sinatra prised away one of Granz's assets, Mo Ostin, who was now installed as president of Reprise. In James Kaplan's *Sinatra: The Chairman*, Mo Ostin claims: 'Frank was absolutely incensed. I don't think he ever got the facts straight. I don't think he ever learned Granz went to Rudin first to see if they could close a deal and then when he couldn't, he went back to MGM.'

Reprise would go on to house some of the most influential names in rock 'n' roll, giving them the artist-friendly environment Sinatra had craved. However, the transition wasn't made easy by Capitol. This was a cut-throat business and they felt let down by Sinatra. Alan Livingston and Capitol had signed Frank Sinatra when he was at a professional and personal low. Let go by CBS, Ava Gardner had left him, he was broke and he couldn't get a gig, let alone a recording contract.

Reprise began recording in 1960, yet didn't release anything until 1961. Sinatra had two more albums and a single in his contract with Capitol, so by the time he got to release his Reprise debut, *Ring-A-Ding-Ding*, Capitol owned so much Sinatra product that they flooded the marketplace with reduced-price albums. Consequently, shops wouldn't take any more Sinatra stock, making it close to impossible for Reprise to generate cash. It had to cut its prices to compete with Capitol.

Unlike most of their competitors, Reprise didn't have the luxury of owning its own

FANORAK FACT

When Capitol boss Alan Livingston briefly left the company to join NBC as vice-president in charge of TV, NBC wanted an hour-long weekly Western series. He came up with a pilot for *Bonanza*.

studio, which also meant exorbitant recording costs and studio bills. It did, though, have one major asset: Sinatra. As well as being a singing superstar, he was also in demand as a Hollywood actor. When it started to get too tight financially, Sinatra reluctantly listened to offers. By the summer of 1963, Warner Bros. came in, buying two-thirds of Sinatra's stake in the record company.

Warner Bros. knew, with Sinatra, they were buying one of the finest entertainers of the twentieth century. Having made his acting debut in 1943 with *Reveille With Beverly* and *Higher and Higher*, in 1945 he won a special Academy Award for a short film, *The House I Live In*, about racial and religious understanding, made to quell attacks on African-Americans, Jews, Italians, Chinese and Irish – anyone viewed as foreign – as the country recovered from the war.

After the war, Sinatra's popularity dipped, and he lost his movie contracts. In 1953, he made a dramatic comeback, winning the Oscar for Best Supporting Actor in *From Here to Eternity*. He was back on form after signing with Capitol, and having found a mature sound, a lush, jazz-based canvas working with top music arrangers. Ol' Blue Eyes was back, in the studio and on screen, releasing hit after hit as well as being nominated for another Academy Award for *The Man with the Golden Arm*. By the time Warner Bros. bought Reprise in 1963, they were getting something of a special package, which included not only Sinatra but also Duke Ellington.

Reprise benefited greatly from Warner Bros., but the deal cut both ways. Warner Bros. used Reprise to release newer, untried artists, while distributing smaller label imprints such as Bearsville (Todd Rundgren) and Brother Records (The Beach Boys). Sinatra would see his 'crooner label' Reprise slowly fade as the business moved towards a more contemporary sound.

Sensing a need to diversify, Mo Ostin knew that Reprise needed more contemporary rock acts. With a change of

> **FANORAK FACT**
>
> Lee Hazelwood wrote 'These Boots Are Made for Walking' for Nancy Sinatra, and the session artists were The Wrecking Crew. The line came from a Robert Aldrich comedy western caper starring Frank Sinatra and Dean Martin.

focus, he wanted more energy, so he embraced the rock underground. One of his first signings was The Kinks. By the end of 1965, they'd had six Top 40 US hits. In 1967, the Monterey County Fairgrounds in California held a three-day festival. Captured by filmmaker D.A. Pennebaker, the Monterey International Pop Festival ushered in the 'Summer of Love'. Ostin was there and signed Hendrix.

By fighting so vehemently to have an artist-friendly label, Sinatra, through Reprise, changed the way the music industry treated artists. By the mid-to-late 1960s, artists wanted to sign with Reprise. Now they all wanted artistic freedom. Such creative and independent philosophies are expensive. You need artists working, recording and making albums to pay for the relaxed environment.

Despite having to sell to Warner Bros. early in its tenure, the label's focus was always about music and the artists. It's a fine balance; artists by their definition are mercurial, recalcitrant and unreliable. Artists thrived at Reprise, perhaps understanding their luck at being on a label that allowed them creative space.

The deal with Warner Bros. was crucial as it gave Reprise the full backing, marketing and distribution of a major label. Warner Bros. also welcomed Sinatra into its film studios. Furthermore, the label received cash, secured crucial staff, such as Mo Ostin, and gave Sinatra a place on the Warner Bros.–Reprise board. Sinatra had maintained his initial concept of the artist-friendly label. Ostin brought in young producers and A&R guys whom he mentored and trusted, like Lenny Waronker and Ted Templeman, and the label thrived with The Doobie Brothers, Little Feat, James Taylor, Neil Young, Gram Parsons, Joni Mitchell, Captain Beefheart, Dean Martin and Nancy Sinatra, as well as the previously mentioned Hendrix and The Kinks.

FANORAK FACT

Sinatra had tried to enlist in the army but failed because of a perforated ear drum. When he was born, weighing 13lb, forceps were used and damaged his ear. He also tried to gain entry as an entertainer in the United Service Organization, which entertained the troops, but he was rejected because the Federal Bureau of Investigation had started a file on him.

In the 1970s, Reprise continued its winning run with best-selling acts Black Sabbath, Jethro Tull, Frank Zappa and the Mothers of Invention, Ry Cooder, Randy Newman and Fleetwood Mac. Mo Ostin went on to become Warner Bros.'s chairman and his prodigy, Lenny Waronker, became president (of the label, not the USA). By 1976, Warner Bros. had deactivated Reprise and most of the acts on it (apart from Neil Young and Frank Sinatra) were moved to the main Warner Bros. label.

Finally, over the last few years, Reprise has continued to reinvent itself as a Warner Bros. sub-label, releasing acts from across the parent company's smaller labels. Reprise continues to prove its relevance creatively and commercially with several key artists. Green Day were signed to Reprise by Rob Cavallo in 1993. Their Ramones–Buzzcocks–Kinks–Cheap Trick formula, along with albums like *American Idiot*, *21st Century Breakdown* and *Revolution Radio*, have delivered over 85 million album sales worldwide. Cavallo became vice-president of Reprise, then moved to take charge of A&R at Warner Bros. before becoming the boss of the company. Blues legend Eric Clapton also celebrated three decades at Reprise with the release of a box set in 2017.

The label has housed Jeff Lynne, Nico, Morrissey and J Mascis of Dinosaur Jr., and today is still home to acts appreciative of the founder Frank Sinatra's vision for creative freedom. Bands and artists like Michael Bublé, Josh Groban and the late Tom Petty sit alongside My Chemical Romance, Mastodon, Depeche Mode and Smashing Pumpkins. It's difficult to imagine Sinatra crooning with many of those bands, yet as an artist, he'd defend their right to creative ownership. Reprise is owned by Warner Music Group.

PLAYLIST: MY TOP 5 ALBUMS

Neil Young: *After the Goldrush*
Gram Parsons: *Grievous Angel*
Frank Sinatra: *Frank Sinatra at the Sands*
Green Day: *American Idiot*
Neil Young and Crazy Horse: *Ragged Glory*

ROUGH TRADE RECORDS

Founder: Geoff Travis

Influential: The Smiths, The Fall, Stiff Little Fingers, Cabaret Voltaire

ROUGH TRADE ORIGINATED AS a record shop. Geoff Travis, a music-obsessed Cambridge graduate, opened the shop in 1976 in Ladbroke Grove, Notting Hill (at 202 Kensington Park Road, to be precise). Travis had been hitchhiking across the USA, collecting records and dreaming of a music career. His inspiration came from a visit to a shop in San Francisco called City Lights Bookstore, an independent bookshop and publisher, specialising in the arts and progressive politics, and for some fifty years, a mainstay of alternative culture. You can see why it would chime so readily with the young Travis, independent, alternative, ethical and politically left-leaning. The shop's masthead reads 'A Literary Meeting Place'.

If San Francisco's most famous bookstore was a literary gathering point, the Rough Trade shop became a musical hub. In 1976, it was a favourite haunt for punks and music fans whose taste couldn't be served by the mainstream. They were able to hang out in safety most of the day, if need be, without being harassed, and could tune in to whatever was playing on the gargantuan shop sound system. At this time, it would be underground punk imports (this was before the Sex Pistols exploded on the scene) and reggae imports for the Jamaican population who lived around this poorer part of (pre-gentrified) Notting Hill. Soon, Travis would take the next logical step and form an independent label and achieve his ambition of releasing records.

The first release was by Metal Urbain, erroneously described as the 'French Sex Pistols', with a song called 'Paris Marquis'. Although they didn't live up to expectations, they were and always will be the first band on Rough Trade. Then there was a Jamaican reggae singer, Augustus Pablo.

In 1978, Richard Scott from Rough Trade created a distribution network called 'The Cartel' in collaboration with other like-minded independent regional distributors across the UK: Sandy McLean's Fast Forward in Edinburgh, Probe in Liverpool, Red Rhino in York and Revolver in Bristol, among others, which would supply product to the shops in their area. By pooling their resources, they had a fighting chance when it came to competing with the majors and getting records from (at the time) smaller regional labels like Factory and 2 Tone into the major shopping chains like HMV, Virgin and Our Price.

It was the label's third release, the debut EP by Sheffield's Cabaret Voltaire, which made people take notice, and by the release of Stiff Little Fingers' 'Alternative Ulster', things had reached a tipping point. In 1979, Rough Trade's first album release, *Inflammable Material*, made it to number 14 in the album charts, selling 100,000.

After Stiff Little Fingers took off, people started to wake up to this hippy cartel cooperative idea. It might not be as ridiculous as it sounded. Rough Trade continued, issuing singles by Monochrome Set, Subway Sect, and Swell Maps, among others.

We are learning by now that fate intervenes in just about every record label discussed. In the case of Rough Trade, it was the day Johnny Marr and Mike Joyce showed up, only to be told Geoff Travis was too busy to see anyone. They hung around but were eventually told to leave. While outside, they saw a van up a back lane delivering vinyl to the warehouse and made their way in there. They saw Travis and noticed he was busy. Biding their time, they eventually seized their chance. Marr handed Travis his band's demo while reminding him not to dismiss it; this wasn't any normal demo.

This happened on the Friday. By Monday, Travis had contacted them and offered The Smiths a trial one-single deal. The demo of 'Hand in Glove' was released in May 1983, with a live version of 'Handsome Devil'. The single was played by Radio 1's John Peel and they were invited to do a session, which generated press in the *NME* and *Melody Maker*. The single reached the indie charts, though failed to make the UK Top 40. But the single sold consistently over a prolonged period. Usually, this points to a strong, grassroots, word-of-mouth following. Travis moved quickly to offer The Smiths a record deal. More prestigious sessions followed, including with Kid Jensen (one, in August 1983, created a media furore when 'Reel Around the Fountain' was banned).

With the singles 'This Charming Man' and 'What Difference Does It Make?' reaching numbers 25 and 12 respectively, followed up by the debut album *The Smiths,* which reached number 2, Geoff Travis wasn't only running Rough Trade and releasing records. Now he was a label boss, handling one of the hottest bands in the world and navigating their career through uncharted waters and high-octane turbulence. Amid the commotion, Geoff Travis and his label were getting noticed.

Even at this early point, it was evident the band had something and the fans got it. Morrissey and Marr were a melody of harpers, a murmuration of starlings, a muster of peacocks; find your own collective noun, preferably one that alludes to contradiction. With Morrissey as the focal point and Marr's tunes, the fans were transfixed. Morrissey had an angular handsomeness; his sexual ambiguity hardly made him the archetypal frontman. Marr seemed to be playing complex, lush, majestic hooks and chords with a natural simplicity. Mike Joyce's drumming and Andy Rourke's bass playing barely missed a beat or note. Their music would reference writers from Virginia Woolf to Oscar Wilde, from Shakespeare's *Anthony and Cleopatra* to George Elliot's *Middlemarch*. Artwork would refer to Joan Cocteau's 1950 film *Orphée* and reveal a vast array of stars including Elvis, James Dean and Charles Hawtrey.

Morrissey played the role of spring-heeled messiah, part Alan Bennett wordsmith, part New York Dolls aficionado, and it enthralled and beguiled millions. Fans of obscure movies, 1960s entertainers and haters of authority understood. Morrissey's hero worship catapulted the band into a different sphere, one beyond the indie confines of Rough Trade. They had quickly built a devoted following, yet fought in vain to remain darlings of the indie world.

The band's output was prolific, but their relationship was fractious and, internally, the group was imploding. This didn't stop them from racking up an implausible number of albums in a short period: four wonderful studio albums, *The Smiths* (1984), *Meat is Murder* (1985),

The Queen Is Dead (1986) and *Strangeways Here We Come* (1987). There were also three Rough Trade compilation releases, *Hatful of Hollow* (1984), *The World Won't Listen* (1987) and *Louder Than Bombs* (1987; Rough Trade and Sire), and the live album, *Rank* (1988).

Most of Morrissey's Penguin Classics memoir, *Autobiography*, finds myriad ways to slaughter Rough Trade. This, perhaps, is unfair as Geoff Travis and Rough Trade would always have had the best intentions for the band. Rough Trade was renowned for having a post-punk socialist philosophy ... and loads of committee meetings. They had a meeting before the meeting, to discuss what was happening at the main meeting, then a meeting after the meeting about the meeting. They were more like civil servants than a record company.

To the public and those involved in music, they wouldn't be the types to take advantage. Their early years are full of examples of this, including an anecdote about Daniel Miller of fledgling label Mute. On one occasion, Rough Trade gave Daniel Miller £300 to press an additional batch of 2,000 singles of 'Warm Leatherette'. They knew it would sell and their buyers would want it, so it would be beneficial. When Miller explained his lack of storage space would prove prohibitive, Rough Trade facilitated the distribution of merchandise through them.

The Cartel could be run along the lines of a democratic cooperative, but a record label can't work that way. Travis stuck with bands he liked, not necessarily ones that made money (The Smiths perhaps the exception); bands such as Television Personalities, The Go-Betweens, Aztec Camera, The Pastels, Prefab Sprout and The Fall.

In 1989, Rough Trade Distribution would become insolvent as a result of bad management, tax problems and uncollected debts. The final blow came when a company that owed it money collapsed, bringing Rough Trade Distribution down with it. Rough Trade,

> **FANORAK FACT**
>
> The Smiths recorded a demo in December 1982 in Drone Studios with the songs 'What Difference Does It Make?', 'Handsome Devil' and 'Miserable Lie', which was rejected by EMI. The version of 'What Difference Does It Make?' has a low-sung vocal.

the label, could have continued as it was a separate entity, but Travis refused on moral grounds, handing over the company's assets to debt collectors.

Travis resurrected the company as Rough Trade Records in 2000, releasing Arcade Fire, The Strokes and The Libertines. During his break, he had continued to work at Warner Music UK subsidiary, Blanco Y Negro as well as forming a management company, which looked after Pulp and The Cranberries. Jeannette Lee came into the business at this time as a partner (she had previously managed Public Image Ltd).

Rough Trade Records was owned by Travis, Lee and partners Sanctuary Records as part of the Zomba Group until 2002 when BMG bought the business. In 2007, Sanctuary sold Rough Trade to the Beggars Group, which, in effect, made Rough Trade independent again.

Music by Alabama Shakes, The Decemberists, Parquet Courts, Jarvis Cocker and Warpaint proves there's life and some committee meetings in the old dog yet.

The Smiths' bass player Andy Rourke's death was announced in May 2023; he died of cancer, aged 59. Johnny Marr said of his friend, 'Andy will be remembered as a kind and beautiful soul by those who knew him, and as a supremely gifted musician by music fans.'

PLAYLIST: MY TOP 5 ALBUMS

The Smiths: *The Queen Is Dead*
The Sundays: *Reading, Writing and Arithmetic*
Stiff Little Fingers: *Inflammable Material*
Television Personalities: *And Don't the Kids Just Love It*
The Smiths: *Meat Is Murder*

ROULETTE RECORDS

Founders: Morris Levy, George Goldner, Joe Kolsky and Phil Khals

Influential: Tommy James and the Shondells, Jimmi Rodgers, Dinah Washington

FOR ANYONE WITH A love of music, social history and controversial record labels, let me introduce Roulette Records. The contentious label's story could be written up for a Netflix drama. It was formed in 1957, when producer George Goldner and nightclub owner Joe Kolsky joined forces. Kolsky was a 50 per cent owner of Goldner's other labels, Gee, Rama and Tico. Goldner had business ties with Phil Khals and Morris Levy, who owned the famed nightclub Birdland. Levy was brought in and installed as president, and soon, Goldner was selling his interest in the labels to Levy due to gambling debts, and they became part of Roulette. Goldner formed two new labels, End and Gone, in the 1960s, which he would also sell to Levy, who folded them into Roulette.

The heads of A&R were Hugo Peretti and Luigi Creatore. Peretti wrote the songs and Creatore was the producer. They were left to get on with it. Levy was the creative director, from the classic school of notorious music industry bosses, known for his ruthlessness. There is no getting away from the fact that Roulette was 'allegedly' run by New York mobsters. Despite its unorthodox approach, the label seldom ran at a loss. They were businessmen and

> ## FANORAK FACT
>
> The comic actor Joe E. Ross, famed for playing MSgt. Rupert B. Ritzik on *The Phil Silvers Show* and voicing 'Botch' in *The Hair Bear Bunch* and 'Sergeant Flint' in *Hong Kong Phooey*, released a song on Roulette in 1966.

liked to make money. We can therefore assume there were no issues securing radio airplay. Whatever their business approach, the label was run well. Roulette covered its genres – rhythm and blues, country, jazz, classical, and even comedy and soundtracks.

By the end of the 1950s, Roulette was having hit singles with Buddy Knox. He was the label's initial release with 'Party Doll'/ 'My Baby's Gone', followed up with 'I'm Sticking With You'/ 'Ever Loving Fingers'. Knox displayed the same Texan charm as Buddy Holly and had a great backing group called the Rhythm Orchids. Roulette also had acts like Jimmy Bowen, The Playmates and Jimmie Rodgers. He was a respected folk-pop singer from the Pacific Northwest, who was hugely successful. He signed in 1957 after auditioning for Roulette. With one of those everyman voices, he was a great singer and had a similar elegiac warmth as Glen Campbell. They recorded a single in two hours in Bell Sound Studios, New York City. That song was called 'Honeycomb' and went to number 1. He had seven songs that sold over a million, including 'It's Over', which Elvis would cover. Rodgers also had hits with 'Kisses Sweeter Than Wine', 'Secretly' and 'Oh-Oh I'm Falling in Love Again'. He stayed at Roulette until 1962 before signing for Dot Records. Ronnie Hawkins had hits with a reworked cover of Chuck Berry's 'Thirty Days' and Young Jesse's 'Mary Lou'.

Peretti and Creatore left to work as freelance producers for RCA in the 1960s before forming Avco. Despite hit singles, it took years for Roulette to have a chart album success. That was a Murray the K compilation called *Murray the 'K's' Sing Along with the Original Golden Gassers*, for which he fronted a compilation of Roulette or Gee artists. After the DJ's album hit big, more compilations followed with their Golden Goodies series, making the most of the dance craze of the day. Levy created a label called Adam VIII, which hit the headlines when he released a John Lennon album and the former Beatle sued.

FANORAK FACT

Ronnie Hawkins was rejected by Sun Records but was big in Canada and had a backing band there called The Hawks, featuring Levon Helm, Robbie Robertson and, eventually, Rick Danko, Richard Manuel and Garth Hudson. They would back Bob Dylan and become The Band.

Mo Levy was Roulette Records; despite being a co-founder of the label, it was his. He ran it from 1957 to 1989. He made his money as the founding partner of Birdland and the Roulette Club. His business enterprise spanned music publishing, multiple labels, a distribution company, record-pressing plants, tape-duplicating plants and a record shop chain of eighty-one stores. At one point he had ninety different companies and employed 900 people. His story is epic – a poor kid from the East Bronx does good, sort of. He was also targeted by the Federal Bureau of Investigation in investigations into organised crime across the music industry. He was said to have swindled artists, mostly Black R&B acts, out of their royalties by falsely claiming a writing credit. Tommy James from Tommy James and the Shondells claimed that Roulette was a front for the Genovese family. James claimed that they kept royalties from many of their hit songs (written and produced by Ritchie Cordell), including 'Hanky Panky', 'I Think We're Alone Now', 'Mirage', 'Mony Mony' and 'Crimson and Clover'. He claimed they were owed $30–40 million in royalties. Levy was eventually convicted of extortion in 1990 after losing his appeal. While awaiting sentencing Levy died of cancer. Roulette was sold to EMI and Rhino Records, thus followed some lengthy corporate juggling and complex fiscal manoeuvring. Best of all though, the artists finally got paid.

FANORAK FACT

Songwriter and producer Ritchie Cordell produced the 1983 Ramones album *Subterranean Jungle*.

PLAYLIST: MY TOP 5 ALBUMS

Tony Bennett and the Count Basie Orchestra: *Strike Up the Band*

Count Basie: *Basie at Birdland*

Tommy James and the Shondells: *Crimson and Clover*

Dinah Washington: *Back to the Blues*

Jimmie Rodgers: *The Number 1 Ballads*

SIRE RECORDS

Founders: Seymour Stein and Richard Gottehrer

Influential: Madonna, Ramones, Talking Heads

SIRE HAS ALWAYS HAD me in its spell. It might have been the logo: the distinctive yellow with the blue-purple circle top and centre split with the S. The distinct yin and yang. It's seductive and strutting, stoic, stylish and super cool, and sums up the driving force behind the label, the famous music business figure Seymour Stein. Sire is also about Madonna, the Ramones and Talking Heads; the New York connection. There's also my lifelong love for New York and stories of long-lost family scattered from Long Island to Brooklyn.

From the outside, it looks to music fans and vinyl lovers as if the artists have a natural affiliation with the label, as if they've found their rightful home. However, it's down to the work put in and the relationship cultivated between artists and label bosses. Bands need to place their trust and hope in savvy music industry guys, and in Sire's Seymour Stein and Richard Gottehrer they had people with their best interests at heart. Successful bands get this balance and association sorted from the start.

Sire was originally set up as Sire Productions when Seymour Stein and Richard Gottehrer pooled resources at the end of 1966, and morphed into Sire Records in 1967. Stein's background was one of old-school music business-based enthusiasm from an early age. He was simply a pop music fan and made it his mission to get involved in it. When he was 13, he went to *Billboard Magazine* to do a school project and write out every single chart song; it's something an obsessive young pop fan would do. It's a love of serial numbers, the labels themselves, reading about bands and the hits over the years.

Those in charge at *Billboard* saw something in his dedication and determination, in the way he worked. The charts' editor, Tom Noonan, gave him a job as his assistant. Then the magazine's music editor, Paul Ackerman, sent him out to review gigs.

Stein worked there all through high school and got paid. Instead of going to college, he started full-time at *Billboard*. From there, he went on to work for George Goldner at Red Bird Records, then at King Records for Syd Nathan while James Brown and Freddy King were on its roster.

Richard Gottehrer was a songwriter and producer, part of the FGG songwriting team with Bob Feldman and Jerry Goldstein. Together, as FGG, they penned The Angels' 'My Boyfriend's Back', a number 1 on the *Billboard* Hot 100. The team members also created a band called The Strangeloves who wrote, produced and had a hit with 'I Want Candy'. They also produced 'Hang on Sloopy' by The McCoys. FGG were based on the tenth floor of the Brill Building, and Stein, who was working at Red Bird Records, Leiber and Stoller's label, was on the floor below. Gottehrer and Stein would meet in the elevator regularly and got on well. When both their jobs reached a creative impasse around the same time, they decided to team up and form a company.

Stein and Gottehrer worked well together. Their approach was simple, effective and proved fruitful. Gottehrer was an experienced producer and Stein simply had what he called 'the ears of a music fan'. Sire made a name for itself by releasing underground UK bands to the US market. When Stein worked for *Billboard*, he noticed that many top UK acts failed to break into the lucrative US marketplace. Instead of having to pay for recording, Sire went directly to the majors in London and spoke to their export divisions, and slowly built up a roster of acts by acquiring the US and Canadian distribution rights. Through an extensive range of licensing agreements, Sire had deals in place with bands such as Climax Blues Band and Barclay James Harvest. Thanks to a distribution deal with Polydor Records, Sire had a breakthrough hit in 1972 with the song 'Hocus Pocus' by Dutch group Focus.

FANORAK FACT

When Stein signed Madonna to Sire, the deal was for $15,000 for three singles and an option for an album.

By the mid-1970s, Gottehrer wanted to get back to his preferred environment, the recording studio. He left Sire, amicably, to become an independent producer, though remained friends with Stein. Both were engrossed by the energy and excitement at their regular haunt, a dingy punk club in the Bowery called CBGB, and at 213 Park Avenue South, Max's Kansas City with bands like Richard Hell and the Voidoids, the Ramones, Blondie and Talking Heads. All these bands were playing while New York was into disco and record shops were selling out of prog rock. Stein and Gottehrer felt energised by what they saw – groups inspired by Bowie, The Velvet Underground and the 1960s rockabilly and garage sound.

Gottehrer was soon in the studio working with Blondie, sensing they had the potential for an international smash. He produced their first two albums, *Blondie* (1976) and *Plastic Letters* (1978). He also produced Richard Hell and the Voidoids' seminal and hugely influential *Blank Generation*.

Meanwhile, Stein was finding it difficult to sell his new bands, the Ramones and Talking Heads. The major stumbling block for bands emerging from the CBGB and Max's Kansas City scene was the unwillingness of American audiences to accept them. The Ramones were embraced by punk fans in London. They played high-profile shows in 1976 at the Roundhouse and Dingwalls, and enjoyed the blessing of the Sex Pistols, The Clash and The Damned, which brought the support of the music press. With journalists raving about them, next time they played full UK theatre tours. When they returned to New York, though, the Ramones would still be playing small clubs.

Seymour Stein looked at the poor sales and was miffed. He realised the confusion was based on the mainstream American audience not fully understanding the term 'punk'. They figured bands who came from the punk scene were punk rock. The term didn't accurately describe Talking Heads or the Ramones.

What Stein did was simple and bordering on genius. He cleverly rebranded the concept by using the term 'new wave', expertly purloining the French cinematic movement, the Nouvelle Vague of the 1960s. This rebranding made people more open to the Ramones and Talking Heads. Once mainstream US pop audiences understood that his bands weren't spitting, snarling upstarts out to cause a riot, they began to sell.

Stein spent a considerable time working from the UK, where he loved the bands. On one occasion, he heard Radio 1 DJ John Peel play 'Teenage Kicks' by The Undertones and knew he had to sign them, and he did. They released two albums on Sire, *The Undertones* and *Hypnotised*, before signing for EMI.

Once he committed to signing the Ramones in 1976, Stein realised he had to move quickly to secure better distribution and exposure. Stein was already using Warner Bros. for distribution and sold a 50 per cent share of Sire to the company in 1978, a deal that lasted until 1995.

Sire was also home to the pop brilliance of Madonna. She came to Stein's attention via the Danceteria DJ Mark Kamins, a popular fixture from the downtown New York City scene who produced Madonna's debut single, 'Everybody'. Stein liked his energy and ideas. Kamins was keen to produce one of Stein's artists, but Stein refused. Instead, he gave him seed money ($18,000) and told him to make demos; he encouraged him to find his own artists, develop them, work with them in the studio and bring him anything interesting. The first couple of things he presented were okay. The third was a demo by Madonna.

Stein was in hospital at the time, yet managed to sign her to Sire in 1982. She had a hit with her third single, 'Borderline', and released her debut album, *Madonna*, in 1983, *Like a Virgin* in 1984 and *True Blue* in 1986. Not a bad day's business from a hospital bed.

When Madonna turned 60, Stein told the *Daily Mail*, in 2018: 'I was awaiting open-heart surgery in New York's Lenox Hill Hospital in mid-1982 when the demo tape

> ## FANORAK FACT
>
> The songwriting team of Billy Steinberg and Tom Kelly, who wrote 'Like a Virgin' for Madonna, also penned 'Eternal Flame' for The Bangles, 'True Colours' for Cyndi Lauper, 'I Drove All Night' for Roy Orbison, covered by Lauper, and 'Alone' for Heart.

arrived. As penicillin dripped into my heart, I slotted it into my Sony Walkman and immediately felt an excitement. I liked the hook, I liked the voice, I liked the feel, and I liked her name.'

Stein was immediately hooked and played it again. 'I liked it all and played it again. I reached over and called up Mark Kamins, the DJ who was hustling this new singer and her song to record companies all over town and asked "Can I meet you and Madonna?"' They showed up that evening and he offered a deal.

Sire also released The Pretenders and two punk albums by The Dead Boys. There was a love of and continued commitment to UK bands like The Smiths, The Cure, Depeche Mode, Soft Cell, Echo and the Bunnymen, Aztec Camera, Madness and The Rezillos. There were places on the eclectic roster for The Flamin' Groovies, The Replacements, Plastic Bertrand and The Saints.

Sire had many great moments. Whether it's the electric shock of a frenzied Ramones performance in an empty club, David Byrne's dislocated, nervy, art school pop with Talking Heads, or the dance floor pop of Madonna – it all comes back to Stein having the ear of both a record company executive and a fan.

Stein, born in Brooklyn in 1942, was feverishly enthusiastic about music and in his many seminars and talks, actively encouraged younger music business people to look to markets in China and India. Continuing to work, he had spent most of 2017 celebrating fifty years of Sire, culminating in a book covering his stellar music career. When Stein died at the age of 80 in April 2023, Richard Williams of *The Guardian* wrote:

> The only thing an A&R man needs, Seymour Stein once said, was a good pair of ears. Stein might have added indefatigable enthusiasm, a streak of opportunism and a shrewd business brain, all of which he deployed in a career that saw him sign the deals that launched the careers of Madonna, the Ramones, Talking Heads and k.d. lang and many others.

Thanks, Richard, and thank you, Seymour.

Ramones: *Ramones*
Talking Heads: *Fear of Music*
Madonna: *Like a Virgin*
Lou Reed: *New York*
The Replacements: *Pleased to Meet Me*

SST

IT MIGHT HAVE BEEN more in keeping with the SST story if it had remained an enthusiastic local label that over-achieved for a few years. This would have allowed everyone to gather forty years later in the pub over a beer to laugh about it. That isn't going to happen though, not anytime soon.

SST has been selected because of its impact but also its shortcomings. The music was the angst-ridden sound of a jilted underground as it morphed and limped from the end of punk rock into hardcore post-punk. There's the joyously bleak yet ferociously powerful music of Black Flag, Minutemen, Saccharine Trust, Hüsker Dü, Dinosaur Jr. and Sonic Youth. The trouble – if there can be trouble with a record label that sold plenty of records – is how far SST took it. They may have gotten it wrong, but at least they tried. SST would, through its anti-establishment punk ethos, pave the way for many bands and have a lasting impact, coming to define the 1980s US underground punk scene.

SST was grappling its way through the sludge and morass. Record labels often reflect life, full of broken promises and false hopes. SST was a thought-provoking, intriguing label. It's not an easy read. It's raw and painful. There's anger and bitterness and frustration. It's the idealistic dream turned into a nightmare.

At one point, by the mid-1980s, SST was the USA's number one indie label. If you were on SST, you were cool. It was a much-cherished label, coveted by bands with tastes veering towards the true independent, and would evolve into the alternative underground scene. SST was hardcore, loud and fun. On Greg Ginn's part in SST, music writer Michael Azerrad said: 'Ginn took his label from a cash-strapped, cop-hassled store-front operation to easily the most popular underground indie of the eighties.'

It would be fair to say the man who formed the label, Greg Ginn, isn't universally loved by artists. However, there's always been something about his randomness, his contrariness and his complete defiance in the face of what he was expected to do, which I get. I understood him in the same way I secretly admired the only punk in the housing estate I grew up in. I admire people with the strength and courage to be different. SST wouldn't follow the tried-and-tested route.

Labels tend to have a formulaic structure because it works. It's important to build up the sound, brand and identity. You can't become too radical with continuity; if you do, you alienate an audience. Ginn might be a genius. It's perhaps the way he's wired, being able to change direction, flip style or, in this case, band, quite easily. But eclecticism is a tough sell.

Born in Tucson, Arizona in 1954, Greg Ginn grew up in Long Beach, California. When he was 12 years old, Ginn, a radio ham, ran a mail-order business selling surplus second-hand reconditioned army radio equipment. The business was called Solid State Tuners.

In 1976, Ginn formed a band called Panic, and in January 1978 they recorded a demo with eight songs. There was some interest from Bomp! Records. But the label kept prevaricating, so, after a year of waiting, Ginn started his own. The band name was changed to Black Flag and they released the *Nervous Breakdown* EP themselves.

FANORAK FACT

Island Records sued the label over Negativland's misuse of U2's 'I Still Haven't Found What I'm Looking For'.

In keeping with the punk spirit of the time, Greg Ginn thought, 'How difficult can it be?' In the *Yellow Pages*, he found a local pressing plant and had records pressed. He then had his cartoonist, now artist, brother Raymond Pettibon do the artwork for the cover. He was similar stylistically to cartoonist Robert Crumb. Ginn named the label SST after his radio equipment business.

After Black Flag's EP, Ginn released Minutemen's debut EP, *Paranoid Time*. They released their second EP, *Jealous Again*, and went for it. Over the next few years, the label took off. SST went nationwide, with Hüsker Dü from Saint Paul, Minnesota, the label's first band outside California, followed by Meat Puppets, from Phoenix, Arizona. Their releases were punky and eclectic but underpinned with that surfing, skateboarding and stoner culture in the Los Angeles and West Coast scene, which during the 1980s eventually morphed into hardcore punk.

You were able to follow what was happening in the music press, usually by reading *Sounds*, all the way back in Airdrie, in W.H. Smiths. SST appeared dangerous and exciting. Police were showing up at Black Flag gigs, riots were breaking out; the label's offices were having their phones bugged. Black Flag had become a conduit for punk rock in its truest sense. The authorities were fearful of insurrection from hardcore bands. This only served to strengthen the label's standing. SST was now the go-to punk and new wave label.

This was counterbalanced by a continual barrage of self-harming business moves. In a portent of what lay ahead, Ginn secured a deal with MCA to allow a co-release of Black Flag's debut album, *Damaged*. Normally he would have preferred a smaller distributor, knowing it would use speciality record stores. MCA would bring out *Damaged* on its Unicorn Records label. Before the release, though, MCA pulled the deal, citing 'anti-parent' subject matter. SST sued Unicorn, which counter-sued, bringing out an injunction preventing Black Flag from releasing any music until the case was settled. SST released a Black Flag compilation, *Everything Went Black*, and Unicorn took SST to court. Ginn and bassist Chuck Dukowski were put in jail for five days. Unicorn went bankrupt in 1983, which allowed Black Flag to release music again. They made up for lost time with four albums in 1984.

FANORAK FACT

In December 1992, SST opened a superstore in West Hollywood on the corner of Sunset and Larrabee.

So, we have riots and police threatening to close the label down, an injunction ... what else could go wrong? In 1984, Hüsker Dü were on the crest of breaking through from their alternative underground berth with *Zen Arcade*. The label erred on the side of caution, pressing between 3,500 and 5,000 copies. The record sold out within weeks. There was massive anticipation for the album, which was heralded as the must-have indie record of the year by the music press. Yet the album was left out of print for months. Then there were allegations by band members that the label didn't want anyone to get bigger than Black Flag. Hüsker Dü ended up signing with Warner Bros. in 1986.

SST continued to be prolific and popular. Luckily, the label had individuals who knew what they were doing. Most labels have quietly heroic employees working behind the scenes to ensure the music reaches the shelves. In SST's case, co-owner Joe Carducci and soundman, driver and roadie Steve Corbin managed to work with distributors, allowing fans across the world to hear the label's bands.

In late 1985, Minutemen were fresh off a tour supporting REM when D. Boon was killed in a car accident. Minutemen were rightly spoken of by the music press as the next big thing, widely expected to make a major breakthrough and emerge from cult and college level into the mainstream. The surviving members formed fIREHOSE. In 1987, Sonic Youth left, citing the label's recruitment policy, suspect accounting and 'the label's stoner administrative quality'. Dinosaur Jr. released *You're Living All Over Me* and *Bug*, then headed for Blanco Y Negro.

Despite the chaos, Greg Ginn signed great bands and released amazing music. Sometimes sticking so rigidly to the ethos gets in the way of the business. It can be difficult to find the correct balance. If you have a successful indie label, the biggest problem is finding the cash to meet the fast turnaround required to ensure momentum is maintained. Funds are tight and capacity stretched. So for labels such as SST, not to sell to a major at its peak in the mid-1980s was admirable.

> ## FANORAK FACT
>
> The Minutemen's 'Corona' became the theme for the TV show *Jackass*.

We've hardly mentioned any of the bands signed to the label since its inception, some forty years ago. The Screaming Trees were on SST before signing to Epic in 1990, as were Soundgarden, briefly, before heading to A&M. Groups like fIREHOSE, Bad Brains and doom metal exponents Saint Vitus also sold well.

One of many accusations directed at Ginn, as a label owner, member of Black Flag and part of countless SST collaborations, is that he unfairly channelled more time, finance and attention to his own projects. Another is that he refused to trawl the label's vast archive – allegedly a goldmine of unreleased work – because it meant he would have to pay royalties. To Ginn, the bands moving to major labels was a slap in the face for his and the label's 'true indie' ethos. The artists argued they needed to move on to get paid and have their work out there.

SST should be remembered as the label that was a springboard, the missing link between punk bands and the polished, radio-friendly alternative rock of the 1990s and grunge. As a teenager, Nirvana's frontman Kurt Cobain was heavily influenced by SST and he was later known to have listed many of its albums among his favourites. He was the upcoming generation and was inspired by the label's attitude and hardcore punk ethic.

Sadly, SST's legacy four decades later, despite the excellent bands who signed to the label, is one of lawsuits, unpaid royalties and bad accounting. Any discussion about SST is always framed around Ginn's behaviour and mismanagement. Here was an influential label that could have easily existed as a true indie and evolved had Ginn's stranglehold not been so tight or he so stubborn. Depending on your point of view, he's either worthy of praise or criticism. In Michael Azerrad's *Our Band Could Be Your Life*, J. Mascis of Dinosaur Jr. sums up perfectly why his band left SST for Blanco Y Negro: 'I like Greg Ginn and stuff, but they wouldn't pay you.'

PLAYLIST: MY TOP 5 ALBUMS

Sonic Youth: *Sister*
Hüsker Dü: *Zen Arcade*
Minutemen: *Double Nickels on the Dime*
Dinosaur Jr.: *Bug*
Saccharine Trust: *Paganicons*

STAX

Founders: Jim Stewart and Estelle Axton

Influential: Otis Redding, Booker T. & the M.G.'s, Isaac Hayes

MEMPHIS, SEPTEMBER 1988, AND it's a sultry evening. I have been travelling around the USA trying to find myself, musically and, at times, almost literally. I'm standing in front of a neglected church called the Southside Church of God in Christ. I happen to know it used to be another church of sorts, the home of Southern Soul; the church of Stax.

There is a strange, unfamiliar humidity, a heaviness. The air is clammy and oppressive. If I was in Europe, I'd be praying for a thunderstorm to clear the air. I look around; no one else seems to notice. I remember that smell of lightning-produced ozone and nitrogen dioxide, the metallic smell of heat and an electrical spark. The electricity in the air. The birds had stopped singing. They knew. Ancient Romans used augury to interpret the behaviour of birds for omens. The auger took auspices. The birds were now behaving in a mix of Aristophanes and Woody Allen, in a New York accent clearly saying, 'Get inside and ignore the augers, they are conmen!' This was the ominous moment as the storm approaches, then the lightning flashes, there's the booming, resounding, distinctive, violent, snapping hammer of the gods, the whip crack of thunder. When you think of the Stax logo, the fingers clicking to the downbeat, there you have the sound of Stax.

For me, Stax *is* soul music. When I think of soul, it's the music of Otis Redding, Sam and Dave (Atlantic artists leased out to Stax) and the horns and driving beat courtesy of the label's house band, Booker T. & the M.G.'s. Stax has a powerfully unique sound and a distinct history. It's a soul stew made of R&B, Southern Soul and gospel – the soundtrack and marching beat of the civil rights movement.

Stax couldn't have formed at any other time or place. It had to be the hot south, in Memphis, Tennessee, in 1959. The Stax studio had no air conditioning. It was hot, sweaty and muggy. Outside the atmosphere was fraught with racial tension.

Imagine you're in the M.G.'s, there are two Black guys and two white guys. Your African-American friends and fellow musicians aren't allowed to eat or drink beside you. Not only would the Black guys feel aggrieved, but you would also be outraged at their treatment. Again, something else is coming into the mix; it's not only the music, there's anger and rage being channelled through the sound, giving the music a unique edge. No wonder so many great records were made with such powerful, raw emotion, giving us this legendary soul music. It's played from a deep, troubled, visceral and emotional place.

Stax Records was formed by Jim Stewart and his sister, Estelle Axton, in Memphis in 1957. It was originally called Satellite, changing its name to Stax in 1961. Stewart was a banker by day and played country fiddle at night. He was captivated by Sam Phillips' Sun Studios and the fortune he made selling Elvis Presley's contract to RCA. He wanted to take the same approach.

Stewart borrowed money, not from the bank but from Estelle, and together they set up a studio, working out of a garage in Brunswick, Tennessee. The business gathered pace when they moved into a rundown former movie theatre on 926E McLemore Ave. Estelle ran the record shop, Satellite Records, at the front of the building, while the studio was in the back.

> **FANORAK FACT**
>
> Stax is derived from the first two letters of Jim Stewart and Estelle Axton's surnames.

Through a process of keeping it local, their 'build it and they will come' approach proved fruitful. By 1965, Stax had Top 40 hits with Rufus Thomas's 'Walking the Dog', William Bell's 'You Don't Miss Your Water (Till Your Well Runs Dry)' and Booker T. & the M.G.s' 'Green Onions'. Soon, the label was offered a distribution deal by Atlantic Records.

Stax studios had a close connection to the Lorraine Motel, a place where the M.G.s would hang out and where Stax artists stayed when visiting the town. 'In the Midnight Hour' and 'Knock on Wood' were written there. Yet sadly, the Lorraine Motel would become known for the 1968 assassination of Martin Luther King. The motel was bought in 1945 by Walter and Lorraine 'Loree' Bailey, having previously been an all-white establishment. They, as proprietors, would change this and offer a warm welcome to Black people. The motel made it into *The Negro Motorist Green Book*, a compilation of Black-friendly hotels, motels, diners and restaurants.

When I was in Memphis in 1988, I visited the Lorraine Motel. It's located downtown, at 450 Mulberry Street. It was padlocked. Planning signs indicated it was to become a museum. I took photographs. They didn't turn out. It felt right. I had a cold, horrible feeling taking them, as I tried to catch the exact point Martin Luther King's friends had shouted and pointed to the window, where a shot had been fired. In 1991, the Lorraine reopened as the National Civil Rights Museum Complex.

Stax was magical, yet life is flawed – and the good times short. Otis Redding was killed on 10 December 1967, when his plane crashed into Lake Monona, Wisconsin. Six others were also killed: four members of The Bar-Kays – Jimmie King (guitar), Phalon Jones (tenor sax), Ronnie Caldwell (organ) and Carl Cunningham (drums) – along with Redding's personal assistant, Matthew Kelly, and the pilot, Richard Fraser. (Bar-Kays trumpeter, Ben Cauley, survived.)

Redding had been co-writing a song with Steve Cropper, guitarist from Booker T. & the M.G.'s, since August 1967. '(Sittin' On) The Dock of the Bay' would become one of the label's biggest and most identifiable hits. Cropper and Redding had recorded it on 22 November. They had tweaked it with overdubs on 8 December, two days before Redding's death. Redding, keen to improve it, didn't get the chance. It was the *Billboard* 100's first-ever posthumous number 1. The album, *The Dock of the Bay*, became the first posthumous album to reach number 1 in the UK.

By December 1967, this first glorious era of Stax was over. The label had to deal not only with the consequences of Redding's death but also with the void left by the death of four of the young Bar-Kays. They were a group of kids, all aged 19, whom Stax had nurtured and the M.G.'s mentored. They were a much-loved part of the set-up of both the label and the studio, and much was expected of them. The pumping heart had been ripped out of the label. Then along came Warner Bros. and made Atlantic an offer it couldn't refuse.

It was commonplace for smaller independent labels like Stax to sign distribution deals with bigger labels, like Atlantic, which were able to get records into the shops and played on national radio. It was normally a mutually beneficial arrangement. Stax had signed to Atlantic and enjoyed a fruitful relationship. However, in 1967, Warner Bros. bought Atlantic for $17.5 million and triggered a clause in the small print of the Atlantic/Stax contract that meant Atlantic owned the masters of all Stax recordings, including most of the hits, and most of the money. Then, in April 1968, Martin Luther King was murdered.

Jim Stewart stood aside and let Al Bell co-own and run his baby. Bell understood the importance of reflecting on the times and signed Johnnie Taylor. Stax would have its first post-Atlantic hit with Johnnie Taylor's 'Who's Making Love' in 1968. Written by Stax team Homer Banks, Bettye Crutcher, Don Davis and Raymond Jackson and featuring Booker T. & the M.G.'s, it was a pivotal song for the label. Not only did it make number 1 on the *Billboard* R&B chart, it reached number 5 on the *Billboard* chart. More importantly, it signalled a new direction for Stax. It heralded Al Bell's marketing campaign: 'the soul explosion'.

> **FANORAK FACT**
>
> Loree Bailey (her husband named the Lorraine Motel after her) suffered a massive stroke when the bullet that killed Martin Luther King was fired. She died on 9 April 1968, the day of Dr King's funeral.

To kick-start the label and recover from the debacle of losing its back catalogue to Atlantic, in May 1968, Al Bell devised the idea of releasing twenty-seven albums and thirty singles simultaneously. Everyone on the label and their staff were pushed to write, produce and record fresh material. All except Isaac Hayes. Hayes was one of Stax's key songwriters, producers and session men. Al Bell knew he owed Isaac Hayes, after the failure of his debut, *Presenting Isaac Hayes*. Bell had rushed the album, which was recorded in two days and bombed. Bell felt partially responsible for its failure. Hayes was one of the few staff afforded time to work and given creative control, and it paid off. In 1969, Hayes released the critically acclaimed album, *Hot Buttered Soul*.

Coming into the 1970s, Stax hits came from Jean Knight's dance floor favourite 'Mr Big Stuff', as well as Isaac Hayes's 'Theme from Shaft', which won an Oscar in 1971. In 1972, the Wattstax Festival, often described as the 'Black Woodstock', would see 100,000 people watch the Reverend Jesse Jackson host an all-day pop show at Los Angeles Memorial Coliseum, featuring Stax acts. The last Stax hit was Shirley Brown's 'Woman to Woman' in 1974.

Al Bell and Jim Stewart tried everything to prevent Stax/Volt from going into bankruptcy. (Volt was the Stax sister label, which housed Otis Redding and The Bar-Kays. They were released via Atco – which was owned by Atlantic.) Stewart would lose his house trying to keep the label afloat. With Isaac Hayes suing for non-payment of royalties, the label would close in January 1976. By June 1977, eighteen months after the original Stax label had been declared bankrupt, the company's master tapes had been purchased by Fantasy Records, which revived Stax and Volt. Fantasy Records issued box sets and endless compilations. Concord Music Group now owns the label, acquiring it as part of the purchase of Fantasy Records in 2004.

Stax released countless hits and won eight Grammys and even an Academy Award. The original site of Stax Records is now the Stax Museum of American Soul Music, the Stax Music Academy and the Soulsville Charter School. Atlantic? It holds the rights to most of the 1959–68 material – and all the money.

PLAYLIST: MY TOP 5 ALBUMS

Isaac Hayes: *Hot Buttered Soul*
Eddie Floyd: *Knock on Wood*
Sam and Dave: *Hold On, I'm Coming*
Otis Redding: *Otis Blue: Otis Redding Sings Soul* (Stax/Volt)
Jean Knight: *Mr. Big Stuff*

STIFF RECORDS

Founders: Dave Robinson and Jake Riviera

Influential: The Damned, Elvis Costello, Madness

I WAS 10 WHEN I first heard 'New Rose' by The Damned, arguably the first UK punk rock single. 'New Rose' is a colossus of punk pop bubblegum, less a song, more an assault on the senses. It's fun, it's loud. When The Damned's drummer, Rat Scabies, pounds the tom-toms like Captain Caveman, and Brian James surges in with those four chords, it's the MC5 and Stooges and 1960s psychedelic garage rock and pop all wrapped up into this sound they're calling punk. It sounds as fresh as it did on the first hearing. As Andrew Oldham did with Jagger and Richards, The Damned should have been locked in the kitchen and forced to write this type of song forever ... They should have created a factory, a Motown or Brill Building conveyor belt, making punk rock masterpieces.

Stiff was set up in August 1976 in London during one of the hottest recorded summers in history by Dave Robinson and Jake Riviera. It was a punk and new wave label, formed with a loan of £400 from Dr Feelgood's Lee Brilleaux. Stiff Records had daft slogans, mystique and notoriety around Robinson – he had a baseball bat, which he rarely used for baseball, more for intimidation – and Stiff had the music: The Damned's 'New Rose', The Adverts' 'One Chord Wonders' and Richard Hell's 'Blank Generation'.

It's October 1976. It could be the additives in the lime Alpine ginger but I can't shake off 'New Rose' by The Damned. The music filters through and Billy Gilchrist next door is working out the guitar and drums to it. It was in the ether, while you watched the *Banana Splits* and *The Monkees* on TV on a Saturday morning. Then you would return to the psychedelic rock and bubblegum garage of the *Banana Splits* and the mad amphetamine-laced cough-syrup riff of one of the psyche interludes of songs like 'I'm Gonna Find a Cave'. This much-travelled garage classic, written by Jimmy Radcliffe and Buddy Scott and performed by Scott himself, was covered by Billy Lee Riley, Miki Dallon, The Sorrows and Girl Trouble (from Tacoma, Washington, on *Sub Pop 200*). Then you're on to *The Monkees* riffing out on the unapologetic sheer pop majesty of Mike Nesmith compositions: 'The Girl I Knew Somewhere' and 'You Just May Be the One'. All this music is swirling around and better still, someone's brought home a copy.

You make a mental note, as soon as your brothers leave, to sneak upstairs and listen to the record again and again and again and again. As these great, thunderously ear-splitting pop tunes and loud guitars and harmonies and drumming swirl around your imagination, they appear, collectively, to find their place. They emerge in a pattern, taking shape, like a chess move or that point when you finally understand algebra. It makes sense. Connection. Boom.

With 'New Rose', the 1970s were distilled from the glam of Bowie, T-Rex, Slade and The Sweet – and again, it is so important, that added ingredient: psychedelic 1960s garage rock and bubblegum pop – liquidised and crystallised, morphing into another shape and form. The power lines were reset and the rulebook changed. The Damned, with 'New Rose', had nailed it. The perfect performance. It's everything Stiff Records was about. Attitude, fun and rock 'n' roll. However, it didn't chart. Everyone loves it these days, but back then few were buying it. Now, let's get back to the show …

Riviera was tour manager for Dr Feelgood. Robinson started tour managing Hendrix and The Animals before managing Brinsley Schwarz, and knew he wanted to start his own label. He had been slowly working on the template, learning different aspects of the business, experience on the road, working the pub circuit and the studio in The Hope and Anchor. His main inspiration was Chris Blackwell's Island Records.

Stiff was the quintessential outsider. Its unique selling point was standing out from the crowd, taking enormous pride in not playing by the rules. It signed artists, now household names, who didn't look like pop stars; its roster was full of unconventional artists. Stiff Records wasn't to everyone's liking, but it is now; everyone loves them. At the time, Riviera and Robinson annoyed a lot of people, which was the point. They wanted a reaction.

Punk rock was about marketing and exposure. Stiff was operating before social media. The labels that succeeded were those who could throw a line to the papers, create a story out of nothing, anything to gain traction and get known. Stiff famously had Elvis Costello get arrested outside the American Embassy for busking at a CBS music conference.

Barney Bubbles did the artwork for the sleeves and the poster campaigns with slogans like 'If it ain't Stiff it ain't worth a f**k', 'The world's most flexible record label' and my favourite, 'Surfing on the New Wave'. It was funny, it was imaginative. It was controversial, but it was also clever. It got people talking and raised the label's profile.

In 1977, *New Boots and Panties*, Ian Dury's brilliantly sardonic debut album, entered the charts and would stay there for two years. In the same year, Elvis Costello finally had a Top 20 breakthrough with 'Watching the Detectives'. Everything was flying, and Stiff was lined up to sign a big deal with CBS, but then Riviera ended their partnership and went off with Elvis Costello, Nick Lowe and The Yachts, and launched Radar Records.

After the initial anger at Riviera's decision, Robinson was galvanised and worked with Ian Dury and the Blockheads. Two hit singles helped keep the album selling; 'What a Waste' made it into the Top 10 in 1978, while 'Hit Me With Your Rhythm Stick' gave Stiff a whopping number 1 bestseller in 1979 (over 900,000 copies sold in the UK). Hard to define, impossible to ignore, it was old-fashioned and music hall, yet it was fresh, funky and jazzy, new wave, dangerous, fun, ugly and sexy, poetically strange and infuriatingly catchy.

It's a common thread throughout most of the big Stiff moments: there's a strangeness on the records. Ian Dury, Elvis Costello and the Attractions' 'Watching the Detectives', Lene Lovich's 'Lucky Number' and Jona Lewie's 'Stop the Cavalry' are united by their brilliant pop strangeness. They all sound so different.

> **FANORAK FACT**
>
> The Damned recorded 'New Rose' in Pathway Studios, Islington, for £50.

Finally, the label's luck was about to change. On the verge of securing an expansive licensing agreement with Clive Davis at Arista Records, for Ian Dury, his press officer, Kosmo Vinyl, kicked off a blazing row and threw Davis out of the dressing room. As you can imagine, no deal was struck.

The Damned beat the Sex Pistols and The Clash to have a single, album and tour in the USA. The magnificent sales of Madness allowed the label to survive. The band was crucial to keeping Stiff afloat. There was a point between 1979 and 1984 when Madness clocked up eighteen Top 20 hit singles. They also had five albums on the charts. They would later sign with Virgin.

The label had three lucrative and high-profile Stiff package tours: the Live Stiffs Tour in 1977, the Be Stiff Tour in 1978 and Son of Stiff in 1979. It also had Tenpole Tudor's 'Swords of a Thousand Men', Wreckless Eric's 'Whole Wide World', Tracy Ullman's 'They Don't Know About Us' and Jona Lewie's 'In The Kitchen at Parties'. All wonderful pop – and again with that off-kilter strangeness.

The Clive Davis incident, and the CBS deal that fell through, are held up as reasons why Stiff stalled. Despite its outrageous pop ingenuity, Stiff was too volatile to last. Notwithstanding the label's hits, inventive marketing, head-turning publicity stunts and aggressive, old-school approach to radio plugging, Stiff's inherent contrariness was a real issue.

Stiff failed because Riviera wanted the label to remain a smaller indie, while Robinson wanted to become a major label. The friction was consistent. Robinson would spend his way out of a problem and Riviera disagreed with costly artwork, picture sleeves for singles, and package tours that served to create no end of friction between artists. Picture the scene: the introverted Elvis Costello lumped on a bus with The Damned?

When Island bought 50 per cent of Stiff in 1984, owner Chris Blackwell asked Robinson to run both labels. Island found itself in financial difficulties and Robinson

FANORAK FACT

The short-lived Stiff label in the USA released an album with nothing on it called *The Wit and Wisdom of Ronald Reagan* – it sold 40,000 copies.

received Stiff back as part of the deal. A minor rally, with chart hits from Furniture and The Pogues, kept the label running a while longer. It eventually went into liquidation. In 1987, its assets were bought for £300,000 by ZTT, ironically a label Robinson had helped nurture and set up while working at Island.

Music fans will always look at the original label with great fondness. It had hits with The Enemy in 2006. Stiff was reactivated without Robinson in 2007 by ZTT. It only adds to the absurdity of Stiff's story when a label capable of delivering so many classic hit singles failed to gain world domination and evolve into a conglomerate. In December 2017, Universal Music, the world's biggest record company, bought the publishing catalogue of Stiff and ZZT.

PLAYLIST: MY TOP 5 ALBUMS

The Damned: *Damned Damned Damned*
Ian Dury and the Blockheads: *New Boots and Panties*
The Pogues: *Rum, Sodomy & the Lash*
Elvis Costello: *My Aim Is True*
Madness: *One Step Beyond*

SUB POP

Founders: Bruce Pavitt and Jonathan Poneman

Influential: Mudhoney, Soundgarden, Nirvana

WHILE AT OLYMPIA'S EVERGREEN State College, in the early 1980s, Bruce Pavitt wanted to showcase regional bands across the USA. At this point, bands appeared to be sprouting up like weeds in every backyard. The bands had taken the applicable parts of punk rock, the DIY approach, and fashioned these into their own scene, keeping creative control. The trouble was, you couldn't find their records in the shops. Pavitt knew bands were making records, yet no one was giving them shelf space. He started the fanzine *Subterranean Pop* to connect with like-minded fans of underground music. The fanzine sometimes included cassette compilations of independent bands from across the country, and due to the way they were packaged, despite the small scale, they sold well.

This was a time of post-punk regeneration. Lessons had been learned from punk rock's mistakes. There was a subtle changing of the guard, a shift of power. The emphasis had changed. Time to say goodbye to the cartoon vaudeville act, the pantomime parody that punk had allowed itself to become; in with a stronger, leaner model. Say hello to the all-improved, sinewy energy and raw power of bands prepared to redefine the underground punk scene. Bands fuelled on vitamins washed down by hallucinatory cough syrup, favoured by 1960s garage punk bands from Pebbles compilations, were armed with a ferocious, frenzied dynamism and a body that refused to sleep. This would bring a certain piquancy to their music and their live shows. These punks were sussed; they knew their history and were unafraid to love The Beatles, Black Sabbath and Kiss. They were post-punk renegades who whacked you with art, irony and fun, and who also happened to love poetry, literature and pop.

Sub Pop began in 1986 with the release of the compilation *Sub Pop 100*. The Green River EP (featuring the future members of Mudhoney) *Dry as a Bone* came out in 1987 and, after Jonathan Poneman borrowed money to record Soundgarden, their single 'Hunted Down'/ 'Nothing to Say' was released, followed by their EP *Screaming Life* in October.

Until this point, Sub Pop had existed in many shapes and forms: as a fanzine (*Subterranean Pop*), a radio show (*Subterranean Pop* on the University of Washington student radio station, KCMU), a magazine column ('Sub Pop USA' for local newspaper *The Rocket*) and a label releasing cassette tapes. In 1988, Pavitt and Poneman quit their jobs, determined to focus full-time on the label, and raised $43,000 in investment. Pavitt dealt with the signings and artists, the music, with Poneman focusing on the business and legal side.

At the heart of the label was an understanding of the significance of location and geography. For Pavitt and Poneman, an independent record company had to create a scene with a solid geographical base. In the same way food is awarded Protected Geographical Status, Sub Pop would be defined by Seattle. It would run through everything, from branding, scene, t-shirts and record sleeves, to the sound of its artists. Sub Pop used the same producer on most of its output, Jack Endino. He was cheap, fast, effective, experienced and consistent. The Sub Pop philosophy and Endino combined to sculpt the Seattle sound and what the world would soon come to recognise as grunge.

Jack Endino plays down the secret of what defined grunge and the Seattle sound. In interviews, he tends to focus more on the people than the technical wizardry. In 2022, in an interview with Jacob Uitti of *American Songwriter*, Endino explained: 'Recording is a sacred task, and if you're not careful, you can take something beautiful and creative and end up sterilizing it and killing it dead.' Endino is perhaps mellowing with age. 'There's a lot of ways of doing it wrong and wasting time, and my job is to steer people away from that, keep it fun, keep it interesting, and preserve the magic and the spark.'

For the producer, it was about bands listening to everything from 1960s garage punk to 1970s heavy rock, mashed up with 1980s hardcore punk, and being unafraid to have fun, almost parodying it. It was a reflection of most bands, good and bad, he had worked with. Bands with cheap, distorted amps, guitarists playing too loudly and singers having to scream over the guitars, then the drummers crashing in, trying to outdo everyone else.

Mudhoney and Nirvana would be influenced by the Melvins (C/Z Records) then Black Flag (SST). In Mudhoney's case, they focused on the punk/garage hybrid. Then it would be popularised with Nirvana's love of The Pixies, and evolve into what would be described as alternative rock. Later, 'Smells Like Teen Spirit' was a musical mash-up of The Kingsmen's 'Louie Louie' and Boston's 'More Than a Feeling' with the stop-start dynamic used by The Pixies.

In Sub Pop's case, the usual forces came into play. Music, timing, geography, clever branding and luck would bring global recognition. It seemed to be in the blood at Sub Pop – the key players at the start of the label were in bands, working either in the Sub Pop warehouse or in record shops. This might be oversimplifying it, but it was pivotal. People in bands know about music and love to listen to old records, constantly. Then they pick up a melody or a guitar hook. It might be Black Sabbath or The Bay City Rollers or The Beatles or Blue Cheer, The Beach Boys or Badfinger, Big Star or The Bee Gees. It doesn't have to be a band beginning with 'B'; it does help, though. The music, from the start, was forging a sound, and the marketing and action photography by Charles Peterson implied a certain look and fashion, suggesting it was a scene. All of these parts came together for the world to come knocking.

Journalists, commentators and distributors are then required to spread the word and sell the music. They, however, tend to oversimplify the process in search of a word or scene; they like to lump bands together, to 'pigeonhole' them. Where in the record store would you find it? The truth is, sometimes the word goes from being an adjective to a noun because they need somewhere in the shop to put Nirvana, Pearl Jam and Soundgarden when they hit the mainstream.

Initially, Sub Pop showed foresight by reaching across the Atlantic to where indie

FANORAK FACT

When Sub Pop write to bands or artists, the rejection letter starts with the harsh, yet funny: 'Dear Loser'. Cheeky.

punk fans and the UK music press showed early excitement. Nirvana were credited with *Melody Maker*'s 'Single of the Week' in February 1988. The song was from the Sub Pop Singles Club and was a cover of Dutch group Shocking Blue's 'Love Buzz'. This was the first Sub Pop Singles Club release.

In 1989, sensing the UK music press would get what was happening, Poneman and Pavitt paid for the assistant editor of *Melody Maker*, Everett True, to fly out to Seattle. He was the first journalist to cover, in any great depth, the scene around Seattle and Olympia. His vivid accounts, articles and reviews acted as a catalyst in raising the profile of the scene, bringing both Sub Pop and bands like Nirvana, Mudhoney, the Melvins and Tad to a wider audience.

The label also understood it was about branding and Seattle was the essential component in this. Sub Pop filtered it out, like a subtle ad campaign. But it was always with fun. Want to see our bands? Why not come to Seattle? Catch the scene. Enjoy a succulent chocolate rocky road dipped in our aromatic rich roast coffee, then check out our perfectly dislocated blend of punk-pop. From the start, Sub Pop's acts were a mix of punk rock philosophy and indie ethic. 'Dry as a Bone' from Green River was promoted as 'ultra-loose grunge that destroyed the morals of a generation'. There you have classic Sub Pop promotion.

We must cover the one band releasing music that quickly outgrew Seattle and had an unprecedented global impact. Jack Endino produced Nirvana's *Bleach* and they sounded like a great Sub Pop band, but by the start of the 1990s, Seattle had become the home of grunge. For the music industry, the gold rush was on; it was time to find Seattle on the map, get up there and sign anything or anyone who knew, sounded like, or had met Nirvana.

Sub Pop were brilliant at marketing and packaging. Limited editions of a single would push up demand. Releases on green vinyl would be in shops, with the run quickly and unexpectedly stopped, leaving fans with a memorable collector's item.

If you'd been able to see into the future, you wouldn't have given your green vinyl single to the girl with kitsch, charity shop glasses who drank coffee and read poetry. She loved your record collection more than she loved you. Music fans buy to listen. Collectors buy to invest. A rare musical artefact to you became a deposit on a flat for her.

Sub Pop's story can be divided into two phases: the grunge era of Nirvana, Mudhoney and Soundgarden, followed around 2001 by the arrival of The Shins. The first era was a time of confusion, living in the shadow of post-Nirvana aftershocks. Unrest, fall-outs, the business over-stretching; it all culminated in Warner Music Group buying 49 per cent in 1995 in anticipation of the next Nirvana turning up for tea.

It wasn't until the release of The Shins (featuring James Mercer, originally of the band Flake from Albuquerque, New Mexico, now based in Portland, Oregon) that the label's fortunes would change. The Shins allowed Sub Pop to breathe again and evolve into a home for alternative, collegiate, pastoral indie-folk, and melodic bands. Soon, a host of other bands wanted to be like The Shins. Groups like Fleet Foxes, The Postal Service and Fruit Bats were stepping up to be quirky and beardy, while channelling their inner rock god from the psychiatrist's chair, and signing for Sub Pop.

Mudhoney, Soundgarden, Babes in Toyland, Dinosaur Jr., L7 and Hole followed Nirvana into the mainstream. After that, Sub Pop released work by Mogwai, The Vaselines, Father John Misty, Fleet Foxes, Death Cab for Cutie, CSS, The Shins, The Postal Service, Foals, Beach House, Blitzen Trapper and Flight of the Conchords.

Sub Pop's current marketing proclamation is: 'We're not the best; but we're pretty good.' This self-deprecating slogan tells you everything about the label. While accepting that Sub Pop is not a world beater, it's nobody's fool either. There's a subtle reminder to misjudge the label at your peril. By underplaying it, Sub Pop is quietly intending to over-deliver.

As for Nirvana, I think they were special because they had amazing songs and were incredible live but also worked so hard. In 1991, I toured with Nirvana and kept a diary. It was published in 2013. This part was removed:

By the time other labels headed to the Northwest, they didn't even realise it was over. If I could cartoon I'd have the staff from Sub Pop waving and laughing as they say goodbye to Nirvana, leaving on the bus while guys with ponytails from the majors chase after them with money. People refuse to accept that sometimes it's just the right time, that magic moment. I don't think you can manufacture that. Yes, it certainly helped that Kurt got out of Aberdeen and away from a logging community. It most certainly helped if people at a label like Sub Pop were trying to guide and navigate with some smart marketing and producers like Jack Endino were in the studio mentoring you. As much as Kurt was surrounded by liberal people in a college town with a superb radio station playing the Vaselines and the Pastels and there were record stores, coffee shops, bookshops, and great venues. These things cannot be manufactured or replicated. They can be provoked and encouraged but sometimes it's just the perfect coming together, it's just as simple as a fantastically talented band with some great songs. For the so-called patron saints of the slacker generation when I met and knew them in 1991, they worked harder than any band I've ever witnessed in my life. That's why they were so good. I watched them develop 'All Apologies' over soundchecks, stop for interviews, then drive off for a session on Radio 1, return, play a blistering show, sleep and be on a bus the next morning to do it all again.

PLAYLIST: MY TOP 5 ALBUMS

Fruit Bats: *Mouthfuls*
Mudhoney: *Superfuzz Bigmuff*
Sebadoh: *Bakesale*
Beat Happening: *You Turn Me On*
Nirvana: *Bleach*

SUN RECORDS

Founder: Sam Phillips

Influential: Elvis Presley, Howlin' Wolf, Ike Turner, Johnny Cash, Jerry Lee Lewis

STANDING IN THE MEMPHIS heat, outside 706 Union Avenue, on the corner of Marshall, if you stop and look around and take it in, you can truly sense the magic. Despite the clichéd rhetoric you've read in countless books and the thousands of records you've listened to, this is it. You've made it. You're finally here: Sun Records, in the migraine-inducing, muddy and moist heat. It feels like the air you're breathing is perspiring. If you're inclined to follow your instinct and the at times destructive force of nature that literature or art can lead you to, the realisation can be fairly Old Testament.

Suddenly it hits you. That dramatic point in the movie when the scenes abruptly flick – it's jarring and confusing. The situation becomes raw; fight or flight. The calm before the storm. The air tastes similar to the iron from the blood inside your head after a sucker punch. The bottled-up chaos of sin, the blues, rock 'n' roll and country, all converge, obdurate ghosts refusing to accept their fate. This is the same atmosphere and air that permeated the music of Elvis and Jerry Lee, Jackie Trenton and Ike Turner, Muddy Waters and B.B. King. You have reached your journey's end. This is commonly accepted and widely viewed as factually, physically and spiritually the moment rhythm and blues and country music gave birth to rock 'n' roll. This, in my view, is the beginning; where rock 'n' roll, as we know it, originated.

It becomes overwhelming. Out of this unassuming building in front of you, Sun Records was born. You know the story so well. You are reminded of the normality of every struggling artist hoping for a break – Elvis's difficulty until stumbling upon 'That's' Alright Mama' and making a record; Sam Phillips taking it to a DJ called Dewey Philips, who played R&B on WHBQ in Memphis; Philips loving it and playing it constantly. Yet it seems too normal. This should be the Taj Mahal or the Great Pyramid of Giza. Sun Records is unremarkable and prosaic. It's just sitting there. Is it too much to ask Memphis to have a 50ft-high garish neon Elvis with gyrating hips?

At this precise point in my journey, in the sky directly above, I witness the bedazzling geometric form of birds in flight. Whatever's happening, they mean business. They are off somewhere and aren't hanging around. I am another tired and gormlessly bedraggled fan, looking at Sun Studios and watching the strange behaviour of the birds in the sky, just as I would do later that day at Stax (see Stax). The natives aren't to know I'm deliberating, waiting for a sign from the gods. I willingly accept I'm losing the plot and realise it's time to calm down, regroup and buy breakfast.

In 1950, Sam Phillips was a frustrated radio engineer who had just left his job to set up a recording studio. With the slogan, 'We record anything; anywhere, anytime', Phillips started the Memphis Recording Service. He quickly garnered a reputation for promoting and recording Black artists like Rosco Gordon, Little Milton and James Cotton.

Phillips loved R&B and was desperate to share it with a broader, mainstream audience. Phillips was brave too. He wanted to bring what was dismissed as 'race music' to a wider audience at a time when the USA, especially the Deep South, was conservative and racist.

Memphis had a thriving music scene: folk, blues, gospel, country, boogie and swing. Stars were on every corner. Sam Phillips (with the help of Rufus Thomas) found B.B. King and his favourite, Howlin' Wolf. So, he was able to spot talent. He knew what was required from artists and had a keen sense of what would sell and what made a song shine on the radio.

Before Sun Records was launched in 1952, Phillips recorded with Ike Turner on 'Rocket 88' by Jackie Brenston. This is arguably one of the first great rock 'n' roll records, a recording released on Chess Records (see Chess Records). With his label up and running, the first hit came from Rufus Thomas's 'Bear Cat'. Unfortunately, the single, which was a response to Big Mama Thornton's 'Hound Dog', practically bankrupted Sun Records when a lawsuit was hastily filed against it for copyright infringement, requesting royalties and damages.

The next hit was from a vocal quintet, a beautiful song by The Prisonaires, 'Just Walkin' in the Rain'. They were called The Prisonaires for a reason: they were allowed out of Nashville State Penitentiary, in chains, to record the song. But the game changed forever in June 1954 when a teenage truck driver from Tupelo, Mississippi, came into the studio to cut a track. Elvis had arrived at Sun to make a record, a $4 cut, as a gift for his mother. Phillips enjoyed his singing style and recognised a quality, a longing and a sadness in it. Marion Keisker, an assistant at the Memphis Recording Service, claimed it was she who recorded Elvis first, two songs on a 10in acetate disk, called 'My Happiness' and 'That's When Heartaches Begin'. She also claims to have written the now famous note, 'Good ballad singer – Hold.'

Elvis had dropped by on several occasions and was becoming friends with Keisker. It was she who kept telling Sam Phillips to give him another chance. Phillips had Elvis back to the studio a few times to try recording a song called 'Without You', a nostalgic ballad that his publisher friend Red Wortham had written. This didn't work out. The song wasn't suitable and the session petered out.

Marion continued to harass Phillips about another session, this time in front of guitarist Scotty Moore while they had a coffee. Phillips gave in to Marion's insistence, this time suggesting Scotty invite him to his house to go through some numbers in a more relaxed environment, to check him out. Elvis, with Bill Black on double bass, ran through some standards. Scotty reported back to Sam that he was good, he did have a great voice, and he was considering asking him to sing in his band. Phillips decided to bring him in and asked Moore and Black to accompany him.

During this session, the problem remained: Elvis was too nervous. The sessions weren't going well. Something just wasn't clicking; there was no flow or spark. Phillips considered it might be the choice of material. Black and Moore heard something in his voice, a humility, a warmth, a yearning to break free, yet it wasn't transferring to the material.

With the session nearing the end and going nowhere, Phillips heard Elvis, Scotty Moore and Bill Black, hamming it up to a version of Arthur Crudup's 'That's All Right, Mama'. Phillips loved it, told them to play it again and caught a version in a live take. On the intro of the original 45, you can hear the Memphis heat slightly warp the tapes. Phillips, as well as capturing the magic, also loved what he called 'imperfect perfection'. Sun Records released the track in July 1954 as 'That's All Right', with 'Blue Moon of Kentucky' as the B-side.

Sam Phillips had an unwavering vision for Sun Records and it would prove groundbreaking. At a time when other record companies stayed with jazz and easy listening, he was introducing a youthful, exciting white rock 'n' roll singer who happened to sound Black. His unrestrained stage act and music were full of energy, making his live shows gloriously unpredictable. No one knew what was going to happen when the truck rolled into town. It scared the adults and the authorities. They saw the carefree abandonment; rebellion was in the air. The girls were going berserk at his raw sexuality and the boys rebelled at the girls going crazy; however, everyone loved the music. This guy was a phenomenon. Underneath it, too, there was danger: the sound crossed musical and racial barriers in an extremely toxic era. Elvis would be a star and Phillips would be rich.

By 1955, Sun Records needed cash for distribution and Phillips required money to record, invest in and develop his other acts. When Elvis's manager, Colonel Tom Parker, asked Phillips to name his price for Elvis's contract, he suggested the outrageous figure of $35,000 plus $5,000 to cover the royalties Sun Records already owed Elvis.

> ### FANORAK FACT
>
> Sam Phillips was no hick. One of the fledgling businesses he heavily invested in went big too: the Holiday Inn Group.

It's easy for pop historians to question the deal in hindsight, but this is what RCA paid for Elvis – it's the equivalent of about half a million dollars now.

Along with Elvis's 'That's All Right', 'Blue Moon of Kentucky', 'Good Rockin' Tonight' and 'Mystery Train', Phillips produced Carl Perkins' 'Blue Suede Shoes', Johnny Cash's 'I Walk the Line' and Jerry Lee Lewis's 'Whole Lotta Shakin' Going On'. There was also the peerless work of Roy Orbison. Imagine a small indie unleashing the musical equivalent today.

In 1958, Johnny Cash and Carl Perkins left for Columbia. Lewis stayed and had hits, though Phillips grew tired. In 1969, Mercury Records' Shelby Singleton bought Sun Records, tweaking the name to Sun International Corporation; it still operates today.

With Sun Records, Phillips shaped popular music. If it wasn't for his vision, we wouldn't have had Elvis, Jerry Lee Lewis or Carl Perkins, and therefore we wouldn't have had The Beatles. As John Lennon said, 'Before Elvis, there was nothing.'

This is the true legacy of Sun Records. Its impact should be measured by the importance of the artists the label would inspire to form bands. Sun Records was more than an influential label; it redefined the template. Suddenly here was a label boss in the south, willing to take on race, break down barriers and find a wider audience. Phillips was colour-blind; the music was everything. It was always the music that drove him. I firmly believe Sam Phillips was one of the great trailblazers and pioneers of the music industry and deserves more credit. He should be lauded like George Martin and Berry Gordy; instead, he is often belittled as a small-town hick, out of his depth. He was a skilled producer and a great A&R man who positively changed music and society.

Several factors go into making a label succeed. Great music isn't enough. A label also requires a strong, clearly defined identity and aesthetic, an owner willing to take risks and, most importantly, good luck and timing. It also needs the ability to see something unique in an artist, to take a truck driver from Tupelo with warmth and charm, who sings ballads with ease, and transform him into the King of Rock 'n' Roll. When the sessions weren't going well, it was probably Elvis's last chance. When he was relaxed, messing around in the studio, something magical happened. Marion Keisker recognised something in his humility; he was well mannered and she liked his personality, warmth and humour. She convinced Phillips to give him the final chance, intuitively knowing the public would love him. But how did Sam Phillips see such potential? Maybe he was looking at the sky and hoping for a positive sign from the birds.

PLAYLIST: MY TOP 5 ALBUMS

Jerry Lee Lewis: *Jerry Lee Lewis*

Johnny Cash: *All Aboard the Blue Train with Johnny Cash*

Roy Orbison: *Roy Orbison at the Rock House*

Carl Perkins: *Teen Beat: The Best of Carl Perkins*

Johnny Cash: *Original Sun Sound of Johnny Cash*

TRACK RECORDS

Founders: Chris Stamp and Kit Lambert

Influential: The Jimi Hendrix Experience, The Who, Thunderclap Newman, The Crazy World of Arthur Brown, Golden Earring

TRACK RECORDS (ACTUALLY TRACK Record but referred to henceforth as Track) was established in 1966 and considered the pulsating heartbeat of swinging London. It was one of the hippest independent labels of its time and was set up by Chris Stamp and Kit Lambert, the management team behind The Who. They were intelligent and inventive in their mentoring and marketing of the band, but when it came to running a label, things weren't as straightforward.

Stamp and Lambert put everything they had into Track. They worked tirelessly to establish a label and environment that would allow creative freedom for The Who. They also wanted a platform to launch and release material by The Jimi Hendrix Experience. Despite eventually finding success, it always looked as though the task would overwhelm them. These were shark-infested waters and their lack of label experience made them an easy target for the less scrupulous in the industry who seemed born with a penchant for smelling blood.

They also appeared to suffer from protracted legal problems. Stamp and Lambert were embroiled in one particularly costly, tedious and time-consuming court case with producer Shel Talmy. This acted as a catalyst, strengthening their resolve to go it alone and set up Track. Talmy worked as a freelance producer, mainly for Decca, and produced most of The Kinks' early hits. Their benchmark 1960s classic, 'You Really Got Me', inspired Pete Townshend to write 'I Can't Explain'. As soon as he'd completed the song, such was Townshend's eagerness to have Talmy produce it that he famously rang up and played the song, in full, down the phone to him. Talmy not only agreed to produce The Who; he also secured a deal with Decca in the USA and its UK subsidiary, Brunswick, bypassing Stamp and Lambert, and creating ambiguity over who 'owned' the band. Talmy would go on to produce 'My Generation'.

This naivety, or perhaps lack of street smarts, might be explained by the way Stamp and Lambert stumbled into managing The Who. As a way of gaining access into the movie business, they wanted to make a cinéma-vérité documentary, an underground movie that reflected the frustrations of youth culture in London at the time. They thought a great rock 'n' roll band would be the perfect vehicle to bring the film together. After months of searching, they found their muse with The Who (at this point known as The High Numbers), playing The Railway Tavern in Harrow Weald. They became so consumed with the band, that they abandoned the movie project and changed direction by mentoring and managing the group. Their showbiz path changed. Instead of movies they would be part of the music business. They set up a record label primarily to release records by The Who.

Stamp and Lambert knew the band had something special. They created so much raw energy and had a strange ugliness or beautiful strangeness. They were like characters from a Caravaggio painting. The parts didn't seem to fit. Townshend was at art school and the others still worked. There was a real conflict between members of the band. This was authentic. They fought with each other on stage. They had fights with the audience. This though was more than just conflicting personalities and the forcefulness of their explosive live performances. Their shows were tense, fraught and cinematic. Who needed a movie?

The band itself, with Pete Townshend as the potent driving force, was growing in both quality of songwriting and performance; in Townshend they had someone with a compelling stage persona, his own style and sound, inspired by both R&B and rock 'n' roll. With mentoring from

> **FANORAK FACT**
>
> Thunderclap Newman's 'Something in the Air' was initially called 'Revolution' and written for the soundtrack album of the movie *The Magic Christian*.

Kit Lambert, Townshend invented a mad-axeman identity, drawn from an abstract world about annihilation and killing to recreate. It was about driving on, about performance. When Daltrey, Entwistle and Townshend settled on Moon as their regular drummer, the alchemy was complete and the game was on.

The Who's first album *My Generation* (Brunswick UK, Decca US) was a hit but the band were growing increasingly frustrated at being locked into the archaic practices and stringent contractual obligations demanded by established record companies. However, Track's aim of creative freedom was proving costly and taking too much time to set up. When they should have been making money, The Who lost at every turn. They were embroiled in a protracted and costly legal battle with Shel Talmy and Brunswick Records.

By December 1966, Track was still not fully operational and they needed to be. Their next ace up the sleeve was Jimi Hendrix. Kit Lambert approached Polydor, who distributed The Who, with a proposal. He knew they were keen to shake off their easy-listening reputation, and who better to shake off the cobwebs than this left-handed genius from Seattle called Jimi Hendrix? He had been causing a scene amongst London's rock glitterati playing the famous London club, the Scotch of St James. Lambert also suggested that along with Hendrix, they needed to release some product by The Who. So until Track was ready, both acts would have single releases via their distributor, Polydor.

The management team had persuaded Jimi Hendrix, by offering £1,000 for a promotional film for his singles and a higher-than-average royalty. Through their TV connections, they guaranteed appearances on the influential music show *Ready Steady Go*. Hendrix would appear twice on *Ready Steady Go* and stole the show on *Top of the Pops* becoming a household name.

Stamp and Lambert would have to wait until April 1967 before The Who had a hit single released on Track. The song was 'Pictures of Lily,' which reached number 4 in the UK but failed to make an impact in the US. This was followed by 'The Last Time'. In 1967, Jagger and Richards of The Rolling Stones had been charged with drug offences: Jagger with possessing amphetamine pills and Richards for allowing cannabis to be smoked at his house, Redlands, a fifteenth-century moated cottage in West Wittering, West Sussex, purchased for £20,000 in 1966. The case was a circus, the authorities viewed to have overreacted. The two were initially sentenced, Jagger receiving three months and Richards a year, though both convictions were later quashed on appeal. The Who promised to release a Rolling Stones song each month they stayed in prison.

Hendrix's second single, 'Purple Haze', in March 1967, was the first Track single, a phenomenal song to launch a label. Track would later release Hendrix's influential debut album, *Are You Experienced?*

Despite their best attempts, Lambert and Stamp staggered from one legal crisis to the next. This era seems characterized by a culture of litigation, with constant suing and counter-suing between artists and management. Before Hendrix left the USA for London, which would see him become a worldwide star, his manager, Chas Chandler, actively chased down each deal and contract Hendrix had signed. As a working musician, he would sign any contract placed in front of him to get a wage. Every contract they found was bought out and ripped up. One was with Ed Chalpin of PPX, in 1965, while Hendrix was backing Curtis Knight and the Squires. It would prove costly. Signing to Track, while under contract, meant Chalpin was within his rights to claim a settlement – which he did, leaving Track in serious financial trouble.

In 1968, The Crazy World of Arthur Brown had a UK number 1 with 'Fire', produced by Townshend and Lambert. It reached number 2 in the US charts. Brown would later claim he wasn't fully compensated for the single's success. Track also had a hit with Hendrix's *Electric Ladyland*, an album memorable for featuring a cover of nineteen nude women (apparently, Hendrix was never consulted about the cover).

Track generated income by releasing compilation albums – commonplace now, yet unusual in the 1960s. They included The Who's *Direct Hits*, *Electric Jimi Hendrix* and one called *The House That Track Built*. In 1969, The Who released their fourth album,

FANORAK FACT

Jimi Hendrix wrote 'Purple Haze' based on a dream where he walked under the water across the sea bed.

the landmark *Tommy*. This was one of the label's biggest sellers. It was released in the USA on Decca.

Thunderclap Newman were put together for Pete Townshend to show off John Speedy Keen, his friend, chauffeur, drummer and guitarist, and to highlight Keen's skill as a songwriter (he wrote 'Armenia City in the Sky' on *The Who Sell Out*). Not only did Townshend play bass (under the name Bijou Drains), he also brought in Andy Thunderclap Newman, a GPO engineer by day and Dixieland jazz piano player by night. He also recruited future Wings guitarist, Jimmy McCulloch. 'Something in the Air' reached number 1 in August 1969, and appeared on the 1970 album *Hollywood Dream*, produced by Townshend and released on Track. Again, the album failed to fulfil its potential, partly due to the label procrastinating when it should have been capitalising on the success of the single.

In March 1970, Track released the live Hendrix album, *Band of Gypsys*. In 1972, Dutch band Golden Earring toured with The Who, signed with Track and had a hit with 'Radar Love'. Their 1973 album, *Moontan*, gave the label some much-needed success. In the same year, The Who released *Quadrophenia*, the band's last album of original material.

Through a mix of financial mismanagement, contractual issues and a refusal to pay royalties, the label slowly fell apart. In 1974, The Who released one more album, a compilation, put together by John Entwistle, called *Odds and Sods*. By 1975, Golden Earring were the only act on the sinking ship and they soon left. Two more albums already recorded were released, one by The Heartbreakers, and the other by Shakin' Stevens, before the label ceased to operate.

If you could choose a time and a place to play in a band or work at a label, why not London in the mid-1960s? Imagine working with Hendrix and The Who and partying with The Beatles and The Stones? For many, the label was merely a subsidiary of Polydor, but the Track logo and the label design epitomised the spirit of one of the most exciting moments in British pop history.

Track, however, was so badly run that even The Who ended up suing *their own* label over unpaid royalties. Close inspection of the 1967 accounts show that the label did make money. From its base in

Old Compton Street, Soho, it spent lavishly: £20,000 on advertising, £16,000 on wages, £8,000 on travel and £5,000 on phone calls. This was an eye-watering amount for the time. Track was revived in 1999 by established music industry figure and manager, Ian Grant.

PLAYLIST: MY TOP 5 ALBUMS

The Jimi Hendrix Experience: *Axis: Bold as Love*
Johnny Thunders and the Heartbreakers: *L.A.M.F*
The Who: *Who's Next*
Thunderclap Newman: *Hollywood Dream*
The Who: *Quadrophenia*

TROJAN

Founders: Lee Gopthal and Chris Blackwell

Influential: Harry J. All Stars, Dave and Ansel Collins, Jimmy Cliff

YOU WILL FIND THE familiar logo of Trojan in just about everyone's record collection. The label's story is one of initial single success, but due to some simple mistakes, Trojan quickly found itself in trouble. The label was releasing singles but not developing artists for the long term. It also failed to grasp the sound its core audience craved, going into liquidation in 1975.

Since the late 1970s, when a young eagle-eyed fan started cataloguing the label's recordings, the musician, producer, writer and Jamaican music expert Laurence Cane-Honeysett has, almost by default, overseen the company, and now runs it. He is part archivist, part boss; he has navigated through buyouts and bankruptcy while dealing with a whole new marketplace. Initially under the auspices of Universal and now BMG, the label still survives and prospers.

Trojan's importance in spreading reggae, rock steady, dub and ska to a global marketplace should not be underestimated. Trojan, in the same way that 2 Tone would do later, united Black and white. The label was initially set up in July 1967 as a subsidiary of Island Records (see Island Records) by Chris Blackwell, to showcase the successful producer Arthur 'Duke' Reid. Surprisingly, the idea failed and was shelved. However, the name would come in handy the following year. Blackwell made money with Island when he licensed and produced 'My Boy Lollipop'. With capital

FANORAK FACT

Every one of the records produced by Judge Dread was banned by the BBC.

from that, he teamed up with his competitor Lee Gopthal at the distribution company Beat and Commercial Records.

With Island's extensive catalogue of Jamaican acts and B&C's distribution and Music City shops, it was the perfect set-up. The old label name, Trojan Records, was dusted down (it was also rumoured that the name was recycled as they had so many Trojan stickers from the first incarnation) and began issuing a variety of reggae labels to highlight music from a vast array of reggae producers – names such as Duke Reid, Edward 'Bunny' Lee, Robert 'Dandy' Thompson, Harry Johnson, Leslie Kong and Lee 'Scratch' Perry.

The label was named after Duke Reid's nickname, 'the Trojan', based on his sound system and the name of the truck required to transport his speakers. Reid was considered one of the main producers at this time, along with Coxsone Dodd. The label's timing was perfect, coinciding with the emerging skinhead scene and a working-class youth movement that adored Jamaican music. This would see an explosion and rapid growth in the popularity of Trojan, which in 1969 had a minor hit with 'Red Red Wine' by Tony Tribe, then 'Longshot' by The Pioneers and 'The Liquidator' by Harry J. All Stars. It was Dave and Ansel Collins' 'Double Barrel' that gave Trojan its first UK number 1. Suddenly, the label was hot as it had a few Jamaican hits simultaneously.

By 1970, Trojan was having hits with artists like Lee 'Scratch' Perry's Upsetters, Bob and Marcia, Desmond Dekker, Jimmy Cliff, Harry J. All Stars, Dave and Ansel Collins, and The Maytals. The label had taken off because the skinheads and mods loved the raw dancefloor sound; now the white working-class fans were buying along with the growing UK West Indian population. The label continued to feed demand, serving the audience what they wanted. It also started to highlight artists who were stars in Jamaica, who then

FANORAK FACT

Jimmy Cliff's 'Vietnam' was said by Bob Dylan to be the best protest song on the Vietnam conflict. The song also inspired Paul Simon to travel to Jamaica to record in Dynamic Studios, using the same backing band for his song 'Mother and Child Reunion'.

became major acts: Judge Dread, Dandy Livingston, Dennis Brown, Gregory Isaacs, and Bob Marley and the Wailers.

By 1972 Chris Blackwell had decided to end Island's association with Trojan, selling his share of the company as Island Records focused on Bob Marley. Despite the label originally concentrating on single releases from top producers, it moved to release a series of highly popular compilations.

My strongest recollection of holding a Trojan single was Ken Boothe's 'Everything I Own'. I remember the Trojan logo and playing the song; it was 1974. Yet this hit was hardly representative of the label. The production was smooth and polished. Nina Simone's 'Young, Gifted and Black', recorded by Bob and Marcia, and Horace Faith's 'Black Pearl' were also kinder on the ear. There were overdubs and added strings to make the records playable for the BBC. However, the production costs were astronomical and eventually took their toll. By trying to open up its product to a wider base, in 1975 Trojan went into liquidation. Ironically, the people who loved the music most – its core audience, West Indians, skinheads and mods – preferred the raw, unpolished sound. The assets were picked up by Marcel Rodd of budget album specialist Saga Records. Saga didn't take on the debts, so artists who had earned the label money with hit singles were still left unpaid.

In 1985, avid record collector and accountant (a great combo for any aspiring record company executive) Colin Newman bought Trojan and got to work rereleasing its numerous rock steady, reggae and ska classics in triple CD box sets. Newman brought in Steve Barrow, a reggae aficionado, journalist and writer who compiled albums and wrote sleeve notes for Island and then Trojan. They saw the music's commercial appeal and licensed it to Adidas, UEFA and TDK for use in ad campaigns. The label was then bought up by the Sanctuary Records Group in 2001, but the group had financial problems and in 2007 Universal Music bought 90 per cent of Sanctuary. Universal sold its back catalogue to BMG.

FANORAK FACT

Desmond Dekker's album has his name misspelt as 'Dekkar'.

Trojan still survives through a mixture of luck and timing, but most of all because of the distinctive feel, power and sound of the music, and because those involved over the years, Newman, Barrow and Laurence Cane-Honeysett, just get it.

PLAYLIST: MY TOP 5 ALBUMS

Desmond Dekker: *This Is Desmond Dekkar*
Duke Reid: *Golden Hits*
Harry J. All Stars: *Liquidator*
The Maytals: *Monkey Man*
The Ethiopians: *Reggae Power*

VERVE RECORDS

Founder: Norman Granz

Influential: Ella Fitzgerald, Count Basie, Cole Porter

THE DICTIONARY DEFINITION OF *VERVE* **PERFECTLY** captures the label's intent and attitude. It depicts a spirit of vigour, enthusiasm, energy, vitality, vivacity, dash, passion and forcefulness. It's a perfectly nuanced name for a jazz label, formed by Norman Granz in 1956. Verve was principally created to house Ella Fitzgerald, whom Granz also managed. He started with the Jazz 4000 series. Granz knew Fitzgerald's career had stalled and required a change of direction. The change was decisive, clear and effective. Verve released *Ella Fitzgerald Sings the Cole Porter Songbook*.

Verve Records' roster is simply a roll call of jazz greats: Ella Fitzgerald, Nina Simone, Count Basie, Cole Porter, George Gershwin and Irving Berlin. This era has often been called the Golden Age of American music, a term that accurately captures the stunning quality of the artists on Verve's roster.

To say Norman Granz was a key figure in the history of jazz would be to grossly understate his significance. If jazz had been the New Testament, it would have been Mathew, Mark, Luke and Norman. Not only was he a renowned producer (apart from Fitzgerald, he also managed Oscar Peterson), he was instrumental in reshaping and marketing the way jazz was presented and perceived. He took it from smoky, seedy clubs into concert halls. People were now happy to pay to sit and enjoy watching these wonderful artists. He also fought against racism at a time when it was extremely dangerous to do so.

Norman Granz had been an experienced label owner, setting up Clef (Gene Krupa, Duke Ellington and Oscar Peterson) in Los Angeles, in

1946, before forming Norgran (Buddy Rich, Stan Getz and Bud Powell) in 1953. He combined the two labels into Verve in 1956. Granz loved live improv jam sessions and the virtuosic statements the great jazz minds brought to the stage; the range and skill of the musicians, who, when under pressure and pushed, created wonderful flourishes. The shows captured the public's imagination.

Granz was a visionary and realised, as early as the mid-1940s, that the stunning skill and highly influential bebop, played by prodigious musicians such as Charlie Parker, would be transformed if he could market, present and showcase their talent correctly. It could be argued that Norman Granz was responsible for moulding Parker into a figure lauded and hailed by many, especially the cool jazz hipsters and the Beat Generation. Parker was respected because, under Granz's tutelage, he was viewed on a more intellectual level.

In 1944, while working on an award-winning short film, *Jammin' the Blues*, Granz organised a concert at the Philharmonic in Los Angeles, dubbed 'Jazz at the Philharmonic' (JATP), which was extremely popular. The fans loved the way Granz featured battles between big names in swing and bop. This show would eventually go on the road in the USA and tour across the world. The timing couldn't have been better. Granz started recording the performances when there were developments in the quality and popularity of vinyl with the LP record.

The formula was simple. Due to the excitement around the live records, the sales of the albums helped pay for the concerts; they in turn generated more live recordings, leading to greater record sales and more demand for live shows.

FANORAK FACT

Inside every Verve inner record sleeve released in the 1960s was written, 'The Jazz of America is on Verve'. A perfect précis.

As with Blue Note, Granz placed a significant amount of time and focus on getting the branding, artwork and concept right for the appropriate artist. His stylised look was adopted for each of the labels. The images on Clef, Norgran and Verve were strong, cool and distinctive. It was about the sound and the look, supported by the illustrations of artist David Stone Martin and the photography of Herman Leonard and Phil Stern.

The son of Ukrainian immigrants, living in a mixed neighbourhood in Los Angeles, Granz had witnessed first-hand how many of his friends were racially mistreated. Now as an adult, he would see millions returning home from the war, who should have been welcomed as heroes but were treated as second-class citizens. Of his stable of artists, Granz famously said, 'I insisted that my musicians were to be treated with the same respect as Leonard Bernstein or Jascha Heifetz because they were just as good – both as people and as musicians.'

Granz was among the most significant figures in the music industry of this era who fought against racial segregation. He saw at close hand how badly Black friends and artists were being treated. He became responsible for stopping racial segregation in many of the venues. He would pay the musicians and make sure they travelled well. Dizzy Gillespie famously said, 'With Norman, you travelled first-class, stayed at first-class hotels and never played anywhere there was segregated seating.' Gene Krupa was also a fan of Granz, though Gene was more about the green, the drummer claiming he made more on a two-week tour with Granz than during eight weeks in a jazz club.

Verve was also a label of creative relationships. One of the longest was Duke Ellington's collaboration with composer Billy Strayhorn, a great composer and arranger whom many won't have heard of. Strayhorn was stylish, sophisticated, uncompromising, Black and gay. He continued to work and produce great music, but is seldom spoken of compared to contemporaries like Johnny Mercer, George Gershwin and Irving Berlin.

Not everyone was a fan of Granz, though: he split opinion and upset several people. Some, especially Mel Torme, found him ignorant. Sinatra fell out with him over a deal that broke down when he tried to buy Verve (see Reprise). But generally his artists loved and respected him. He was a strong powerful presence, an ex-marine who kept fit, the type of figure who would be abrasive if his artists weren't being treated well. He famously said, 'If you don't get what you want, be prepared to walk. And don't look back.' It embodies his loyalty and belief in his artists.

When touring Jazz at the Philharmonic, Granz set in place many of the same methods used in modern touring today. Preparation and planning were everything. The local DJs in each town and city were incorporated into the deal, promoting the gigs and playing the music of those appearing, while actively endorsing the gigs and offering chances to win tickets on air. Tour itineraries were set out and planned with military precision; Granz scheduled travelling times, insisted on soundchecks and ensured the crew were looked after and fed. Hotels would be booked in advance, everything was professionally done and everyone had to adhere to the itinerary.

What makes Granz's story remarkable is the astonishing lack of recognition afforded to someone who gave so much to jazz over fifty years. During his career, Granz would eventually create five jazz labels. He was one of the most important impresarios in the music business, yet few outside the jazz world would even know his name.

Verve, especially with both Ella Fitzgerald's Songbook series (eight in total) and the Jazz at the Philharmonic series, were Granz's finest hour. Norman Granz didn't only own Verve, he ran the label, took charge of A&R, managed and produced artists, oversaw the marketing, distribution, contracts and kept a close eye on the accounts. The lack of accolades and grudging treatment from the press tend to be attributed to his manner and contempt for them. They considered him arrogant and haughty, as he hated his artists to be criticised and would remain distant and standoffish towards the jazz press. Granz was, however, the perfect label boss and manager. He believed in getting the best deals for his artists and made sure they were treated properly in the studio, and when they toured, travelled and performed.

In 1960, Granz sold Verve to MGM, where the label also released pop and rock 'n' roll artists like The Righteous Brothers and Frank Zappa. They were issued on

FANORAK FACT

Jazz at the Philharmonic played two shows in London in February 1953. American jazz musicians hadn't played in the UK since before the war because of a dispute between the UK and US musicians' unions. Granz got around the problem by donating the takings to the victims of a disastrous flood, endearing himself to the UK's jazz lovers.

blue labels to differentiate them from the black (jazz). *The Velvet Underground and Nico* was released in March 1967 on Verve/MGM. It would become one of the most influential rock albums ever.

Granz continued in the role of promoter and manager, returning to jazz labels in 1973 with the Pablo label. In 1987, he sold this to Fantasy Records. Granz died in Geneva, on 22 November 2001, aged 83.

PLAYLIST: MY TOP 5 ALBUMS

Charlie Parker: *Charlie Parker with Strings: The Master Takes*

The Ben Webster Quintet: *Soulville*

Nat King Cole and Les Paul: *Complete Jazz at the Philharmonic 1944–1949*

Ella Fitzgerald: *Ella Fitzgerald Sings the Cole Porter Songbook*

Oscar Peterson Trio: *Night Train*

VIRGIN RECORDS

Founder: Richard Branson

Influential: Mike Oldfield, Sex Pistols, Human League

THERE'S FOOTAGE OF A young, bespectacled Richard Branson organising and editing a magazine called *Student*. He left school, aged 16, to create this business. The intention was simple: to provide an alternative voice for a new generation, covering popular culture, film, music, social issues and the Vietnam War. By the age of 17, he was running a magazine with a circulation of 100,000. He has, in his inimitable way, been providing a creative alternative ever since.

When he decided to move into the music business, Branson's original idea was straightforward:

> Back in 1970, my friends and I noticed a gap in the market for selling cut-price records by post, so we launched Virgin Mail Order. What started as a relatively small operation grew into something phenomenal. Demand got so high that just one year later we opened our first Virgin Records store on Oxford Street.

Virgin Records was formed in 1970. The business was originally a mail-order music company. They would track down, buy and fill vans with cheap, discounted records, end-of-the-line runs and imports, and post them on to the customer for profit. This proved fraught on at least two memorable occasions. One morning, they awoke to find a postal strike had left their fledgling business empire practically bust. On another occasion, Branson was arrested by the taxman for not paying import duty and was ordered to pay a £60,000 fine, which his mother picked up. This altogether unconventional business practice resulted in a night's bed and breakfast, compliments of H.M. Prison Service.

Simon Draper, Branson's distant cousin, was from South Africa, a DJ and music fan who in the late 1960s was able to source imports via mail order of acts like Jimi Hendrix, The Doors, Bob Dylan and Soft Machine, who were all banned in his homeland. On his arrival in London, with £100 in his pocket, he sought out 'cousin' Richard and the next day was put in charge of the mail-order business and ordering stock for the new Oxford Street shop, located at the cheaper end of the street. Draper's enthusiasm and knowledge made him a key figure in establishing Virgin Records. He was pushing underground acts like Robert Wyatt, Hatfield and the North, and Ivor Cutler. He also was a fan of the German experimental rock bands Can and Tangerine Dream.

When his record shop in Oxford Street went well, Branson opened a second store in Liverpool. Once he figured out there was money to be made in multiples and the resulting economies of scale, Branson quickly opened another twelve stores across the UK. My vivid memory of Virgin Records was of rarely buying anything. The shop was cool, the staff were rude, and you could spend hours walking around, flicking through records and checking out girls. But the vinyl was cheaper and more tasteful elsewhere.

Thinking out of the box, or the back of the van, or now the back of the shop, Branson visualised the whole picture. He understood that more could be made by owning the process, from artist to recording to manufacturing to selling. With funding from the exclusive private bank Coutts, he set about converting an Oxfordshire mansion into a state-of-the-art residential recording studio, called the Manor. From there, hearing demo tapes of Mike Oldfield's *Tubular Bells*, he offered to find him a record deal. Six labels were approached, but no one shared Branson's

FANORAK FACT

Virgin was almost called Slipped Disc until Tessa Watts (one of those involved at the beginning with *Student* magazine) mentioned in conversation that they were virgins in business and the name stuck. Watts would later, as head of publicity at Virgin, oversee the career of the Sex Pistols.

excitement. Branson and Draper's belief in Oldfield's haunting sound drove them to create a label to release it.

The label launched in May 1973, with the simultaneous release of four albums, Mike Oldfield's *Tubular Bells*, Gong's *Flying Teapot*, Faust's *The Faust Tapes* and an obscure jam session called *Manor Live*.

Branson always had driving ambition; he sometimes appeared scatter-brained and lacking focus, but his unique selling point as label owner was Richard Branson. His eccentricity was part of the deal. If you asked the man on the street to name Virgin Records' biggest star, they would reply Branson.

In New York, the Ramones were only playing small, if prestigious venues. Despite rave reviews and cheerleading from *The Village Voice* and *Rolling Stone*, US fans were not smitten by the punk thing (see Sire Records). However, in the UK, due to the support and praise of writers like Charles Shaar Murray and Nick Kent, by the time the Ramones arrived, punk had evolved into a scene. On 4 July 1976, the 200th birthday of the USA, the Ramones played to 2,000 people in the Roundhouse, with The Flamin' Groovies and The Stranglers as support acts.

The audience went crazy. Present at the Roundhouse gig were most of London's punk cognoscenti – members of The Adverts and The Damned were there. However, contrary to some gargantuan urban mythology, the Sex Pistols and The Clash were not present. The Clash were playing their first-ever gig that night, supporting the Sex Pistols in The Black Swan pub in Sheffield.

In 1977, Virgin was a progressive rock label, hippies fronted by the affable, fun-loving boss. Their biggest seller thus far was *Tubular Bells*. The artwork and logo for the label were created by artist and prog-rock album designer, Roger Dean. The Sex Pistols' decision to sign with Virgin was a major story: public school hippies and nihilistic punks did not seem natural bedfellows. It was like Nirvana signing with Stock, Aitken and Waterman. Branson, though, sensed it was the perfect appointment to raise the label's profile, shake off the cobwebs and do what the great rock impresarios of the past did – come at it from leftfield with something unexpected. Sensing it was a great opportunity to keep ahead of the pack, Branson knew everything would change when the Sex Pistols signed in May 1977.

In October 1976, the Sex Pistols had signed to EMI for £40,000. Three months later, EMI claimed that, due to the controversy and adverse publicity they had generated, their contract would be terminated. In March 1977, the band signed to A&M, outside Buckingham Palace, for £75,000. Six days later, they were sacked due to pressure from US owners Herb Alpert and Jerry Moss.

Enter Branson, the colourful label boss ready to shake off Virgin's hippy image by piggybacking on the band's notoriety. It was a gamble that proved a smart move – to offer the most notorious band in the UK, perhaps even the world, a deal. The timing was perfect. If ever there was a moment to attach his label to an act, it would be May 1977 and the Sex Pistols. The publicity around the band had already upset and captivated millions in equal measure. 'God Save the Queen' was released to coincide with the Queen's Silver Jubilee celebrations. It was immediately banned by radio and TV. Shops refused to handle the record. The vinyl manufacturers refused to make it. The outcome? It sold 200,000 copies in one week, reaching number 2 in the charts.

On 7 June, the official day of Jubilee celebrations, Branson hired a boat and the Pistols played on the Thames, opposite the Houses of Parliament – a deliberate act of punk provocation. Julian Temple captured on film the Metropolitan Police's ham-fisted attempt to put a stop to the stunt. The band's manager, Malcolm McLaren, seeing another chance to cement the band's notoriety, remonstrated with the boys in blue. Twelve officers set about him with truncheons as Temple filmed the mêlée. Within hours, the whole circus was being beamed into every home in the land, and Virgin's image had changed forever. Job done.

Around 1979, punk rock had to be hidden like porn. My friend's older brother had one particular single planked in an album, and we used to play it when his mum and dad were out. The idea of a band even being called the Sex Pistols was exciting enough. The single was unique in many ways.

FANORAK FACT

'God Save the Queen', despite selling 200,000 copies in one week, was kept off the number 1 spot by Rod Stewart's 'I Don't Want to Talk About It'.

'Something Else' / 'Friggin' in the Riggin' reached number 3 in the UK charts and was the band's biggest-selling single (328,000 copies).

I remember explaining to my pal that this was a double-A side and 'Something Else' wasn't their song but an Eddie Cochran cover. You sensed, even then, aged 12, that the initial danger and impact of the Sex Pistols was gone. This wasn't Johnny Rotten singing, I explained; this was Sid Vicious. We both agreed it was quite punk rock that Sid was dead now, nonchalantly discussing his overdose as if it was a storyline from *Coronation Street*. When we heard 'Friggin' in the Riggin'', we couldn't stop laughing. We played it constantly. Full of cursing and rebellion, the Sex Pistols were crazy shagging pirates. To Catholic boys growing up in a housing scheme in West Central Scotland, this was our epiphany. There was a big wide world out there, full of fun, and we had to pretend we didn't know it existed. We laughed and laughed and didn't care. If you looked at the crucifix and the pictures of Mary on the wall, Jesus was tapping his foot and Mary was giving us the fingers.

As punk evolved into a broader sound, post-punk bands signed for Virgin: X-Ray Spex, The Ruts, Penetration, XTC, Skids and Magazine. John Lydon's lauded Public Image Ltd and the Sex Pistols' ringleader and Svengali, McLaren, also worked with Branson and Virgin into the 1980s.

Mention should be made of a prolific reggae imprint, Front Line. Often overlooked in the Virgin story, it was formed in 1978. Front Line produced an astonishing forty-six albums and twenty-six singles.

Virgin made good with Sheffield's Human League. Their third album, after *Reproduction* and *Travelogue*, was *Dare* (1981) which gave Virgin its first worldwide smash with 'Don't You Want Me'. *Dare* was everywhere, a popular Christmas gift. If you bought the album in the USA, it was called *Dare!* (Virgin licensed the album to A&M in the USA and they added an exclamation mark.) The album reached number 3 on the *Billboard* charts, with 'Don't You Want Me' reaching number 1. Virgin became the new wave,

FANORAK FACT

The riff for 'Pretty Vacant' was ripped off from Abba's 'SOS'.

synth-pop label and paved the way for bands like Japan, Simple Minds and Culture Club.

In 1983, Virgin bought Charisma, which came gift-wrapped with Genesis, bringing the solo sales of both Phil Collins and Peter Gabriel. Branson also signed Stevie Winwood and Roy Orbison, resurrecting both their careers.

It wasn't all plain sailing. Branson would have a few plummeting balloons to deal with both in business and the Atlantic – the ocean, not the label. In 1992, a high-profile cash scramble to keep his Virgin Atlantic airline afloat resulted in him reluctantly selling Virgin Music to EMI for £510 million, ending his relationship with the label.

When Universal Music Group bought EMI in 2012, it took over Virgin EMI. It has established stars like Keith Richards, Sir Paul McCartney and Neil Diamond, along with the younger acts Corinne Bailey Rae, Jake Bugg and Slaves (now Soft Play).

Sir Richard has taken 'brand' Branson into the race to build spaceships. However, he was such a presence that he will always be inextricably linked with Virgin Records. Branson made a return to the record industry in 1996, fronting a new label, V2 Records (he owned 5 per cent while Morgan Stanley owned the rest). V2 was sold for £7 million in 2006 to Universal Music Group, which sold it on to PIAS Entertainment Group in 2013.

PLAYLIST: MY TOP 5 ALBUMS

Sex Pistols: *Never Mind the Bollocks*
Human League: *Dare*
Skids: *Days in Europa*
Simple Minds: *Sons and Fascination*
XTC: *English Settlement*

WARNER BROS. RECORDS

Founder: James Conkling

Influential: The Faces, Talking Heads, Tom Petty and the Heartbreakers, Frankie Valli

THERE'S SOMETHING WONDERFULLY DECADENT in the fading glamour of the artwork of the Warner Bros. label. It's impossible to pick up its vinyl and not be transported to an imaginary movie scene in Hollywood. The artwork on this particular era of the label's vinyl is known by collectors as the 'Burbank Palm Trees'. I remember picking up albums by The Faces, Rod Stewart's solo material and 'December 1963 (Oh, What a Night)' by Frankie Valli and the Four Seasons, and seeing tree-lined boulevards; it all looked so sophisticated, a million miles away from Scotland's cold summers and perpetual low-lying winter sun.

Warner Bros. Records has its roots in Warner Brothers, the Hollywood studio started by Jack, Albert, Sam and Harry Warner, which became Warner Bros. Pictures. The company that bought over and incorporated Loony Tunes, with Daffy Duck and Bugs Bunny, was the same company that would, eventually, find itself as a major player in the music business. When you consider the company's positioning in the heart of the entertainment industry, with a clear understanding of giving people what they want, it took Warner Bros. a remarkably long time to set up a popular music label. By 1947, Ahmet Ertegun and Herb Abramson had set up Atlantic. By 1950, Jack Holzman had formed Elektra. Yet it took until 1958 before Warner Bros. Records was set up in Burbank, California. Even then, there was a sense of trepidation and nervousness as the business tried to keep up with MGM and Paramount.

It's argued that the formation of Warner Bros. Records was down to a comical incident when, in 1957, one of its studio stars, an actor called Tab Hunter, had been signed to Dot Records, despite having an exclusivity deal with Warners. Hunter was the classic all-American, square-jawed, blonde, romantic lead. The owner of Dot Records, Randy Woods, realised Warner Bros. didn't have a record company. Warner Bros. were so infuriated with the situation that they moved to set up a label and get their star back. By the time they'd re-signed Hunter, the deed was done and he'd scored two hits with Dot Records. The first was a massive smash hit, with Ric Cartey and Carole Joyner's 'Young Love', in January 1957, which stayed at number 1 for six weeks, selling over a million copies on the US charts. The next release was 'Ninety-Nine Ways', which reached number 11. To make matters worse for Warners, Dot Records was owned by their movie-making rival, Paramount.

Warner Bros. had been considering the label idea well before Tab Hunter signed to Dot, and had tentatively made moves to form a record division from 1956, when Harry and Albert Warner sold up and left the board. They were replaced by bankers Charles Allen and Serge Semenenko and investor David Baird, who favoured expansion into the fast-developing music business. Semenenko was most vocal about the urgency to set up their own label, highlighting the futility of making deals to release their soundtracks with other companies. However, there's no doubt the situation with Dot Records and Tab Hunter accelerated the process.

James B. Conkling, former president of Columbia Records, was hired as boss. He was a respected figure within the music industry, more a safe pair of hands than an influential, exciting risk-taker. He was more attuned to middle-of-the-road music at a time when the label should have been embracing rock 'n' roll. When Warner Bros. finally set up their record label and recaptured Tab Hunter, the moment was gone and he only recorded a few average albums. His success with Dot wasn't replicated. The song 'Jealous Heart' performed poorly and peaked at number 62 on the charts. It was the label's only chart entry of 1958. But at least the business was up and running.

For the first few years, Warner Bros. floundered, looking out of its depth and out of touch. Jack Warner thought the label had principally been set up as the movie studio's soundtrack label. Any movie made for Warner Bros. would be released as a soundtrack. Any of its signed movie or TV stars who could hold a tune would be releasing singles. It felt like a wasted opportunity. Warner Bros. had the money, the wherewithal and the setup, but didn't have the edge to take advantage of the current rock 'n' roll trend and modern tastes.

However, when Warner Bros. applied its movie industry savvy to the music business, it achieved results. If it wanted a star to sign for its studio, it would throw money at them. In this case, the big-money signing was The Everly Brothers. This was a coup at the time and sent a clear message. A respected and popular international act had signed to Warner Bros. Records. The publicity around Don and Phil signing the first million-dollar deal entirely changed the label's perception. With this one move, Warner Bros. was suddenly hip and had proved it could compete.

The Everly Brothers delivered. By April 1960, their first song for Warner Bros., 'Cathy's Clown', written by Don and Phil, had sold 8 million copies and was the label's biggest-selling record. In the UK, The Everly Brothers had eighteen hits in the 1960s on Warner Bros. The next big-name signing for Warner Bros. was Bill Haley and the Comets.

As the 1960s saw sweeping social change, Warner Bros. cashed in on the growing folk wave by signing Peter Yarrow, Noel Paul Stookey and Mary Travers, who ingeniously came up with the name Peter, Paul and Mary. The folk trio were hot; they had their first hit with 'Lemon Tree', then reworked The Weavers' song, 'If I Had a Hammer (The Hammer Song)'. A few more mid-reaching releases followed, and in 1963 they released 'Puff the Magic Dragon'. Later in the year, they followed up with two Dylan songs, 'Blowin' in the Wind' and 'Don't Think Twice (That's Alright)'. Peter, Paul and Mary were consistent throughout the rest of the decade, finally making it to number 1 with their last hit, John Denver's 'Leaving on a Jet Plane', in 1969.

FANORAK FACT

The B-side to Napoleon XIV's 'They're Coming to Take Me Away' was the same song played backwards. Even the Warner Bros. label was backwards too.

A strategic move to more album-selling acts would see Warner Bros. Records buy up Sinatra's Reprise in 1963. What followed provided grounds for optimism with Joni Mitchell, Neil Young, Randy Newman and Arlo Guthrie, all huge LP-selling artists. Reprise's extensive deals in distribution with the UK acts meant that The Kinks, Hendrix and Fleetwood Mac were picked up by Warner Bros.

Petula Clark delivered at the start of 1965, hitting big with 'Downtown'. She would go on to provide hit after hit for the next three years. In 1966, Clark had four hits and then The Marketts scored with 'The Batman Theme', though changes would soon be afoot.

In 1967, the last brother standing, Jack, sold Warner Bros. to Seven Arts Ltd for $32 million. The label became known as Warner Bros.–Seven Arts and a few months later bought out Atlantic. The Seven Arts deal came with Warner Bros. Records and Reprise and a chunk of Loony Tunes. Crucially, it meant Mo Ostin and Joe Smith would be at the helm. Ostin brought a fresh vibrancy, and from here on in, the label began to focus on a more refined, contemporary roster.

In the 1970s, Warner Bros. Records, as most of us know and love the label, found some steam. It was now a genuine, bona fide major record company, one to be reckoned with. Suddenly it had Deep Purple, Black Sabbath, Alice Cooper, The Grateful Dead, The Faces, America, James Taylor, and Seals and Crofts. By the mid-1970s, the label was finally ahead of the curve.

Music can bring joy and delight, the simple pleasures. If 1974 was about The Faces and Rod Stewart, 1976 was about one single and I played it constantly: 'December, 1963 (Oh, What a Night)' by The Four Seasons. I was infatuated by this song. I would copy the drummer who sang at the start. It was unusual to see a singing drummer: Ringo, Mickey Dolenz and Kevin Godley from 10CC sometimes. You could name a few others – Dave Clark, Karen Carpenter and Don Henley. Not too many when you consider the history of music. I'd go upstairs and find two Funk and Wagnalls' dictionaries, use wooden spoons to count out notes, and try to sing at the same time like the drummer Gerry Polci. I knew when I was 9 that 'December, 1963 (Oh, What a Night)' was destined to reach number 1. I told everyone about the song; I was convinced it was a hit, and sure enough, it reached the top in the UK, USA and Canada.

I would've hated me as a child. The Four Seasons then followed that success with a song of undoubted quality called 'Silver Star', which sounded marvellous, like two different songs stuck together.

The label has remained influential, a central force through to the present day, and continues as a wholly owned subsidiary within the Warner Music Group. In May 2019, Warner Bros. Records was rebranded as Warner Records and people were none too pleased. *Variety*'s Michele Amabile Angermiller called it perfectly: 'If there's one thing the music industry takes very seriously, it's an iconic logo. So when Warner Bros. Records announced a major rebranding earlier today — complete with a new name, Warner Records — the biz responded swiftly and viscerally on social media.'

PLAYLIST: MY TOP 5 ALBUMS

Fleetwood Mac: *Rumours*
Van Morrison: *Astral Weeks*
Tom Petty and the Heartbreakers: *Into the Great Wide Open*
The Association: *Birthday*
The Four Seasons: *Who Loves You*

XL RECORDINGS

Founders: Richard Russell, Tim Palmer and Nick Halkes

Influential: The Prodigy, Radiohead, The White Stripes, Adele

IF YOU HAD TO write a swish bit of ad agency copy to describe Richard Russell's company, it would be something like: 'XL Recordings: Just outside of everything'. It sums up the label Richard Russell has steered to extraordinary success. XL Recordings has been quietly and successfully making serious waves for over three decades.

Initially, XL was run by Tim Palmer and Nick Halkes. It was set up as a niche specialist dance and rave label. Russell was a DJ and a fan of garage, drum 'n' bass and jungle. He began his journey simply to find the music he wanted to hear. This led him to Groove Records and like-minded people in Palmer and Halkes ... he joined a year later, in 1990.

Around the late 1980s, any dance DJ worth their salt from across London frequented Groove Records. Palmer was an influential dance and acid-house specialist. Then, for the discerning music fan, collector or DJ, it was about one thing: carefully flicking through each record, in the hope of hunting down an elusive 12in import. Then you had the excitement of playing it. Now, it would be flicking through CDs or a discarded box of a dead man's vinyl in a charity shop, purely for bragging rights.

Palmer realised from the nature of sales at Groove Records that money might be made licensing records from the USA. XL was set up, initially as an offshoot of Citybeat Records, a more commercial dance label owned by Beggars Banquet. At this point, for the label's eventual boss, Richard Russell, it was about imports, white labels and hip-hop mix tapes, which he sold at Camden Market.

When you listen to Russell speak about his formative years and being a fan of the vibrant independent rap scene in New York, you get a sense of his passion, infatuation and knowledge; he's a music fan. Like most record-loving fans and collectors, he wasn't interested only in the music, but also in the concept and notion of the record itself. It was about the information: the logo, the date and the serial number. Where was it made? Who engineered it? Who produced it? Dance music was production and label-based, from the street to the underground rave scene. The label was as crucial as the music. This enthusiasm for music took him to the source, to New York and Greenwich Village, to work in a record store called Vinyl Mania. Ironically, there he bumped into Palmer, who was checking out stock to import back to his shop in London.

In 1991, the label received a ten-song demo from an enthusiastic chap called Liam Howlett. Four of the songs from the demo would make The Prodigy's four-track EP, *What Evil Lurks?* Their next release, 'Charley', made it to number 3 in the charts. With SL2's 'On a Ragga Tip' released in 1992, suddenly XL was overshadowing the main label, Citybeat. The Prodigy's 1992 debut, *Experience*, was the first of their three albums on XL. Well received in the UK, it was ignored elsewhere. Their second, *Music for the Jilted Generation* (1994) reaffirmed the band's desire to be viewed as a punk dance band, the techno Sex Pistols.

In 1996, they released the game-changing single, the visceral and intoxicating 'Firestarter', netting a number 1 single in the UK charts. They had a much-coveted spot on the touring music festival Lollapalooza. Most importantly, the warning flare of 'Firestarter' preceded the 1997 album, *The Fat of the Land*, which saw the band achieve global recognition. The album entered the charts at number 1 in the UK and the USA, establishing the band as a unique international dance act. The album reached number 1 in twenty-seven countries.

This period saw changes in personnel at XL. In 1993, Hawkes left for EMI to set up the dance imprint Positiva Records. Palmer retired from the music business, leaving Russell in charge. He continued to be inspired by working closely with The Prodigy. He loved their punk rock attitude and the way they refused to do interviews and turned down TV performances. The less they gave, the more the press and fans wanted. They stayed resolute and played it on their terms. With The Prodigy taking off, he had the capital to license House of Pain's 'Jump Around'. He signed Basement Jaxx and, more significantly, Badly Drawn Boy. This was an imaginative signing, making it clear the label was opening up and broadening its roster. Badly Drawn Boy's 2000 release, *The Hour of Bewilderbeast*, won the Mercury Prize.

A more diverse A&R stance saw Russell bring in The White Stripes; they released *White Blood Cells*. The label also repackaged and released the band's previous two albums, *The White Stripes* and *De Stijl*. In 2003, The White Stripes hit number 1 on the UK album charts. The same year saw grime artist Dizzee Rascal release *Boy in da Corner*. He would also win the Mercury Prize.

Mathangi Arulpragasam, the rapper, singer and visual artist better known as M.I.A., was introduced to the world via XL, with her 2005 debut *Arular* and 2007's *Kala* hitting big and finding global acclaim. By 2008, both Friendly Fires and The Horrors had signed.

If Liam Howlett's demo was responsible for launching XL Recordings, then the signing of Adele, in 2006, shifted the label's narrative, catapulting XL into the stratosphere. Millions immediately tuned into Adele's authenticity and loved the instinctive nature of the songs, a peculiarly charming mixture of strength and vulnerability. After signing Adele, Russell shrewdly refused to push her, allowing her time for development, believing she would deliver. Following the success of the first album, *19*, Russell continued to not place unnecessary pressure on Adele. Instead, he allowed the artist time to feel her way through the uncharted waters and deal with the stress and pressure this level of fame brings.

Adele's follow-up, *21*, reached number 1 in thirty countries. Her records continue to sell: *21* had sold over 32 million copies at the last official count. In November 2015, *25* would sell 7.5 million copies in a calendar year. Through 2016, as she toured the world, the album was hitting sales of over 25 million.

The release of Jack White's solo album, *Blunderbuss*, displaced Adele's *21* from the charts – no mean feat by White. Russell

FANORAK FACT

The Prodigy got their name from Howlett's Moog Prodigy synthesizer.

enjoyed working with White in particular. In interviews about The White Stripes or Jack White's solo work, you sense that Russell liked him as a person and valued him as a talented artist. In a wider context, within the music industry, White is viewed as a virtuoso, someone able to write, play guitar, drums and piano, sing, engineer and produce.

With Adele's global success and phenomenal sales, the label's fortunes changed beyond belief. However, Russell remained resolutely focused; it was still about putting out great music. In 2006, the label signed Thom Yorke, who released *The Eraser*. Then, when Radiohead brought out their 'pay-what-you-want' album, *In Rainbows*, Russell signed them to XL for the physical release of the album's vinyl and CD. In May 2016, Radiohead released their critically received album, *A Moon Shaped Pool* on XL Recordings.

In keeping with the DIY attitude and ethos of hip-hop and punk – and inspired by labels like Motown – XL created a studio in the garage of its label at Ladbroke Grove. This was tailored for the band XX (on Young Turks, an XL imprint set up by Caius Pawson in 2006), who thanked XL by winning yet another Mercury Prize, the third band on the label to do so.

There's a strand that runs through Russell's signings. It's that word again – authenticity – artists with a clear vision who are strong-willed. He wanted artists to be charismatic and talented, but they should have an opinion too. He wanted strong individuals such as Liam Howlett, Adele, Jack White, Badly Drawn Boy, M.I.A, Dizzee Rascal and Radiohead. Russell continued to work as a producer with Damon Albarn, Bobby Womack and the late, great Gil Scott-Heron on his first album in sixteen years, the brilliant *I'm New Here*. (Gil Scott-Heron passed away in May 2011.) These aren't the type of stars who need constant supervision and intrusion; they're serious people, who know their jobs as artists.

Initially, Richard Russell was a fan who, through his enthusiasm, was given a job running around for XL, distributing vinyl, and doing promo and some A&R work. He ended up becoming the boss and signing Adele. However, for a modern label, Richard Russell and XL's artist-led approach harks back to the days of guys like Ahmet Ertegun, Mo Ostin and Norman Granz. When asked to explain the label's winning formula, Russell shuffles uncomfortably before reasoning that he trusts his artists. He tries to sign people strong enough to make a great album. He shouldn't need to intercede, and usually, the interference is minimal.

When the late writer Martin Amis was asked to describe his father Kingsley's somewhat lax parenting skills, he summed it up in two words, 'amiably minimalist'. This describes Russell's approach to his artists. Instead of taking advantage of his trust, they respond positively. They know he's there if they need him. He knows what he's doing, smiling as he looks on.

XL Recordings: Just outside of everything.

PLAYLIST: MY TOP 5 ALBUMS

Gill Scott Heron: *I'm New Here*
The White Stripes: *White Blood Cells*
The Prodigy: *The Fat of the Land*
Adele: *21*
Beck: *Modern Guilt*

BIBLIOGRAPHY

Unless otherwise indicated, all quotes are from my personal conversations.

BOOKS

Cope, Julian, *Copendium: An Expedition into the Rock 'n' Roll Underworld* (Faber and Faber, 2012)
Harris, Larry, *And Party Every Day: The Inside Story of Casablanca Records* (Backbeat Books 2009)
Kaplan, James, *Sinatra: The Chairman* (Anchor Books, 2016).
McGee, Alan, *Creation Stories: Riots, Raves and Running a Label* (Pan Macmillan, 2014)

OTHER SOURCES

American Songwriter
Columbia University Alumni
Daily Record
Daily Mirror
Design Week
Evening Standard
Forbes Magazine
God Is In The TV
The Guardian
The Independent
Irish News

Magnet Magazine
National Public Radio (NPR)
New Musical Express (NME)
New York Times
The New Statesman
News.com.au
Philadelphia Inquirer
Record Mirror
Rolling Stone
Variety

INDEX

See Contents for main labels.

GENERAL

ARTISTS

BANDS

ALBUMS

The destination for history
www.thehistorypress.co.uk